About the Publisher

The New York Institute of Finance

... more than just books.

NYIF offers practical, applied training and education in a wide range of formats and topics:

* *Classroom training:* evenings, mornings, noon-hour
* *Seminars and conferences:* one-, two, and three-day introductory, intermediate-, and professional-level programs
* *Customized training:* need-specific programs conducted on your site or ours; in New York City, throughout the United States, anywhere in the world
* *Independent study:* self-paced learning—basic, intermediate, or advanced
* *Exam preparation:* NASD licensing (including Series 3, 6, 7, 24, 27, 63); C.F.A.; state life and health insurance

Subjects of books and training programs include the following:

* Account Executive Training
* Brokerage Operations
* Currency Trading
* Futures Trading
* International Corporate Finance
* Investment Analysis
* Options Trading
* Securities Transfer
* Selling Securities
* Technical Analysis
* Treasury Management
* Yield Curve Analysis

When Wall Street professionals think ***training****, they think NYIF.*

For further information, please call or write to us. Please specify your areas of interest—classroom training, custom programs, independent-study courses, exam preparation, or books—so that we can respond promptly to your inquiry.

New York Institute of Finance
70 Pine Street
New York, NY 10270–0003
212 / 344–2900
FAX: 212 / 514–8423
TELEX: 238790

Simon & Schuster, Inc. A Gulf+Western Company
"Where Wall Street Goes to School"™

ASSET PLAYS:

PROFITING FROM UNDERVALUED STOCKS

New York Institute of Finance

LIBRARY OF CONGRESS
Library of Congress Cataloging-in-Publication Data

Asset plays : profiting from undervalued stocks / by the New York
Institute of Finance.
p. cm.
Includes index.
ISBN 0-13-049819-X : $35.00
1. Stocks. 2. Investments. I. New York Institute of Finance.
HG4661.A87 1988
332.63'22--dc19 88-9708
CIP

A Division of Simon & Schuster, Inc.
70 Pine Street, New York, NY 10270–0003

Printed in the United States of America

10 9 8 7 6 5 4 3 2 1

New York Institute of Finance
(NYIF Corp.)
70 Pine Street
New York, New York 10270–0003

Contents

CHAPTER 2
Asset Plays—Definition and Categories, 45

CHAPTER 3
How to Locate Asset Plays, 81

CHAPTER 4
Basic Techniques for Analyzing Asset Plays, 99

CHAPTER 7

Techniques for Purchasing Stock in Asset-Play Companies, 253

Index, 269

Introduction

In the sober aftermath of 1987's Black Monday, increasing numbers of individual investors, as well as the traders and account executives representing them, have become leery of speculation and inclined to substitute security for profit. For those willing to do some homework, however, there exists a means of identifying stocks that combine the dual promises of long-term profits and relatively low risk. The key to such successful stock choices is nothing more than a return to solid value—the identification of companies that are sufficiently asset-rich to ride out a market crash as well as decline, but whose assets are not *yet* reflected in the market price of the stock.

An example:

In 1983, Woolworth's stock was trading at $17 per share. In 1987, even after Black Monday, it was trading at well over $90 per share—considerably more than a quadrupling of value in only four years. Why?

Effective management might have played a role, as might have other elements. But undoubtedly the primary reason for such a dramatic increase in value was that the five-and-dime chain owned prime downtown real estate in New York and other cities across the country—an asset whose value was not reflected in the company's financial statements and thus was not recognized in the market price of its stock.

The wise investor who had bought Woolworth's stock in anticipation of such a rise in value would have been performing an asset play.

Asset plays come in a variety of shapes and sizes involving many elements besides real estate ownership. They range from acquiring stock in large capitalized—"Big Cap"—companies undergoing "restructuring" or operating in a "depressed" industry, to buying shares in companies whose stock is closely held and thinly traded. They exist in all parts of the market, from stocks listed on the New York Stock Exchange to those traded in the Pink Sheets. The only common denominator to "asset-play" investing is identifying and buying assets at a discount.

This book shows you, step by step, how to identify asset plays—that is, how to find stocks that are trading below their "real" value:

- Where to get needed information
- What to look for in a company's financial statements
- How to speak with the company's management to get the "inside" story
- Successful approaches and techniques for choosing and trading asset-play stocks
- What the "spread" tells you when the time comes to place your order
- How to identify fund managers and others who are "players" in this arena
- How to assess the rate of return you can expect from investing in asset plays

Possessed of such knowledge, the individual investor will be able to make asset plays and reap three primary benefits unavailable with virtually any other market investment:

1. Because such stocks are as yet undiscovered by the market, they typically elicit little interest from institutional investors and traders. In the usual situation, these large organizations, armed with computer-generated analyses and research department reports, are better able to get in and out of the market when it counts, leaving the individual to enter too late or stay in too long. In the unusual situation of asset plays, the individual is not unequally pitted against resource- and knowledge-rich investment giants.
2. Again because of the institutional investors' relative lack of interest, stocks acquired in an asset play are less vulnerable to program trading and therefore less susceptible to losing points through the automatic sell orders so integral to the 1987 crash.
3. Because the price of stock purchased in an asset play depends largely on the company's hidden assets and only partly on its trading value, the investor is further shielded from market downturns. Even in such a drastic situation as Black Monday, asset-play stocks dropped by only a few points—leaving them still greatly increased in value over the purchase price of the early investor—while others plummeted by the tens of points.

By analogy, asset-play investing is at the stage option trading was at twenty years ago: a specialized market niche on the threshold of becoming an area of dynamic growth and interest. Written "from the ground up" in such a way as to be useful to the complete novice as well as the experienced pro, *Asset Plays: Profiting from Undervalued Stocks* provides any serious reader ground-floor entrance to an investment arena in which, like so many others, early entrance is a key to considerable profit.

As with any investment analysis approach, some "homework" is necessary. You must be able to read a company's financial statements. If you've never done that before, Chapter 1 shows you—in everyday language and with clear illustrations—how to interpret a company's "financials." On the other hand, if you are an experienced analyst, you might skip Chapter 1 and get right into the how-to part of the book, beginning with Chapter 2.

In fact, do not be daunted by the financial statements included in this book. (They are, by the way, genuine documents with only the company and corporate officers' names changed.) You need not wade through every page of every statement. They are included in their entirety simply to make you accustomed to working with such statements and to enable you to pick out the relevant elements.

Financial Statement Analysis

CHAPTER 1

Intelligent investment decisions are made after careful consideration of available information: facts about world events, domestic news, industry reports, and corporate announcements. Most investors also rely on financial information released by the company to aid them in their judgments to buy or sell.

Information that comes from the corporation itself is also subject to an investor's interpretation, despite the well-known axiom that "figures don't lie." A corporation with $1 million in total assets and at least 500 stockholders is obliged to file financial information with the Securities and Exchange Commission (SEC) under the Securities Exchange Act of 1934. (Exempt from this rule are banks and insurance companies regulated by state or federal authority, whose rules parallel the SEC's anyway. Also excluded from reporting requirements are corporations engaged in religious, education, fraternal, or other eleomosynary enterprises.) These corporations must report significant events and changes as they occur periodically and must file an audited financial statement with the commission annually. At about the same time, similar information is distributed to the company's shareholders. However, the information is "raw," without explanation or analysis. Shareholders and prospective purchasers are expected to know and understand the techniques the company uses to keep the investment community informed.

This is often a difficult task because accounting is not a precise science. It is a sophisticated art, using various methods to present the same basic information and arrive at different conclusions. Despite the fact that most companies follow the standards of the FASB (Financial Accounting Standards Board), there is still enough leeway for accounting practices to vary from company to company, even within the same industry. Frequently, the difference in approach depends upon management's judgment; sometimes it depends upon the preferences of the auditor who prepares the statements. In any case, anyone who analyzes such information should realize that these documents are only part fact and part opinion.

Nevertheless, valuable insight into the health and wealth of a corporation is often readily apparent from careful examination of that institution's financial reports. A shareholder or registered representative need have only fundamental knowledge of accounting terms, procedures, and analysis in order to interpret such data competently. This chapter presents and identifies basic information in understandable lay language.

The Balance Sheet

Periodically, a corporation needs to demonstrate to its shareholders what the company is worth. The company simply lists everything it owns (assets) and everything it owes (liabilities). *Assets* are items of value—things that a company *owns* or has *owed to it*; assets are a corporation's possessions, or its pluses! *Liabilities* are the company's obligations—its debts, what the companies *owes*. The difference between assets and liabilities represents the company's net worth or the stockholders' net ownership, called *stockholders' equity*. This tabulation of assets, liabilities, and net worth is known as a *balance sheet*. The basic balance sheet equation is

$$\text{Assets} = \text{Liabilities} + \text{Stockholders' equity}$$

Both sides "balance," of course, because a corporation's stockholders have a stake in their corporation equal to the amount by which the corporation's assets exceed its liabilities. Expressed another way, what a company owns (assets) minus what it owes (liabilities) is equal to its net worth. The net worth (stockholders' equity) represents the value of the shareholders' investment in the corporation: It is the amount of money invested in the business by stockholders, plus the profits that have *not* been paid out as dividends.

Since a firm's financial state is continually changing, the balance sheet must be dated. The balance sheet's date shows on what day the tabulations were made. The assets, liabilities, and stockholders' equity are listed at their values *at the close of business* on the date shown at the top of the statement. A *simplified* balance sheet appears in Table 1-1.

Table 1-1.

BALANCE SHEET
ROXBURY MANUFACTURING COMPANY
December 31, 19X8

Assets	
Cash	$ 75,000
Marketable securities	150,000
Accounts receivable	375,000
Inventory	400,000
Total current assets	$1,000,000
Property, plant, and equipment	$ 605,000
Prepayments	20,000
Intangibles	10,000
Total assets	$1,635,000

=

Liabilities	
Accounts payable	$ 200,000
Accrued expenses	150,000
Accrued taxes	50,000
Total current liabilities	$ 400,000
Bonds—8%, due 19Z5	500,000
Total liabilities	$ 900,000

+

Stockholders' Equity	
Preferred stock—6% ($100 par)	$ 75,000
Common stock ($10 par)	300,000
Capital surplus	100,000
Retained earnings	260,000
Total stockholders' equity	$ 735,000
Total liabilities and stockholders' equity	$1,635,000

The value of the items owned—of the assets—can be figured many different ways. In actuality, the amount of money received from buyers, should all the assets be sold (liquidated), may differ dramatically from the values shown on the balance sheet. The shareholders' (stockholders') equity therefore represents the amount of money that *would* go to the preferred and common stockholders if all the company's assets were sold at the values at which they are carried on the balance sheet and if all liabilities were paid off as well. Thus, in another form, the balance sheet equation is

$$\text{Shareholders' equity} = \text{Total assets} - \text{Total liabilities}$$

Let us "build" a sample balance sheet for a typical manufacturing corporation, a block at a time, explaining each item separately.

Assets

A corporation's assets are traditionally listed, by type, in the following order:

Current assets
Fixed assets
Sundry assets
Intangibles

Current assets. These are items that a company owns or has owed to it and that, in the normal course of business, will be converted into cash within a year or less. This category includes:

- *Cash.* In addition to bank deposits, these are the bills and coins in the corporate "till." Such deposits are usually of the demand type, such as *checking* account balances.
- *Marketable securities.* Cash that the company does not need immediately it puts to work by investing it, usually in short-term instruments such as Treasury bills. The value of such investments is shown on the balance sheet at the *lower* of their cost or their market value; in the vast majority of cases the market value of the securities is higher than their cost, so cost usually appears on the balance sheet. An indication elsewhere, possibly in a footnote, cites the current market value of the securities.
- *Accounts receivable.* Most manufacturing companies sell to wholesalers or distributors. Goods are usually shipped with payment expected within 15 to 90 days. The total amount of billings outstanding represents the amount of money due the company for goods already shipped. Since the *entire* amount of the billings will probably not be collected for various reasons (for example, bankruptcy of the buyer), an estimate of bad debts is made. This *allowance for bad debt* is deducted from the total accounts receivable, and the leftover figure is shown on the balance sheet. This net figure represents an estimate of the amount that will be collected eventually.
- *Inventory.* This category includes raw materials, work in progress, and finished goods. Like marketable securities, inventories are carried on the balance sheet at the lower of cost or market value. Except in very unusual situations, the market value of the inventory is expected to be higher than its cost: A

manufacturing corporation makes its profit selling its finished goods for more than it costs to produce them. Cost accounting for inventory is based on two popular methods: FIFO (first-in/first-out) and LIFO (last-in/first-out). The method that a company chooses can have a dramatic effect on its earnings and on the value of the inventory remaining after a sale.

Example:

Roxbury Manufacturing has three manufactured items in inventory, each one produced in successive months at successively higher costs. During inflationary periods, such a situation is the norm. The first item manufactured (the one longest in inventory) cost $100, the second item cost $110, and the last item cost $120. The company is now selling its products for $300 each. Under FIFO the gross profit is $200, since the item sold is considered to be the first item produced at a cost of $100. The value of the inventory remaining after the sale totals $230. Under the LIFO method, the profit on $300 is based on the last item produced (at a cost of $120), and the gross profit is therefore only $180. The remaining inventory valuation is $210.

During *inflationary* periods, therefore, the FIFO method yields higher profits (and higher taxes!) than LIFO. FIFO also results in higher inventory evaluation. During *deflationary* periods, the results are just the opposite. Figure 1-1 gives you a visual aid in remembering the effects of LIFO over FIFO during inflationary periods.

Total Current Assets. The sum of these four types of current assets is the corporation's *total current assets.* Now more detail can be added to the current asset portion of the sample balance sheet in Table 1-1. Compare the section below with the first section in that figure. Note that some corporate balance sheets might show such additional items as notes receivable and/or prepaid expenses. Prepaid expenses are explained in this chapter.

Figure 1-1. Inventory cost accounting.

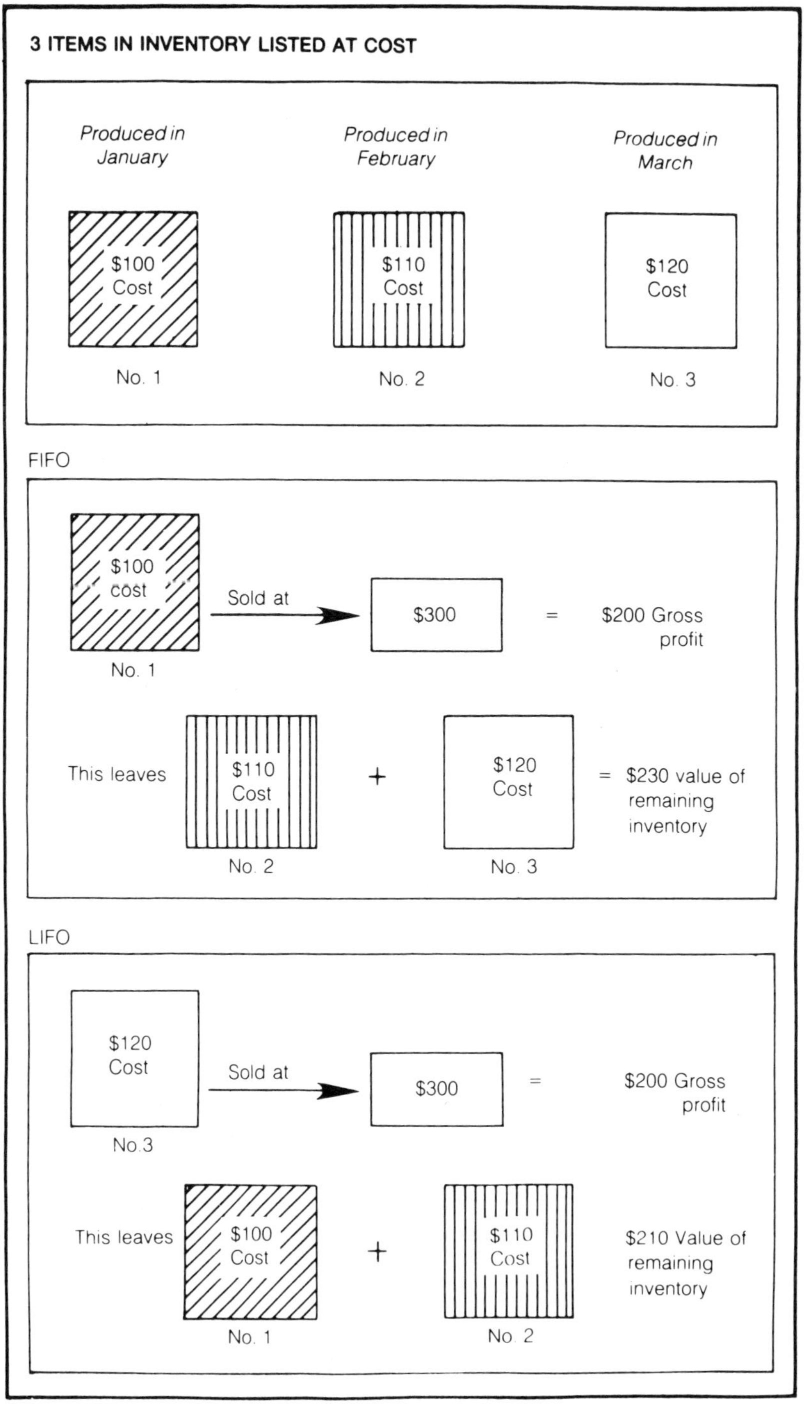

Current Assets	
Cash	$ 75,000
Marketable securities at cost (Market value—$156,000)	150,000
Accounts receivable ($390,000 less $15,000 allowance for bad debt)	375,000
Inventory (first-in/first-out)	400,000
Total current assets	$1,000,000

Current assets are in constant motion! When a company sells its products, an appropriate amount is deducted from inventory and goes into accounts receivable. When buyers pay their bills, accounts receivable become cash and the cash may then be used to pay debts. Or, a company may add to inventory and thus repeat the cycle.

Also, when an item is sold for more than its inventoried value, the difference (that is, the *gross profit*) automatically increases the total current assets by the amount of the profit. (How this profit is reflected is demonstrated on the *other* side of the balance sheet later.) Since both sides must balance, this profit is reflected by a corresponding increase in shareholders' equity. The company has made a profit, and the shareholders are therefore better off!

Quick Assets. The total current assets that may be *quickly* converted into cash, should the company deem it necessary, are called *quick assets.* The only item under current assets that is *not* considered very liquid is inventory. Therefore, to figure *quick assets,* merely subtract inventory from total current assets.

Example:

Cash	$ 75,000
Marketable securities	150,000
Accounts receivable	375,000
Inventory	400,000
Total current assets	$1,000,000

Subtracting inventory ($400,000) from the total ($1,000,000) leaves a figure of $600,000 for quick assets. Of course, the same amount may be derived by adding together cash, marketable securities, and accounts receivable—if these figures are all you have to work with. The formulas are as follows:*

$$\begin{aligned}\text{Quick assets} &= \text{Total current assets} - \text{Inventory}\\ &= \$1{,}000{,}000 - \$400{,}000\\ &= \$600{,}000\end{aligned}$$

or

$$\begin{aligned}\text{Quick assets} &= \text{Cash} + \text{Marketable securities} + \text{Accounts receivable}\\ &= \$75{,}000 + \$150{,}000 + \$375{,}000\\ &= \$600{,}000\end{aligned}$$

*Note that many of the concepts depicted by the formulas cited throughout Chapter 1 are also discussed in later chapters of the book in a varied form.

Fixed assets. The items of value used in current operations that can be expected to generate revenue are referred to as *fixed assets*. Included in this category are such items as improved land, buildings, furniture and fixtures, machinery, tools, and transportation equipment—sometimes referred to collectively as *property, plant,* and *equipment*. These assets are normally not considered as items to be sold but rather as "tools of the trade" with which the manufactured product is produced, displayed, and transported. Most fixed assets are listed on the balance sheet as *cost minus accumulated depreciation*. For our typical manufacturing corporation the fixed assets are $605,000, as shown on the balance sheet under property, plant, and equipment. (See Table 1-1.)

Depreciation. As fixed assets grow older, they decrease in value due to ordinary wear and tear, action of the elements, or obsolescence. Since the balance sheet attempts to list everything owned by the corporation at current value, the value at which fixed assets are shown declines as the assets get older. When a fixed asset is acquired by the corporation, it is *not* charged as a business expense in the year it is purchased. Since a fixed asset is expected to last quite a few years, the company charges it as an expense, *a little bit at a time*, spread over the years it is supposed to be usable to the company. By way of analogy, assume you as an individual wanted to spread out a personal expense of $5,000 for a car. Instead of considering your car expense for one year to be $5,000 and nothing for each additional year you own the car, you might consider your expense to be $1,000 a year for five consecutive years, thus spreading out the expense. Spreading out the expense is what is done by a corporation! The amount by which the fixed assets are lowered each year is the portion of the cost of fixed assets charged as an expense for a given year; that portion is called *annual depreciation* and is listed as such.

Fixed assets may be depreciated by three principal methods:

1. Straight-line
2. Sum-of-years' digits
3. Double declining balance

When a fixed asset is purchased, the company determines how long the asset is expected to be used (*useful life*). It also determines the value that it expects to receive when the asset is scrapped (*salvage value*). The cost of the asset is considered to be the initial price *minus* the salvage value, because the salvage value will be received some time after the item is purchased. In most cases, this net cost figure is the amount depreciated over the item's useful life, not the full price paid. The simple equation is

$$\text{Net cost} = \text{Actual cost} - \text{Salvage value}$$

Depreciation for tax purposes is not computed in the same way as depreciation for financial accounting purposes.

In each of the following examples for determining the amount of depreciation, the fixed asset is purchased for $40,000;

it is expected to have a useful life of five years and a salvage value of $10,000.

$$\begin{aligned}\text{Net cost} &= \text{Actual cost} - \text{Salvage value}\\ &= \$40{,}000 - \$10{,}000\\ &= \$30{,}000\end{aligned}$$

Straight-line depreciation is the simplest and most commonly used method. To determine the amount of each year's depreciation, divide the *net* cost of the item (actual cost − salvage value) by the number of years of useful life.

$$\begin{aligned}\text{Annual depreciation} &= \frac{\text{Net cost}}{\text{Years of useful life}}\\ &= \frac{\$30{,}000}{5} = \$6{,}000\end{aligned}$$

Fixed assets are carried at *cost less accumulated depreciation.* At the end of the item's first year of use, the fixed asset section of the balance sheet shows:

Fixed Assets		
Cost	$40,000	
Accumulated depreciation	− 6,000	
		$34,000

The annual writeoff (depreciation) is the same in years 2 through 5. At the end of the second year, the *accumulated depreciation* is $12,000 ($6,000 from year 1 plus $6,000 from year 2), and the balance sheet shows:

Fixed Assets		
Cost	$40,000	
Accumulated depreciation	− 12,000	
		$28,000

By year 5, accumulated depreciation totals up to $30,000, and the asset has been "written down" to a carrying value of $10,000, its salvage value. The total picture in chart form is shown in Table 1-2.

Table 1-2. Straight-line depreciation.

Year		*Annual Depreciation*	*Accumulated Depreciation*	*Asset's Balance Sheet Value*
1	$30,000 ÷ 5 =	$6,000	$ 6,000	$34,000
2	30,000 ÷ 5 =	6,000	12,000	28,000
3	30,000 ÷ 5 =	6,000	18,000	22,000
4	30,000 ÷ 5 =	6,000	24,000	16,000
5	30,000 ÷ 5 =	6,000	30,000	10,000

Note that each year's depreciation is 20% of the net cost of the fixed asset since you are working with a useful life of 5 years (100% ÷ 5 = 20%).

Tax depreciation for federal income tax purposes is determined using the accelerated cost recovery system (ACRS). Taxpayers who are entitled to depreciate fixed assets and other capital equipment now have a choice of straight line and ACRS. In addition, the IRS also distinguishes between real property—what you and I would call real estate—and personal property, which you and I would call equipment such as automobiles, computers, and other similar items.

Sundry assets. This is a *miscellaneous* category, generally including unimproved land, prepaid expenses, deferred charges, and other items that are usually considered investments for the future. *Prepaid expenses* include payments for materials or services in *advance* of their receipt or use, such as early rent payments and insurance premiums. *Deferred charges* are used to "charge off" major expenses, such as those incurred in the introduction of a new product or the formation of a new subsidiary company.

Example:

A company spends $1,000,000 to purchase a ten-year lease in a given year. It includes $900,000 in the sundry assets section so that the *total assets* section shows a decline of only $100,000 that year; that is, the company considers $900,000 of the total amount spent as an asset in terms of having a lease. The balance sheet shows cash minus $1,000,000 and sundry assets plus $900,000. The company then reduces the $900,000 in each subsequent year for the next nine years so that it spreads out the $1,000,000 cost for the lease over a ten-year period.

Intangible assets. Included in this category are items of value that have no physical existence, such as patients, franchises, and goodwill. Such items are very difficult to quantify. Traditionally, intangibles are the last item shown on the asset side of the balance sheet.

Liabilities

Let us now turn our attention again to the *right* (debit) side of the balance sheet. Here are listed the corporation's debts and, further down, the stockholders' equity.

Current liabilities. Now shift to the *other* side of the balance sheet to look at the debts of the corporation that are scheduled for payment within one year. This quick comparison determines in a shorthand way, as accountants do, whether enough money is available to stay in business: Since current assets, at least in theory, represent the source from which current liabilities are paid, you want to know how the debts compare with the assets.

Current liabilities might include: *accounts payable,* the amount the company owes to its business creditors; *accrued expenses,* amounts owed to its salespeople in salaries and wages, interest on debt, and all other unpaid items; *accrued taxes,* federal, state, and local taxes owed, social security (FICA) deductions, and local government levies withheld from employees; *notes payable,* monies owed to banks, to other lenders, or on outstanding bonds that are due to be paid within the year. The current liabilities section of the balance sheet of our typical manufacturing corporation reads:

Accounts payable	$200,000
Accrued expenses	150,000
Accrued taxes	+ 50,000
Total current liabilities	$400,000

Relating current assets to current liabilities

Working Capital. The relationship between current assets and current liabilities is quite important. After all, a corporation must be able to keep current on its obligations. At a minimum, there should be an excess of current assets over current liabilities. This excess, called *working capital,* represents the amount of money that would be left from the current assets if all current liabilities were paid off. This important figure is derived by subtracting current liabilities from current assets, thus:

Working capital = Current assets − Current liabilities

A company's ability to meet its obligations is measured, at least in part, by the amount of its working capital. Working capital is also known as *net working capital* or *net current assets.*

Example:

Assets		*Liabilities*	
Cash	$ 75,000	Accounts payable	$200,000
Marketable securities	150,000	Accrued expenses	150,000
Accounts receivable	375,000	Accrued taxes	50,000
Inventory	+ 400,000		+
Total current assets	$1,000,000	Total current liabilities	$400,000

For our typical corporation:
Working capital = Current assets − Current liabilities
= $1,000,000 − $400,000
= $600,000

Current Ratio. Working with a *dollar* figure for working capital is difficult, especially when comparing one company with another. Dollars alone do not tell the whole story. A company may have only a modest amount of current liabilities, requiring a relatively small amount of working capital. Or its current liabilities may be very large, requiring many more dollars of working capital for safety's sake. Of primary importance, therefore, is the *proportion* by which current assets exceed current liabilities. This ratio, called the *current ratio,* is arrived at by dividing current assets by current liabilities. Thus:

$$\text{Current ratio} = \frac{\text{Current assets}}{\text{Current liabilities}}$$

Using the figures from the previous section on working capital:

$$\text{Current ratio} = \frac{\$1{,}000{,}000}{\$400{,}000} = 2.5$$

The current ratio, 2.5, means that our typical corporation can cover its current liabilities two and a half times over. In other words, for every dollar of current liabilities, it has 2½ dollars of current assets.

This current ratio is expressed in a variety of ways:

2.5 or 2½ or 2.5 × or 2½ times or
2.5 to 1 or 2½ to 1 or 2½/1

A "good" current ratio, for the typical manufacturing company, is 2 to 1 or higher. For a company with easily collectible receivables, like a public utility, a current ratio as low as 1 to 1 may be acceptable.

Quick Asset Ratio. An even more stringent test of a company's ability to meet its current obligations is the *quick asset ratio,* also called the *liquidity ratio* or *acid test ratio.* This ratio indicates the relationship between *quick assets* and current liabilities:

$$\text{Quick asset ratio} = \frac{\text{Quick assets}}{\text{Current liabilities}}$$

Example:

Using the ongoing figures for our corporation:

$$\begin{aligned}\text{Quick assets} &= \text{Total current assets} - \text{Inventory}\\ &= \$1{,}000{,}000 - \$400{,}000\\ &= \$600{,}000\end{aligned}$$

$$\text{Quick asset ratio} = \frac{\text{Quick assets}}{\text{Total current liabilities}}$$

$$= \frac{\$600{,}000}{\$400{,}000} = 1.5$$

The quick asset ratio of 1.5 indicates that our corporation had one and one half times the total of its short-term liabilities in quick assets alone. A "safe" quick asset ratio for the average manufacturing concern is 1 to 1. In other words, the corporation should have enough *quick* assets to pay off all the current liabilities.

Fixed liabilities. The fixed liabilities appear below current liabilities on the balance sheet. The major item, ordinarily, is the corporation's funded debt, usually outstanding bonds maturing more than one year in the future. This category may also include long-term promissory notes, bank loans, and other obligations.

Bonds are carried on the balance sheet at their par value. Keep in mind that the actual market prices of the company's own bonds *could* be either at a premium (above par) or at a discount (below par). The coupon rate and maturity date are usually indicated for each bond outstanding. The liabilities section of the balance sheet of our typical manufacturing corporation looks like this:

Liabilities	
Accounts payable	$200,000
Accrued expenses	150,000
Accrued taxes	+ 50,000
Total current liabilities	$400,000
Convertible debentures	+ 500,000
8% interest, due 19Z5	
Total liabilities	$900,000

Shareholders' Equity

The difference between the corporation's total assets and total liabilities is referred to as *stockholders' equity* or net worth. The final section of the balance sheet therefore represents the stockholders' equity, which is the stake that the stockholders, both common and preferred, have in their corporation. This section itemizes the amount of equity or *ownership* of the *true owners* of the corporation, the shareholders. The items in this category are

1. Preferred stock
2. Common stock
3. Paid-in capital (capital surplus)
4. Retained earnings (earned surplus)

Preferred stock. Like common stock, *preferred stock* is an equity security. Holders of such stock are considered to be owners of the corporation in contrast to bondholders who are considered creditors. Fittingly, preferred stock, which is ordinarily senior to common stock with respect to dividends and liquidation rights, is listed first. Such stock is "carried" *not* at its market value, but at its total par value, which in most instances is approximately equal to the amount the company received when the stock was first sold to the public. This listed figure usually approximates the amount that the preferred shareholders are entitled to receive if the company is dissolved. Most balance sheets detail information about any preferred stock listed, such as par value, convertibility (if any), dividend rate, and the number of shares authorized, issued, or outstanding.

Example:

Preferred stock	$75,000
6% Cumulative—$100 par	
Authorized, issued, and outstanding	
750 shares	

All 750 authorized shares of preferred stock are issued and outstanding.

750 Shares × $100 Par = $75,000 Book value
(Total par value)

Each share of $100 par preferred stock is entitled to a dividend at 6% of the par value each year. In other words, 6% of $100 equals a $6-per-share annual dividend. The balance sheet indicates that such dividends are cumulative. In the event that any preferred dividends are "skipped," the company may not pay dividends on the common stock until all back dividends on the preferred stock (arrearages) have been paid.

Common stock. The balance sheet shows the number of shares of common stock outstanding and their par value. At one time, par value represented the price at which the shares were first sold by the corporation, but that is no longer true. After the initial offering, par value has very little real significance. For our purposes, let's consider the amount shown on the balance sheet as "common stock" to represent the company's "seed money"—the amount of money, at *par value,* that the company first received from the sale of stock. In recent years, because stock transfer taxes are based on par values, corporations are assigning par value well below the price at which the shares are sold. Today, par value has little or no meaning in terms of the value of the shares.

Example:

Common stock $10 par	$300,000
Authorized, issued, and outstanding 30,000 shares	

Paid-in capital. This item, also called *capital surplus,* shows the amount of money the company received from the sale of shares of common stock to the public *in addition* to the par value.

Example:

Roxbury Manufacturing starts in business by selling 20,000 shares of stock at their original par value of $10 each. After this initial offering, the common stock section of the balance sheet shows $200,000. At least at this point in time, there is *no* paid-in capital. If, at a later date, the company issues another 10,000 shares at $20 each, the "extra" money received—the amount *over* par value—is indicated in the paid-in capital section of the balance sheet. The *basic* amount received ($10 par value) is added to the common stock account. The overage (the $10 which *exceeded* par value) goes into the paid-in capital account.

Common stock $10 par	$300,000
Authorized, issued, and outstanding 30,000 shares	
Paid-in capital (capital surplus)	100,000

This entry indicates that the owners of the business invested a total of $400,000 in common stock, of which $100,000 exceeded the total par value of $300,000. Generally, therefore, the *total* of these two accounts (common stock and paid-in capital) indicates the amount of money the company has received through the sale of its common stock to investors.

Retained earnings. Also known as *earned surplus*, this section shows the amount of profit that the company retains in the business *after* paying any dividends on the common stock. In a sense, retained earnings represent profits that have not yet been paid out to the common stockholders in the form of dividends.

Example:

A company is formed by selling a share of common stock at $100 per share to ten different people. The total amount collected is used to purchase goods at wholesale for subsequent resale. An early balance sheet is as follows:

Assets		*Liabilities*	
Inventory	$1,000		-0-
		Stockholders' Equity	
		Common stock $100 par	$1,000

At this point, total assets ($1,000 in inventory) equal total liabilities (zero) plus stockholders' equity ($1,000). The company then sells the inventory for a total of $2,000 and uses all the cash to purchase still more inventory.

Situation is now:

Assets		*Liabilities*	
Inventory	$2,000		-0-
		Stockholders' Equity	
		Common stock $100 par	$1,000
		Retained earnings	$1,000

The $1,000 earned profit, over and above its initial investment, appears in the retained earnings account.

The total of $2,000 under stockholders' equity, however, does not mean that the shareholders will receive $20 back for their $10 investments. These retained earnings are *not* cash: The profit has already been reinvested in additional inventory. Since the average balance sheet lists many items at *other than* their liquidation values, the chances of the shareholders' receiving cash equal to the net worth (shareholders' equity) portion of the balance sheet are small. Remember that shareholders' equity represents the amount that the stockholders *would* receive, *if* all assets were sold at the values at which they are carried on the balance sheet (book value) and *if* all liabilities were paid off at their balance sheet figures.

Example:

A company is formed through the sale of 1,000 shares of preferred stock at $100 per share and 500,000 shares of common stock at $1 per share. It uses some of the cash received to purchase machinery and raw materials, but it does not pay for all the items in full. Our balance sheet looks like this:

Assets		*Liabilities*	
Cash	$160,000	Accounts payable	$ 50,000
Inventory	+ 85,000		
		Stockholders' Equity	
Total current assets	$245,000	Preferred stock $100 par	100,000
Property, plant, and equipment	+ 405,000	Common stock $1 par	+ 500,000
Total assets	$650,000	Total liabilities and stockholders' equity	$650,000

At this early period of the company's development, it has no profits and therefore no retained earnings. But it operates successfully over time and increases its assets by $200,000 through sales and its liabilities by only $50,000. The difference between the value of the newly acquired items and the additional debt—$150,000—represents a "gain" for the company's owners. At least in theory, the stockholders are "worth" $150,000 more, a profit shown as retained earnings. Keep in mind that the $150,000 thus "earned" is spread out among various assets. To realize this sum in cash, the company would have to liquidate some assets. The balance sheet now looks like this:

Assets		*Liabilities*	
Cash	$ 80,000	Accounts payable	$ 60,000
Accounts receivable	135,000	Accrued expenses	+ 40,000
Inventory	+ 140,000	Total liabilities	$100,000
		Stockholders' Equity	
Total current assets	$355,000	Preferred stock $100 par	100,000
Property, plant and equipment	470,000	Common stock $1 par	500,000
Prepaid expenses	+ 25,000	Retained earnings	+ 150,000
Total assets	$850,000	Total liabilities and stockholders' equity	$850,000

The balance sheet balances! If the company decides to liquidate, it realizes $850,000 in cash from the sale of the assets, at least in theory. If it next pays off all obligations ($100,000 for all liabilities), it would have a total of $750,000 (less taxes on gain) to be distributed to the owners of the company, its shareholders. The preferred stockholders are entitled to receive par for their stock ($100,000), leaving $650,000 for the common stockholders. The common-stockholders' stake in the company can be found by adding together the common stock listing ($500,000), paid-in capital ($0), and retained earnings ($150,000). The sum of these three figures shows the *common* stockholders' equity.

On the other hand, let us assume the company decides to continue operations for future profits. To reward the stockholders, it decides to distribute a dividend. Since the term "retained earnings" means earning retained in the business, any distributed earnings in the form of dividends *decreases* retained earnings.

Balance Sheet Analysis

This section analyzes the balance sheet by looking at capitalization and book value. You have already compared current assets with current liabilities in the first section of this chapter.

Capitalization (Capital Structure-Invested Capital)

A company's *capitalization* is simply the sum of the balance sheet values for the corporation's bonds, preferred stock, and common stock. All *three* elements of the common stock are added: common stock, paid-in capital, and retained earnings. Thus, capitalization represents the money invested in the company by the *original* purchasers of the bonds, preferred stock, and common stock. It also reflects retained earnings, which is the capital that has *not* been paid out as dividends but that rather has been reinvested in the company. Capitalization thus tells us how a company got its funds and, secondarily, how it is handling them.

Capitalization is expressed in terms of three ratios, one each for bonds, common, and preferred stock. Each of these *capitalization ratios* represents the proportion of money collected through each vehicle to the *total* capitalization amount, assuming the total amount is equal to 100 percent.

In Table 1-3, Roxbury's capitalization is shown to be \$1,235,000, calculated as follows:

Bonds	+	Preferred stock	+	Common stock	+	Capital surplus	+	Retained earnings	=	Capitalization
\$500,000	+	\$75,000	+	\$300,000	+	\$100,000	+	\$260,000	=	\$1,235,000

The *bond ratio* is derived by dividing total capitalization into the funded debt, usually outstanding bonds maturing five years or more in the future.

$$\text{Bond ratio} = \frac{\text{Bonds}}{\text{Total capitalization}}$$

Example:

Set the balance sheet in Table 1-3.

$$\text{Bond ratio} = \frac{\$500{,}000}{\$1{,}235{,}000} = 0.405 \text{ or } 40.5\%$$

The *preferred stock* ratio is found by dividing total capitalization into the par value of the preferred stock.

$$\text{Preferred stock ratio} = \frac{\text{Preferred stock}}{\text{Total capitalization}}$$

$$= \frac{\$75{,}000}{\$1{,}235{,}000} = 0.061 \text{ or } 6.1\%$$

The *common stock ratio* is found by dividing total capitalization into *all three parts* of the common stock account.

$$\text{Common stock ratio} = \frac{\text{Common stock} + \text{Capital surplus} + \text{Retained earnings}}{\text{Total capitalization}}$$

$$= \frac{\$300{,}000 + \$100{,}000 + \$260{,}000}{\$1{,}235{,}000} = 0.534 \text{ or } 53.4\%$$

All three capitalization ratios add up to 100%.

Table 1-3.

BALANCE SHEET
ROXBURY MANUFACTURING COMPANY
December 31, 19Y3

Assets		*Liabilities*	
Cash	$ 75,000	Accounts payable	$ 200,000
Marketable securities	150,000	Accrued expenses	150,000
Accounts receivable	375,000	Accrued taxes	50,000
Inventory	400,000	Total current liabilities	$ 400,000
Total current assets	$1,000,000	Bonds—8%, due 19Z5	500,000
Property, plant and equipment	$ 605,000	Total liabilities	$ 900,000
Prepayments	20,000		
Intangibles	10,000	*Stockholders' Equity*	
		Preferred stock—6% ($100 par)	$ 75,000
		Common stock ($10 par)	300,000
		Capital surplus	100,000
		Retained earnings	260,000
		Total stockholders' equity	$ 735,000
Total assets	$1,635,000	Total liabilities and stockholders' equity	$1,635,000

There are certain capitalization ratio "yardsticks." For example, if the bond and preferred stock ratios combined exceed 33% of the total capitalization, an industrial company is generally considered by industry standards to have a highly leveraged capital structure. This condition may be considered speculative. Banks that use large amounts of borrowed money and public utilities that are very capital intensive will generally have debts far in excess of 50%. In this case, highly leveraged capitalization ratios are not speculative.

Figure 1-2. Breakdown of Roxbury's capitalization ratios.

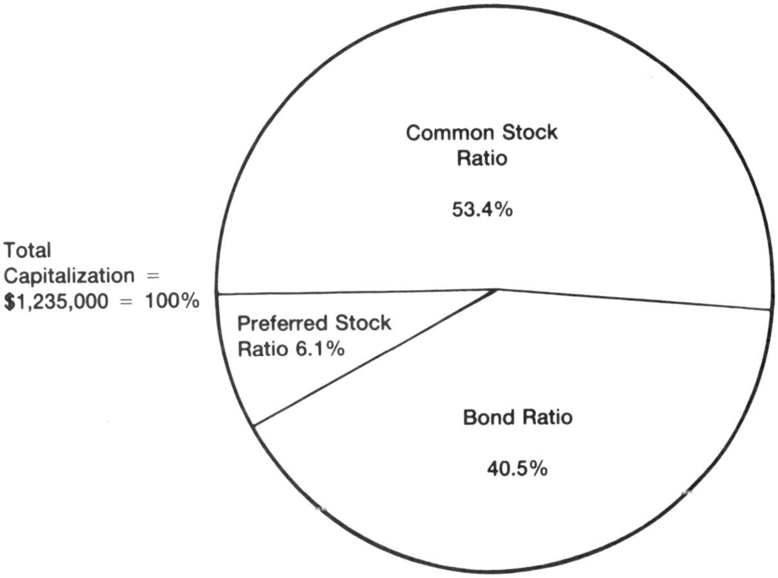

Book Value

The net tangible assets backing each share of common stock is known as *book value*. Calculating book value is easy: Since the balance sheet always shows the theoretical value of the common stockholders' equity (common stock + paid-in capital + retained earnings), just subtract the *intangibles* (if any) and divide by the number of outstanding common shares. The formula, applied to the sample balance sheet from the previous section on capitalization, is as follows:

$$\text{Book value} = \text{Common stock} + \text{Capital surplus} + \text{Retained earnings} - \text{Intangibles} \div \text{Number of shares of common stock outstanding}$$

$$= (\$300{,}000 + \$100{,}000 + \$260{,}000 - \$10{,}000) \div 30{,}000$$

$$= \$21.67 \text{ per share}$$

The book value per common share represents the amount of cash that would be available for each share of common stock if all the assets (excepting intangibles) are sold *at the values at which they are carried on the balance sheet* and if all liabilities, bondholders, and preferred stockholders are also "paid off." For our purposes, assume that the company must pay the bondholders and preferred stockholders the total par value of their securities as shown on the balance sheet. (However, accountants would most probably use the higher value between the total par value as shown on the balance sheet and the total market value based on the call price of their securities.)

A company's book value can be of great significance, despite the fact that, in the real world, liquidating the company at balance sheet values is virtually impossible. An increasing book value is generally considered to be a healthy sign for a company; a decreasing book value may indicate a weakening financial situation. To the securities analyst, whether a company's book value is *increasing* or *decreasing* is especially significant. While normally a company's *book value* and its *market value* bear no correlation (with some exceptions, mostly for financial service companies, such as insurance firms), these values do usually move in concert. For example, the "bid" shown in the newspaper for mutual funds is actually the book value of a share of the fund!

Summary Comment

The balance sheet reflects the company's financial position at a particular point in time—what it owns, what it owes, and what the shareholders are worth. It is like a snapshot of a subject "on the run"—the action is frozen, and the values are reflected as of the close of business on the balance sheet date.

While one balance sheet can be very revealing, a *series* of balance sheets, possibly covering the previous five or six years of operations, can be of even greater significance. The *trends* are extremely important. Is this year's current ratio better or worse than it has been over the last several years? Is the book value per common share going higher or lower? A study of the ratios *over a period of a few years* can reveal much about the company's future prospects.

Income Statement

Construction

Corporate annual reports traditionally show a balance sheet representing the corporation's financial picture on a particular day, usually the final day of the company's fiscal year. Most annual reports contain another financial statement in addition to the balance sheet—the income statement. The *income statement* (also known as the *profit and loss statement*), a statement of income and expenses usually over the *entire* year, shows how much the company made or lost during the year. A typical, simplified, income statement appears in Table 1-4. (Assume 30,000 shares of common stock outstanding.) Review that statement briefly before we examine it entry by entry.

Note: The tax rate used in these examples is 50%—for simplicity's sake. The tax rates may change but the principles of financial analysis remain the same.

Table 1-4.

STATEMENT OF INCOME
ROXBURY MANUFACTURING COMPANY
January 1–December 31, 19Y3

Net sales		$2,000,000
Cost of goods sold	–	1,590,000
Selling, general, and administrative expenses	–	154,000
Depreciation	–	56,000
Operating income		$ 200,000
Other income	+	7,500
Total income (EBIT)		$ 207,500
Interest on bonds	–	40,000
Taxes (50% rate)	–	83,750
Net income		83,750
Preferred dividends	–	4,500
Earnings available for common stock		$ 79,250

Net Sales. The *net sales* listing shows the amount of money that the company took in as the result of its manufacturing activities. "Net" reflects the fact that returned goods and discounts have been taken into account. Were this a nonmanufacturing enterprise (such as an airline or utility), this item might be called *operating revenues.*

Cost of Goods Sold. Think of this item as "factory" costs. It includes such factors as the costs of maintaining the manufacturing facilities, raw materials, and labor.

Selling, General, and Administrative Expenses. This item includes the cost of running the *sales* office of the company: office payroll, salespersons' commissions, advertising, and other such nonmanufacturing expenses.

Depreciation. The annual depreciation of the fixed assets appears in this category. You may consider this a *noncash expense* because the assets may have been paid for long ago but are being "charged off" in small increments each year.

Operating Income. Subtracting the operating costs from net sales gives operating income. We call it operating income because it is "factory" profit, and we have not yet considered other investments, rents, royalties, or income from sources other than manufacturing.

Other Income. The income the company receives as dividends and/or interest on the marketable securities it may own appears here. This item may also include other sources of income not related directly to the firm's operations, such as the sale of real estate (above book value) or rental income or unused land held for future use.

Total Income. Also known as *earnings before interest and taxes* (EBIT), this category is self-explanatory.

Interest on Bonds. Almost as self-explanatory is the amount of money that the corporation pays out each year to service its outstanding bonds.

Taxes. Federal and state income taxes, for our purposes, can be figured at roughly 50%. Thus, 50% of ($207,500 – $40,000) gives us $83,750 in taxes. (The 50% rate has been eliminated by the Tax Reform Act of 1986, but it is kept here because representation of taxes on the income statement remains the same—and 50% is a simple calculation.)

Net Income. This item is also known as *net profit*. All income and all expenses have now been weighed against each other. Only the stockholders remain to be satisfied.

Preferred Dividends. Note that the corporation deducted its bond interest payments *before* figuring its tax liability. Preferred dividend payments, however, are *not* a deductible item and do not lower taxes.

Earnings Available for Common Stock. Some call these net earnings, because they may be reinvested in the company and/or paid out to the common stockholders as cash dividends. Any amount *not* paid out as dividends, at least in theory, increases the retained earnings accounts.

Analysis

Just as balance sheet ratios measure a company's financial strength, so too do important income statement ratios reflect a company's state of affairs. In the following analyses, use the income statement shown in Table 1-4.

Expense Ratio (Operating Ratio). The *expense ratio*, also known as the *operating ratio*, is an excellent measure of corporate efficiency and should therefore be compared with the results of prior years. An increasing expense ratio could indicate a company's loss of control over cost.

$$\text{Expense ratio} = \frac{\text{Operating costs}}{\text{Net sales}}$$

$$= \frac{\text{Cost of goods sold} + \text{Selling, general, and administrative expenses} + \text{Depreciation}}{\text{Net sales}}$$

$$= \frac{\$1{,}590{,}000 + 154{,}000 + 56{,}000}{2{,}000{,}000} = 0.9 \text{ or } 90\%$$

Margin of Profit Ratio. The complement of the expense ratio, this ratio shows the percentage of the sales dollar *not* eaten up by operating costs. It is derived by dividing operating income by net sales.

$$\text{Margin of profit ratio} = \frac{\text{Operating income}}{\text{Net sales}}$$

$$= \frac{\$200{,}000}{2{,}000{,}000} = 0.10 \text{ or } 10\%$$

Note that the margin of profit ratio plus the operating ratio equals 100%.

Cash Flow. Realizing that one of the operating expenses—depreciation—is "artificial," you might ask how much actual cash the company has available before it pays out any money on preferred or common stock cash dividends. Depreciation is not actually "spent," at least not in the current year, and therefore cash flow is equal to the sum of net income and annual depreciation.

$$\text{Cash flow} = \text{Net income} + \text{Annual depreciation}$$

$$= \$83{,}750 + 56{,}000 = \$139{,}750$$

Interest Coverage. When examining a company you want to know how well it provides for the payment of interest on its outstanding bonds. To find out, divide total income (EBIT) by the interest on the bonds:

$$\text{Interest coverage} = \frac{\text{Total income (EBIT)}}{\text{Interest on bonds}}$$

$$= \frac{\$207{,}500}{\$40{,}000} = 5.2 \text{ times}$$

Interest coverage of over four times is usually considered a safe margin for the protection of a company.

Preferred Dividend Coverage. Another question is: How well are the preferred dividends covered by earnings? To find out, simply divide the net income by the preferred dividend requirements.

$$\text{Preferred dividend coverage} = \frac{\text{Net income}}{\text{Preferred dividends}}$$

$$= \frac{\$83{,}750}{\$4{,}500} = 18.6 \text{ times}$$

The calculation shows that the earnings cover the preferred dividends 18.6 times over.

Primary Earnings per Share. The earnings per share ratio is probably the most widely used measure of how well a company's fortunes are faring. As a result, it is also the most widely advertised measure—the "bottom line." This most important measurement is determined by dividing the net earnings (which is equal to net income minus preferred dividends) by the number of common shares outstanding.

$$\text{Primary earnings per share} = \frac{\text{Net earnings}}{\text{Number of shares of common stock outstanding}}$$

$$= \frac{\$79{,}250}{30{,}000} = \$2.64$$

The expression "earnings per share" has practically been replaced by the more modern expression *primary earnings per share.* The newer term reflects earnings as they would be if all "common stock equivalents" were issued and outstanding as common stock, thus diluting "ordinary" earnings per share by 3% or more. Common stock equivalents include warrants, stock options, and *certain* convertible bonds and convertible preferred shares. Common stock equivalents, if they exist, are clearly labeled. Corporations now report primary earnings per share so that the investing public does *not* have to refigure the "ordinary" earnings per share. Nor does the public have to determine which convertible items are considered common stock equivalents. When earnings are figured to include *all* possible additional shares of common stock, whether common stock equivalents or not, then such earnings are reported as "fully diluted."

Fully Diluted Earnings per Share. A corporation may have convertible bonds and/or convertible preferred stock outstanding. Investors realize that earnings per common share would be affected if such securities were to be converted. Fully diluted earnings reflect the per-share results as they *would* be if all *potential* common shares were added to the outstanding common stock. Under this method all warrants, stock options (options issued *privately* by the corporation), and convertible issues are considered as exchanged for additional common stock.

It is beyond the scope of this text to determine which common stock equivalents are included in the primary earnings per share and which are reserved for fully diluted earnings. Suffice it to say that fully diluted means just what it says: All potential common shares are included.

Table 1-5 contains the same basic figures as those in Table 1-4, but they have been recalculated on the assumption that the outstanding bonds are convertible and that they *have been* converted. The bonds are convertible into 20,000 additional shares of stock, and, again, the corporate tax rate is 50%. Assuming that the convertible bonds are exchanged for common stock, the interest on bonds entry disappears. With that deduction of $40,000 gone, the income *before* tax rises from $167,500 to $207,500. At a tax rate of 50%, the tax burden under fully diluted conditions is $103,750 instead of $83,750, thus *raising* net earnings from $79,250 to $99,250. Again assuming that the bonds are converted, we must take into account the additional shares thus created. If 30,000 shares were outstanding before the conversion, then the fully diluted earnings figure is calculated by dividing the "new" net earnings by 50,000 shares of common stock (30,000 outstanding + 20,000 after conversion). Of course, all these changes affect the "ordinary" earnings per share of the corporation:

$$\text{Fully diluted earnings per share} = \frac{\text{Earnings available for common stock}}{\text{Number of shares of common stock outstanding after conversion}}$$

$$= \frac{\$99{,}250}{50{,}000} = \$1.99$$

Table 1-5.

INCOME STATEMENT
(Fully Diluted)
ROXBURY MANUFACTURING COMPANY
January 1–December 31, 19Y3

Net sales		$2,000,000
Cost of goods sold	–	1,590,000
Selling, general, and administrative expenses	–	154,000
Depreciation	–	56,000
Operating income	$	200,000
Other income	+	7,500
Total income (EBIT)	$	207,500
Taxes (39% rate)	–	103,750
Net income	$	103,750
Preferred dividends	–	4,500
Earnings available for common stock	$	99,250

Other Analyses

Payout Ratio

Most corporations pay out at least a part of their net earnings to common shareholders through cash dividends. The percentage of earnings so distributed is known as the *payout ratio.* As a rough guideline, growth companies may be expected to have low payout ratios (10%), compared with a typical manufacturing company payout of approximately 50%. This ratio is derived by dividing the total common dividends paid by the total net earnings, which is net income minus preferred dividends.

$$\text{Payout ratio} = \frac{\text{Common stock dividends}}{\text{Net income} - \text{Preferred dividends}}$$

Example:

A corporation with $1,000,000 in net income pays $50,000 in preferred dividends and $375,000 in common stock dividends. Its payout ratio is

$$\text{Payout ratio} = \frac{\$375{,}000}{\$1{,}000{,}000 - \$50{,}000} = 0.395 \text{ or } 39.5\%$$

Yield on Common Stock

To determine *current yield,* divide a security's annual dividends (or interest) by its current market price.

$$\text{Current yield} = \frac{\text{Annual dividend rate}}{\text{Market price}}$$

Generally speaking, companies with greater prospects for growth have lower yields, because growth companies usually reinvest most of their earnings in their own businesses.

Example:

A common stock has a current market price of 42 and pays annual dividends of $1.80. Its current yield is 4.3%, calculated thus:

$$\text{Current yield} = \frac{\$1.80}{\$42} = 0.043 \text{ or } 4.3\%$$

Inventory Turnover Ratio

We can measure how effectively the company is selling its products by determining how often its supply of inventory is manufactured and sold. Of the several methods for calculating this ratio, the simplest (and least accurate) is as follows:

$$\text{Inventory turnover ratio} = \frac{\text{Net sales}}{\text{Year-end inventory}}$$

This method is presented because it is simple and workable. Other methods use the cost of goods sold, rather than net sales, as the numerator and the *average* inventory, rather than year-end inventory, as the denominator. As a general guide, a "good" inventory turnover ratio for an average manufacturing company is 6 times per year.

Example:

A corporation's annual report shows net sales of \$14,000,000 (on the income statement) and an inventory of \$2,682,000 (on the balance sheet). The inventory turnover is 5.2 times, determined as follows:

$$\text{Inventory turnover ratio} = \frac{\$14{,}000{,}000}{\$2{,}682{,}000} = 5.2 \text{ times}$$

Price-Earnings Ratio

The *price-earnings (P/E)* ratio is one of the most significant measurements. It is also called the price multiple. It relates a corporation's profitability to the market price of its common shares, thus affording a measure of the *relative* "expensiveness" of the common stock. Typically, growth stocks have high P/E ratios; companies with poorer prospects sell at lower earnings multiples. To obtain this ratio, divide the market price of the company's common stock by the earnings per share:

$$\text{Price-earnings ratio} = \frac{\text{Current market price of the common stock}}{\text{Common stock earnings per share}}$$

Example:

Company A earned \$1.04 per share. Its common stock is selling in the open market at 23¼.

$$\text{Price-earnings (P/E) ratio} = \frac{\$23.25}{\$1.04} = 22.4$$

Each share of common stock is selling for about 22 times the amount of earnings generated by each share.

Return on Equity

An informative measure of management's efficiency is the *return on equity*, derived by dividing net income by shareholders' equity. (Shareholders' equity is the sum of preferred stock, common stock, paid-in capital, and retained earnings.)

$$\text{Return on equity} = \frac{\text{Net income}}{\text{Shareholders' equity}}$$

Example:

Refer to Tables 1-3 and 1-4. For a corporation with net income of $83,750 and shareholders' equity of $735,000:

$$\text{Return on equity} = \frac{\$83{,}750}{\$735{,}000} = 0.114 \text{ or } 11.4\%$$

Return on Invested Capital

A measure of how well the company is utilizing its entire capitalization is the *return on invested capital.* The formula is

$$\text{Return on invested capital} = \frac{\text{Net income} + \text{Interest on debt}}{\text{Total capitalization (invested capital)}}$$

Example:

Again using the balance sheet and the income statement in Tables 1-3 and 1-5, you can calculate the interest on bonds ($40,000) by multiplying the coupon rate, 8%, by the total par value, $500,000. After that, simply fill in the formula:

$$\text{Return on invested capital} = \frac{\$83{,}750 + \$40{,}000}{\$1{,}235{,}000}$$
$$= 10.0\%$$

"Financial Reasoning" Problems

Let us apply our knowledge of accounting by following the effects of a managerial decision on the corporation's financial statements. In each instance, we shall trace the course of events, noting the impact on the company's assets, liabilities, shareholders' equity, and several of the more common ratios.

Stock Splits. When a common stock is split, the *number of shares* of common stock *increases* and the *par value* of the common stock *decreases* in the same proportion.

Example:

A "beginning" common stockholders' equity before a split consists of:

Common stock: at $.40 par value, 600,000 shares authorized, 300,000 shares issued and outstanding	$120,000
Paid-in capital	40,000
Retained earnings	+ 135,000
Total common stockholders' equity	$295,000

In a 2-for-1 split, the number of issued and outstanding shares doubles (from 300,000 to 600,000) and the par value is halved (from $.40 to $.20). The *new* common stockholders' equity looks like this after the split:

Common stock: at $.20 par value, 600,000 shares authorized, 600,000 shares issued and outstanding	$120,000
Paid-in capital	40,000
Retained earnings	+ 135,000
Total common stockholders' equity	$295,000

Because of the 2-for-1 split, the par value changes from $.40 to $.20 but the number of outstanding shares doubles. No *real* change occurs in the balance sheet! The common stock account *still* comes out to $120,000:

300,000 shares @ $.40 per = $120,000 *and*

600,000 shares @ $.20 par = $120,000

Certainly a greater number of shares are outstanding; but, at least in theory, the shareholders are no better off (and no *worse* off!) than they were before the split. Traditionally a flurry of buying follows a stock split. The market theory is that the stock will sell better at a lower price after the split because it is more "marketable." People tend to favor lower-priced issues even though a lower-priced security bears no more intrinsic value than a higher-priced security. The actual net effect of the split is nil, because the book values on the balance sheet do not change.

Stock Dividends. Stock dividends result in the issuance of additional shares, but the par value of the common stock does *not* change.

Example:

Using the same stockholders' equity statement from the previous section, let us restate the figures as they appear after the payment of a 30% stock dividend, that is, 90,000 shares (30% of 300,000):

Common stock: at \$.40 par value, 600,000 shares authorized, 390,000 shares issued and outstanding	\$156,000
Paid-in capital	40,000
Retained earnings	+ 99,000
Total common stockholders' equity	\$295,000

Compare the previous figures with these. The *total* equity does not change. Nevertheless, the common stock account increases by \$36,000 (from \$120,000 to \$156,000), and the retained earnings account decreases by \$36,000 (from \$135,000 to \$99,000). Our common stockholders are no richer or poorer, but the balance sheet changes in that the common stock account increases at the expense of the retained earnings account.

Smaller stock dividends (generally less than 25%) are treated differently: Paid-in capital may also be increased, and the market value of the common stock may be taken into account.

Declaration of Cash Dividends. For the remainder of this section use the balance sheet in Table 1-6.

A board of directors announces a cash dividend payment of \$0.50 per common share approximately two months before the dividends are actually paid out to the stockholders. As a result, the Doktabessie Corporation balance sheet undergoes changes

Table 1-6.

DOKTABESSIE CORPORATION
BALANCE SHEET
June 30, 19Y3

Assets		*Liabilities*	
Cash	$ 165,000	Accounts payable	$ 166,000
Marketable securities	18,000	Accrued taxes	70,000
Accounts receivable	260,000	Notes payable	84,000
Inventory	455,000	Accrued expenses	151,000
Total current assets	$ 898,000	*Total current liabilities*	471,000
		First mortgage bonds: 7½% due 1/1/94	500,000
		Total liabilities	$ 971,000
Property, plant, and equipment:		*Stockholders' Equity*	
Land	$ 75,000	Preferred stock ($100 par, 1,000 shares authorized, issued, and outstanding)	100,000
Buildings	506,000		
Equipment	89,000		
Machinery	164,000		
	834,000	Common stock ($25 par, 12,000 shares authorized, issued, and outstanding)	300,000
Less: Accumulated depreciation	− 217,000		
Net property, plant, and equipment	$ 617,000	Paid-in capital	58,000
		Accumulated retained earnings	290,000
Intangibles	204,000	*Total stockholders' equity*	748,000
Total assets	$1,719,000	Total liabilities and stockholders' equity	$1,719,000

between the time the corporation declares a cash dividend and the time it actually pays it.

The declaration of a cash dividend creates a current liability of $6,000 ($0.50 × 12,000 common shares). Current liabilities must be adjusted to include this *new* obligation, which must be paid out within the next year. An item (probably labeled "dividends payable'') is added to current liabilities, raising the total by $6,000 to $477,000. Where does this $6,000 come from? From the accumulated retained earnings! As you will recall, retained earnings may be thought of as unpaid dividends. Management has now decided to pay some of this accumulated value to the common stockholders. So we now *reduce* retained earnings by $6,000 (from $290,000 to $284,000). The overall ''change'' on the balance sheet is an increase in current liabilities and a decrease in retained earnings.

Since current assets remain the same while current liabilities have increased, several ratios are adversely affected. The dividend reduces the:

- Working capital (net current assets)
- Quick asset ratio (acid test ratio)
- Current ratio

Logically, the dividend also reduces the common stockholders' stake in the company, because part of their accumulated profits is paid out to them! Understandably, the value remaining after they receive their dividends is reduced by the amount of such dividends.

Payment of Cash Dividends. When the Doktabessie Corporation actually pays out the cash dividends, the company is dispersing cash in the amount of the current liability established for such payment. The following changes occur:

- *Cash* decreases and
- *Dividends payable* disappears

Cash is now $159,000 ($165,000 − $6,000), and total current assets decreases to $892,000. The total current liabilities entry goes back to $471,000. Note where the *ultimate* change occurs: Cash is reduced, and the payment comes from retained earnings! The shift was done in two stages:

1. When the dividend is *declared,* retained earnings decrease and current liabilities increase.

2. When the dividend is *paid*, cash decreases and that particular current liability disappears.

Retiring Debt at a Discount. If the corporation's bonds are trading in the open market at a discount, the management may possibly elect to buy them back. Thus they can retire the obligation at a bargain rate rather than pay the holders full par value at maturity.

The Doktabessie Corporation buys $50,000 of its own bonds in the open market for a total of $40,000. The balance sheet changes as follows:

- Cash decreases by $40,000.
- Total current assets and *total* assets also decrease by the same amount.
- Working capital, quick assets, current ratio, and acid test (quick asset) ratio all decline because current assets are reduced while current liabilities remain unchanged.
- Bonds are reduced by $50,000.
- Stockholders' equity *increases* by $10,000 because we have reduced assets (cash) by $40,000 and liabilities by $50,000. Thus we gain $10,000, which is reflected in increased net worth. Since the company has "paid off" a $50,000 debt at a cost of only $40,000, the stockholders have gained!

While the *cash* picture is not as good as it was and although some ratios have declined, the overall effect is "good" in that the stockholders' equity increases.

Retiring Debt at a Premium. The Doktabessie Corporation elects to retire some of its bonds through the exercise of a "call" provision. An early price is usually above par, so our corporation is paying a premium price for the early retirement of part of its debt. Calling $100,000 par value of bonds at a price of 102 ($1,020 per bond) costs the corporation $102,000. The management is eliminating a $100,000 debt (liabilities), but the cost is $102,000 in cash (assets)! It pays the "extra" $2,000 from retained earnings.

Note the effects on the corporation's balance sheet. Cash decreases from $165,000 to $63,000. Current assets, of course, now total only $796,000 and total assets, $1,617,000. On the liabilities side of the balance sheet, the bonds go down from $500,000 to $400,000 and total liabilities from $971,000 to $871,000. Retained earnings reflect the $2,000 "loss" the company suffered and decreases from $290,000 to $288,000. The "new" balance sheet shows:

Total assets	=	Total liabilities	+	Net worth (Stockholders' equity)
$1,617,000	=	871,000	+	746,000

The cash spent also adversely affects working capital, current ratio, quick assets, and the liquidity (quick asset) ratio.

Sale and Lease-Back of Fixed Assets. The Doktabessie Corporation decides to raise cash by selling and leasing back some of its expensive machinery. The corporation sells machinery carried on its balance sheet at $30,000. This sale reduces the property, plant, and equipment from $617,000 to $587,000. At the same time it increases current assets from $898,000 to $928,000 because cash goes up to $195,000.

The effect on the balance sheet depends on whether the sale is made at a price greater or lower than the value at which the assets are carried on the balance sheet. Essentially, if the sale is made for more than the book value of the asset, the corporation makes a "profit." For sales of assets at prices below their book value, the corporation sustains a "loss." In essence, the company is exchanging a *fixed* asset (machinery) for a *current* asset (cash). This shift increases current assets at the expense of fixed assets and thus improves working capital and the current ratio. Since current assets increase while the current liabilities remain the same, the corporation's working capital increases (current assets − current liabilities). The current ratio (current assets ÷ current liabilities) also improves. In short:

- *If the asset is sold at a profit, total* assets increase, and the increase is also reflected in the retained earnings account.
- *If the asset is sold at a loss, total* assets decrease (by the difference between the book value and the sale price of the asset sold).

The decrease also lowers the retained earnings account by the same amount.

Concluding Comments

This chapter explains, in simple fashion, the construction of the two most basic financial statements, the balance sheet and the income statement. You should now understand the basic purpose of each document and be able to examine such statements with an eye toward evaluating a company's future prospects.

These documents detail a corporation's financial position and its earnings. They show the end result of the management's efforts to run a profitable business. Knowing how to interpret this information is absolutely essential to a professional analysis of the company—the key ingredient to enable you to decide whether to buy or sell the company's securities.

Asset Plays–Definition and Categories

CHAPTER 2

How the Current Investment Environment Affects Individual Investors

To better understand asset plays, you should first understand the current investment environment. Institutionalization is the key word in today's stock market. In the past, individual investors were the driving force in the market. Typically, individual investors bought and sold in lots of 100 shares or less and were the main source of business and income for the investment community. For the most part, such investors were long-term holders of a stock once they made a decision to buy and based their decision on the comparatively limited amount of financial information provided them by their broker, investment adviser, or the company itself.

Today's market differs considerably from the market of the past. Pension plans, mutual funds, insurance companies, and trust departments of banks account for more and more of the trading activity in the marketplace. There are a number of large blocks traded on any given day as well as an ever-increasing overall volume of trading. Whereas in the past 100 share lots were considered the norm, today it is not uncommon to see blocks of 100,000 or more shares traded, even in relatively unknown companies. Also, 100 million shares or more are traded every day in the stock market.

For the most part, the brokerage community has shifted its focus from the individual investor to the institutional buyer and seller of stock, leaving the individual investor to his or her own devices. Also, recent studies have shown that market cycles are more volatile, as institutional investors are quicker to sell or buy depending on the quarterly results, as compared to individual investors who typically are long-term holders of stock. Further, the recent waves of mergers and acquisitions and the abuse of inside information by major figures in the investment world may leave the individual investor questioning whether there is a place for him or her in today's stock market.

Where does this institutionalization of the stock market leave the individual investor? Such an investor must consider whether he or she wishes to operate in the mainstream, or look for a special area of the stock market not dominated by institutions. *Asset plays are one such special niche.*

Why Asset Plays Offer an Attractive Alternative to the Mainstream

There are a number of reasons why asset plays can offer a special "niche" in the marketplace. First, for the most part, institutions are unwilling to spend the time and effort to find such situations as asset plays and prefer to concentrate on the IBMs of the investment world. Second, because institutions are typically run by committees, it is easier to suggest investing in a stock known and followed by many professional investors instead of recommending an unknown stock. This "herd instinct" prevents many institutional investors from investing in asset plays. Third, because many institutional investors are heavily regulated, in particular, pension plans and bank trust departments, they are, in many cases, precluded from investing in asset plays. Finally, and probably the greatest bar to institutions investing in asset plays, is the fact most institutional investors require that they be able to accumulate and dispose easily of large blocks of stock without disturbing the market, that is, without causing a rapid rise or decline in the price of the particular stock. Institutional investors require that the stocks they invest in be "liquid," meaning that they have millions of shares outstanding and in the public hands so that they can be easily traded. All of these factors serve to prevent institutional domination of the market for asset plays, thereby making them one of the few arenas in which the individual investor can operate freely.

How to Realize a Profit from Asset Plays

At this point, you are probably asking yourself two questions. First, what kind of return can you expect to earn from investing in asset plays? Second, who will buy the asset plays you have invested in?

Chapter 7 explores the question of what rate of return you can expect from investing in asset plays. Typically, the return should be better than 50% per year and should be in line with the greater risk and effort entailed in identifying and investing in asset plays. Also, the return and risk associated with the various categories and types of asset plays vary, as you will see later in this chapter. Finally, it is best to select a number of asset plays when you invest rather than a single one as the payout period (the number of years until the stock reaches a defined selling price) will vary, and you will not be able to predict with absolute certainty how fast or slow a given asset play will appreciate. Also, asset-play investing is not geared to producing a fixed or defined return as would come from a bank certificate of deposit, corporate bond, and so forth.

Who will be the buyer of an asset play you "discovered" and invested in? Typically as an asset play matures and receives greater recognition, institutional investors will find it acceptable to recommend and invest in the particular situation. The advantage you as an individual investor have over the professional investor is that you can invest in an asset play early and have institutional/professional investors take you out of the situation at the point where it is recognized and probably fully priced. Using the proceeds of one asset play you can move on to another yet "undiscovered" asset play. Even if you are not taken out of the asset play by institutional/professional investors, as the company's earnings and assets grow the price of the stock should appreciate in line with its improved prospects. Also, in recent years many asset plays have been acquired by larger companies or have been the subject of a leveraged buyout. Thus, there are a number of ways in which you can realize a profit from investing in asset plays.

How to Identify Asset Plays

Asset plays come in a variety of sizes and shapes. The one common thread running through all asset plays is *the buying of assets at a discount.*

What does buying assets at a discount mean? It means identifying those stocks whose price does not reflect the underlying value of the company's assets. It means identifying so-called "hidden assets." Hidden assets come in a variety of forms, including cash or cash equivalents, marketable securities, and real estate.

Also, asset plays are traded in a variety of marketplaces. While some asset plays can be found on the New York Stock Exchange, the number is relatively small because such a listing serves to attract the interest of professional and institutional investors. Although a greater number of asset plays can be found on the American Stock Exchange and the various regional stock exchanges, it is in the over-the-counter (OTC) market where the greatest number of asset plays are to be found.

Furthermore, asset plays are not restricted to companies of a particular size or industry. While some large companies may be selling at a discount from their underlying assets, a greater number of asset plays are to be found among the small capitalized companies traded primarily in the over-the-counter market. Asset plays exist in all industries, but many asset plays are companies operating in a specialized business or market niche. The special niche they occupy might range from being the leading manufacturer of ice cream cones to a major manufacturer of burial caskets.

Asset plays tend to sell at a low price to earnings ratio (P/E), at least until they are discovered by professional investors. Studies have shown that historically low price to earnings stocks have provided a greater return to investors over time when compared to the return produced by investing in high price to earnings stocks. One of the reasons given for this pattern is that a stock selling at a high P/E ratio is most likely to have a large institutional following whose buying resulted in its high P/E ratio. In other words, the stock has already been "discovered" by professional investors. High P/E stocks tend to have volatile price movements because institutions are quicker to liquidate a stock at the first sign of a downturn in the rate of growth or in earnings. On the other hand, low P/E stocks generally have less volatile price movements because they are held in "strong hands," that is, insiders and individual investors who for the most part do not turn over their holdings that frequently. In many ways, investing in asset plays is safer because they typically sell at a low P/E ratio and are less likely to be impacted by changes in institutional sentiment.

Categories of Asset Plays

Perhaps the best way to grasp what asset-play investing is all about is to break asset plays down into various categories and describe the key characteristics of each category. This will help you understand such things as what sources of information you can utilize to identify asset plays, what numerical ratios and techniques are useful in analyzing potential asset plays once you have identified them, and who the key players are—both individual and institutional investors—who are active in asset-play investing.

Closely Held Companies

Closely held companies represent the greatest source for potential asset plays. While some closely held companies are listed on the New York and American Stock Exchanges, most are traded in the over-the-counter market. The over-the-counter market is divided into two worlds: those securities traded exclusively via the Pink Sheets (a trade publication that will be described shortly), and an automated system called NASDAQ, which was developed for trading over-the-counter stocks. Starting with a few hundred stocks, NASDAQ (National Association of Securities Dealers Automated Quotation) has expanded to include more than 4,500 stocks. NASDAQ has added liquidity and exposure to the over-the-counter market and, while less so than among stocks traded exclusively via the Pink Sheets, some potential asset plays can be found among NASDAQ listed stocks.

In identifying potential asset plays and, in particular, closely held companies, the Pink Sheets are probably the first source. Pink Sheets (so called because of the pink paper on which they are printed) are published daily by the National Quotation Bureau, a privately owned corporation. The Pink Sheets list in alphabetical order all over-the-counter stocks along with such vital information as the names of the brokerage firms interested in trading the particular stock (referred to as market makers). When available the Pink Sheets also list bid and asked prices representing the price at which the brokerage firm will buy and sell the stock respectively, and weekly volume. Thus, the Sheets are in effect the bible for any individual or professional investor seeking to buy or sell an over-the-counter stock. In 1986, approximately 15,000 stocks were traded exclusively via the Pink Sheets, which included a number of closely held companies representing potential asset plays.

How does a company get its shares traded in the over-the-counter market? For many companies, the over-the-counter market is the first place their stock is traded after they go public via a stock offering. Once traded in the over-the-counter market, a company and its stock can follow a number of routes. Some stocks will decline and languish in the over-the-counter market or wind up bankrupt. Other companies will grow and expand in terms of assets and earnings. In many cases, the managements of such successful companies will decide to have their stock listed on the American or New York Stock Exchange in the hope of obtaining greater exposure and price appreciation for their companies' stocks. As an "asset-play" investor, you will be most interested in those companies that, while successful and well managed, decide not to move to one of the exchanges but rather choose to remain traded exclusively in the Pink Sheets.

There are a number of reasons why a successful and well-managed company might choose to remain a Pink Sheet number. One reason might be that the company's management is more concerned with the business as opposed to how its stock performs in the marketplace. Management might recognize the company's potential for future growth and be unwilling to give up control, but would rather have its stock closely held by management and local investors instead of large institutional investors based in major cities such as Boston and New York. In many cases, the management of these asset-rich companies rests in the hands of a family and is closely identified with a particular region or town. Such companies are not eager to have outsiders having a say in how their business is run. Likewise, many such companies restrict the number of shares they have outstanding so as to discourage institutional ownership of their stock. Because of these factors, many of these closely held stocks represent real buys in terms of the assets and earning power you are getting for the price you pay for a share of stock. In later chapters of this book you will learn how to identify and purchase such closely held stocks; such closely held companies span a variety of industries, regions of the country, and sell at prices ranging from $2 per share to $200 or more per share of stock.

Example:

Consider, for example, Squire Industries ("Squire").*

Exhibit 2-1 shows the relevant information from Standard & Poor's describing the key characteristics of Squire. After reviewing the data, you can see that the company operated 66 parking lots (6 owned and 60 leased) as of February 28, 19Y6 in New York, New Jersey, Pennsylvania, and Ohio.

*Examples are based on actual companies, but almost all case names and some facts have been slightly altered for illustrative purposes. No one should interpret the sample companies as representing or endorsing any real investments.

Further, Squire fits into the category of a closely held company since it had only 383 shareholders as of February 28, 19Y6 and its officers and directors (principally the Harvester family) controlled 56.7% of its 1,148,801 outstanding shares as of May 1, 19Y6.

The balance sheet is the key factor that has to be considered before any determination can be made as to whether a particular closely held company represents an asset play. In later chapters of this book the key financial ratios will be explained further, but by reviewing Squire's balance sheet as of February 28, 19Y6 you can see that the company is not cash rich. Hidden assets come in a variety of forms with undervalued real estate representing perhaps the second most important category after cash and cash equivalents. Squire, through its ownership and lease rights to centrally located real estate (such as parking lots), appears to represent an opportunity to buy prime property at a discount. To confirm this conclusion you would have to look further into the company and from its most recent annual report and 10K find out where specifically the parking lots are located; how long the company has owned or leased the lots; the terms of its leases; and whether the company intends to and is capable of converting the parking lots to alternative and more profitable uses, such as commercial and/or residential dwellings. From a reading of the company's recent press releases you would learn that Squire's management is aware of the hidden value its real estate holdings represent and is moving to capitalize on it while still operating its profitable parking lot operations.

Another factor that has to be considered in the case of any closely held company is whether there is stock available in the marketplace. Squire is traded in the over-the-counter market and listed on NASDAQ. In some ways it is atypical of a closely held company in that there is an active market for its stock and because of this it should be easy to both buy and sell its stock. However, institutional investors would not be interested in Squire because of the small number of shares held in public hands. The large position held by management would in all likelihood discourage a potential acquisition of the company unless management decided to "cash out" its ownership via an outright sale or leverage buyout. Also, the company's stock is currently selling at $13 per share representing a price to earnings ratio of 14 to 1. Thus it appears that the market is pricing the stock on the basis of its existing business (parking lots) as opposed to the value of its underlying assets.

To summarize, Squire fits into the category of a closely held company and represents an asset play based on the following factors: (1) a limited number of shares outstanding held by a small number of investors; (2) control of the company resting in the hands of a few major investors; (3) undervalued assets (in this example, it is real estate whose value is not recognized by the market); and (4) an active management that is seeking to capitalize on this hidden asset by developing it and converting it to more profitable use.

Exhibit 2-1.

Squire Industries, Inc.

CAPITALIZATION (Feb. 28 'Y6)

LONG TERM DEBT—$6,402,711, excl. $1,504,103 curr. portion.

STOCK—	Auth. Shs.	Outstg. Shs.
Common $0.01 par........	*2,000,000	1,148,801

*Incl. 15,183 optioned to employees, with 70,730 for future grants.

LINE OF CREDIT provides up to $6,500,000 to Aug. 1, 19X6, with int. at ½% above prime—$2,916,711 taken down at Feb. 28, 19Y6.

CORPORATE BACKGROUND

Company, at Feb. 28, 19Y6, operated 66 parking lots and garages (6 owned and 60 leased) in NYC (36), N.J. (9), Cleveland, Ohio (3), and Philadelphia (18), and managed 14 lots and garages in NYC (6), N.J. (3), Phila. (3), Mass. and Md. Aggregate parking capacity was apx. 29,220 cars. Co. also operated a car wash in Phila. and a self-service gas station in NYC.

In fiscal 19Y6, parking service revenue accounted for 89.8% of total revenues (91.6% in fiscal 1985), and service station revenue 10.2% (8.4%).

SUBSIDIARIES—wholly owned—
Brewack Realty Corp.
Gailgal Holding Corp.
Leslie Craig Corp.
Laujan Garage Corp.
26 Mad Corp.
3rd & 11th Parking Corp.
King Green Parking Corp.
Greenwhich-Houston Parking Corp.
Marbern Industries, Inc.
Reboy Development Corp.
Second Avenue Commercial, Inc.
Truban Realties, Ltd.
Scott 215 Corp.
Institutional Parking Management Inc.
306 W. 44 Corp.
211 W. 56th St. Garage Corp.
6 & 30 Garage Corp.
29 & 6 Garage Corp.
Mileau Realty Corp.
Medical Parking Management, Inc.
Eighty Second and First Parking Corp.
Jarose Properties, Inc.
73-83 Third Avenue Corp.
8 + 50 Parking Corp.
Elzab Development Corp.
8th Ave. Properties Corp.
47th Street Parking, Inc.
S.P. Parking, Inc.
643 Broad Street Corp.
Medical Parking Management of New Jersey, Inc.
13th & Euclid Corp.
S.I.I. Corp.
12th & Sansom Parking Corp.
23rd & Arch Parking Corp.
Broad Newark Corp.
303 W. 46th St. Corp.
Union Square West Corp.
161 St. Parking Corp.

Company also has numerous other subsidiaries with the name Squire or Squire Corp. in their titles.

Exhibit 2-1 continued

CAPITAL EXPENDITURES, Yrs. End. Apx. Feb. 28: Thou. $
19Y6...... 3,303 19Y5...... 1,219 19Y4...... 2,127

EMPLOYEES—Apr. 20, 19Y6: 798 full time; 143 part-time.

INCORPORATED in N.Y. in Mar., 1968, as Squire Plus, Inc.; present title adopted in 1969.

CHAIRMAN & CHIEF EXEC OFFICER, Lowell Harvester; PRES & CHIEF OPER OFFICER, Sanford Harvester; EXEC V-P, Brett Harvester; V-Ps, Jack Beny, Dan Jeremitsky, John Hogan, Steven Chiappa; SECY & TREAS, A.D. Levey.

DIRECTORS—Lowell Harvester, Sanford Harvester, A.D. Levey, D.R. Schein.

OFFICE—111 Berg Ave., Jersey City, NJ 07306 (Tel.: 201-555-0090). ANNUAL MEETING—As set by directors.

STOCK DATA

STOCKHOLDERS—Feb. 28, 19Y6, 383 (of record). May 1, 19Y6, officers and directors owned or controlled 56.7% of the Com., including 24.6% by Lowell Harvester and 21.1% by Sanford Harvester.

TRANSFER AGENCY & REGISTRAR—Registrar & Transfer Co., Cranford, N.J.

PRICE—OTC bid (NASDAC: SQAI):

19Y5	9½	5½	†19Y4	7	4½
*19Y3	13½	8¼	19Y2	8½	2½
19Y1	2¼	⅞	19Y0	1	⅛
19X9	¾	⅜	19X8	½	¼
19X7	⅜	¼	19X6	½	⅛

*Aft. 10% stk. dvd. June 10; bef. 10¾-7.
†Aft. 10% stk. dvd. July 31; bef. 9¾-6½.

DIVIDENDS—Com. $0.01 par: 19Y2, $0.10 init. June 30; 19Y3, 10% stk. June 10; 19Y4, 10% stk. July 31; 19Y5, nil.

DIVIDEND WAIVED—Directors and their wives and children and a person affiliated with an officer and director and his wife and children waived the cash dividend paid. June 30, 19Y2, on their holdings of 596,845 Com. shs.

EARNINGS AND FINANCES

AUDITORS—Tourche Ross & Co., Newark, N.J.

CONSOL. EARNS., Y-E (Apx.) Feb. 28: Thou. $

	Total Revs.	Inc. Taxes	*Net Inc.	*Sh. Earns.
19Y6	43,430	1,180	1,147	0.99
19Y5	37,147	833	1,129	0.98
19Y4	34,098	895	1,053	1.05
19Y3	24,288	721	690	0.77
19Y2	18,125	480	411	0.46
19Y1	18,418	1,084	1,238	1.38
19Y1	11,542	159	147	0.16
19X9	9,871	94	185	0.21
19X8	8,021	65	162	0.18
19X7	6,894	80	69	0.08

dDeficit.

*Bef. extraord. items (Thou. $): 19Y1, cr436 or $0.48. Sh. earns. are as reported by Co.

ADJTD. EARNS. for June 'Y4 & 'Y3 10% stk. divds.: $

19Y4	19Y3	19Y2	19Y1	19Y0	19X9	19X8
0.96	0.64	0.38	1.15	0.14	0.17	0.15

Annual Report—Consol. Inc. Acct. Yrs. End.: Thou. $

	Feb. 28 'Y6	Feb. 28 'Y5	Feb. 29 'Y4
Parking serv. rev	39,004	34,009	30,649
Service station rev	4,426	3,138	3,449
Total revenues	43,430	37,147	34,098
Cost & exps	38,718	33,879	30,912
Oper. income	4,712	3,268	3,186
Gain on sale of parking facils	—	768	601
Total income	4,712	4,036	3,787
Depr. & amort	1,427	1,021	832
Interest	958	1,053	1,007
Income taxes	1,180	833	895
Net income	1,147	1,129	1,053
*Sh. earns	$0.99	$0.98	$0.92

*Avge. com. & com. equiv. shs.: 19Y6—1,159,937; 19Y5—1,149,487; 19Y4—1,148,598, adjtd. for July 'Y4 10% stk. divd.

Consol. Bal. Sheet Feb. 28: Thou. $

Assets—	19Y6	19Y5
Cash	590	244
Ctf. of depos	—	122
Accts. rec	665	512
Advs. to partnership developer	2,102	—
Oth. curr. assets	134	90
Prepayments	1,780	1,580
Tot. curr. assets	5,721	2,548
Lease acquis. costs	2,052	1,967
*Net property	14,069	11,885
Other assets	2,192	2,048
Total assets	23,584	18,448
Liabilities—		
Revolving loan	2,917	300
Curr. debt mat	1,504	1,531
Accts. pay. & accrs	2,761	2,534
Income taxes	689	—
Deposits on sale of realty	1,238	—
Tot. curr. liab	9,109	4,365
Long term debt	6,403	7,322
Defr. taxes	805	693
Sec. depos	28	22
†Com. stk. p. $0.01	11	11
Paid-in surp	2,733	2,687
Retain. earns	4,495	3,348
Total liabs	23,584	18,448
Net wkg. cap	d3,838	d1,817
dDeficit.		
*Depr. & amort	3,412	2,560
†Shs.:	1,148,801	1,126,736

Companies Undergoing Restructuring or Liquidation

This represents another important category for the asset-play investor.

In light of the recent pace of merger and acquisition activity, a number of companies find themselves with subsidiaries that do not fit into their corporate philosophy. Such a management has a number of alternative routes to select from in deciding how to dispose of an unwanted subsidiary including: the outright sale of the unwanted subsidiary to another company, the sale of such a subsidiary to its existing management in the form of a leveraged buyout, or the distribution of stock in the subsidiary via a spinoff to the parent company shareholders. It is this third category—spinoffs—that can represent a major buying opportunity for the asset-play investor.

Spinoffs can represent a good buying opportunity because in many cases once a subsidiary is free from a large corporate parent and the inherent control and "bottlenecks" that go with such ownership, the performance of the spinoff company may improve dramatically. Also, the subsidiary may have been saddled with an inordinate amount of the parent company's overhead expenses and once free of these expenses profits may substantially increase. Finally, in many cases the market is unable to determine adequately what is the true value of a spinoff. This is where the skills you will develop from reading this book will enable you to determine whether a particular spinoff represents an opportunity to buy assets at a discount.

Along with spinoffs, liquidations represent an important source of potential asset plays. Real estate companies are often candidates for liquidation. As managements grow older and in the absence of any chain of succession, management may decide to liquidate the company. In many of these cases, the parts are worth more than the whole, especially in the case of real estate companies that may be carrying properties at the cost for which they were acquired years ago. Also, such properties may be worth substantially more when put to a different use from what they are presently being used. Investing in liquidations as with investing in spinoffs requires the ability to analyze a company's balance sheet paying particular attention to locating hidden assets and evaluating its holdings, such as real estate, marketable securities, and patents, to reach a conclusion as to the true worth of the company.

Example:

As with closely held companies, the best way to familiarize yourself with the characteristics of a company undergoing restructuring or liquidation is to analyze an example of such a company; this example features the Ernest Hanes Lumber Company ("Hanes").

Exhibit 2-2 consists of the Ernest Hanes' Report to Shareholders which was an integral part of that company's 19Y2 Annual Report. This report contained many signals to alert an asset-play investor to the fact that the company was seeking to redeploy its assets and change the direction of its business. The first paragraph states that the company ". . .has announced a major divestiture program . . .and initiated significant plans for the future." Further on reference is made to the completion of a strategic plan to capitalize on corporate strengths and opportunities.

Once alerted to the fact that management has embarked on a restructuring program, the task of an asset-play investor is to determine if the parts are worth more than the whole. From reviewing Exhibit 2-2, you would learn that Ernest Hanes owns sawmills, a wholesale and retail building products operation, and is an important shareholder in South Wood Company, the owner of significant mineral rights in southern Mississippi. Because of the losses that the company incurred in 19Y0, 19Y1 and, in particular, 19Y2, the stock sunk to a low of $13 per share. Many long-term holders of the company's stock were concerned whether the company would survive. Yet many professional asset-play investors were quick to realize that Ernest Hanes represented an opportunity to buy assets at a discount.

Any investor who had spent the time to determine the value of the company's underlying assets and looked beyond current losses would have concluded that the company's real worth was something on the order of $40 per share, even if management simply liquidated the company. That's the price the stock reached in 19Y5 when earnings recovered as a result of the company's concentration on its retail operations and as Ernest Hanes paid out substantial dividends from the liquidation of certain segments of its business and the spinning off of others to its shareholders. This example shows why it is important to spend time analyzing a company's balance sheet to determine if the company is holding any undervalued or hidden assets such as real estate, operating divisions, or substantial holdings in other companies whose value will surface when they are sold off in the course of a restructuring.

Exhibit 2-2.

Ernest Hanes Lumber Co.

19Y2 Annual Report

After careful and thorough study, our company has introduced a new business plan to strengthen its competitive position in the marketplace and accelerate its return to profitability. We will concentrate on three basic segments: retail, wholesale distribution, and carload trading. Of these, our 25 Home Centers and conventional retail yards offer the greatest long-term potential for improved performance. Redeployment of corporate assets is expected to build profitable growth with an upturn in the economy and restoration of the home building market.

In July 19Y2, we had a successful Grand Opening of our new Home Center.

Exhibit 2-2 continued

To Our Stockholders:

> "Our new business strategy provides for the return of our company to an acceptable level of profitability. To achieve that objective, we will strengthen our leadership position as a distributor and retailer of wood and related products in the metropolitan Chicago market, and maintain a strong wholesale distribution network in other geographic locations. To accomplish our goal, we must focus on customer needs, increased productivity, and expansion of our marketing abilities."
>
> *Ernest Hanes*

The depression in home building and its related industries continued throughout most of 19Y2 and adversely affected our business. The company recorded substantial operating losses, announced a major devestiture program, and initiated significant plans for the future.

Our financial statements have all been restated to include only results from Continuing Operations in retail and wholesale distribution. Manufacturing operations have been accounted for as Discontinued Operations since the end of the second quarter in 19Y2, when we announced the decision to divest that part of the business. Sales from Continuing Operations were $180,533,000, off 8% from 19Y1. A pretax loss of $4,455,000 was incurred as compared with the pretax loss of $2,214,000 in 19Y1. Much lower loss carry-back provisions were available in 19Y2, and the net loss after these carry-back provisions was $3,874,000 or $2.19 per share, compared to a loss of $1,190,000 or $0.67 per share in 19Y1. Discontinued Operations incurred an operating loss of $7,874,000 in 19Y2 compared with a loss of $4,646,000 in 19Y1. In addition, a $19,863,000 Special Charge for estimated losses on the divestiture of mill operations was provided at the end of the second quarter. All of these factors are described in detail the "Management Discussion" section and in the Notes to Consolidated Financial Statements.

The year began with few encouraging signs for a recovery of the economy. The excessive cost of mortgage money, coupled with record low winter temperatures in our northern markets, caused miserable business conditions and resulted in substantial operating losses. The housing industry remained depressed throughout the summer, forcing the temporary closure of some sawmills and curtailed operating levels at others. By fall the economic indicators were moving up, and some optimistic signs were beginning to appear. Declining interest rates triggered a rise in housing starts and initiated a flurry of activity in the lumber industry. Business conditions improved noticeably at our Distribution Centers and Retail stores.

Clearly, the results of the last few years have been inadequate and new

Exhibit 2-2 continued

business directions are indicated. During 19Y2 we completed a strategic plan to capitalize on our corporate strengths and opportunities. Developed by management with the aid of outside consultants, this plan directs a course of action that should assure us of growth and profitability for the future.

Divestiture of Sawmills

The Manufacturing segment of our business demanded particular attention. Lengthy feasibility studies were conducted to assess the potential of our sawmills and determine their future. In May our Board of Directors decided to sell our Western manufacturing facilities. We have continued to operate the mills to assure their value and maintain our tradition as a responsible employer. As part of a prior divestiture program, two of our three sawmills in the South were sold. In February 19Y3, three sawmills in the Rocky Mountain Region were sold, and in March we announced the sale of our St. Anthony, Idaho, stud mill and our mill at Hill City, South Dakota. We are continuing to negotiate the sale of our four remaining manufacturing locations and their related properties.

Our Western mills are almost totally dependent on federal timber bought at auction from the Forest Service, an agency of the U.S. Department of Agriculture. Two closely related events, initiated largely by the federal government, dramatically altered the economics of companies dependent on timber from the National Forests. First, housing was stimulated by low interest rates on the real cost of money and resultantly surged to record proportions. Then, during the same period, and at a singularly inopportune time, millions of acres of public timber were set aside by Congress for single use Wilderness, greatly reducing the volume of timber available.

Faced with the reality of fewer federal timber sales and a diminishing supply of logs, keen competition forced manufacturers to overbid for raw material or close their operations. The timber supply problem swept through the industry in epidemic proportions and our company was caught in the middle of this complicated and highly controversial issue. Finally, the gravity of the timber problem became abundantly clear when the lumber market collapsed under the weight of excessive interest rates.

The decision to divest ourselves of our mills was motivated by the degree of risk and capital requirements involved in lumber manufacturing. We believe it to be more prudent to concentrate on the opportunities which exist in the distribution and retailing of lumber and other building material products.

Wholesale Distribution

We are dissatisfied with the operating results of our Wholesale Distribution Division. Units with marginal potential have been closed and stringent cost controls have been initiated. We intend to change the configuration of our Main Yard complex to return this unit to profitability while maintaining its

Exhibit 2-2 continued

very important source of supply function for our Retail Division. Our carload Trading Group also has been realigned in a more efficient mode. A resumption of adequate business conditions, coupled with these changes, should produce the desired results.

Wholesale distribution is an ever-changing process of matching customer demands at the retail level with the more static capabilities of manufacturing. Competitive conditions change constantly in the various market areas. Knowledgeable people, using efficient and flexible systems, are invaluable corporate assets in such an environment, and our company has gifted men and women who possess these competitive strengths.

Our twelve Distribution Centers are strategically located to capture their share of the business within their respective market areas. Each is capable of providing customers with quality products, expert service, and highly competitive prices. Our Trading Group specializes in nationwide buying and selling of commodity products to dealers, distributors, and industrial accounts. Deregulation of the freight industry by the federal government altered distribution patterns substantially. Our company established reload centers to take advantage of the logistics involved in the cost-efficient transportation and marketing of lumber and other wood-related commodities. As we expand our purchasing network, we will continue to make a market for the lumber products from our former mills, as well as from those which are owned by other manufacturers.

Emphasis on Retailing

In 19Y2 our Retail Division demonstrated its ability to perform under adverse conditions. Our stores recovered from the unprecedented first quarter losses, and operating profits slightly exceeded the prior year's results. Our fine staff handled the business well under the circumstances. We are confident that retail sales and earnings will improve as the economy strengthens and as we implement our new business strategy. The present challenge is to initiate the changes which are necessary to reach our earnings potential.

Marketing and demographic studies reinforced the fact that the Greater Chicago Area is a large but relatively mature market. A fundamentally strong demand still exists for new home construction and basic do-it-yourself products. The "Hanes" name remains a familiar household word, a distinct advantage. Our customers continue to recognize us as a valued source of top-quality, name-brand merchandise, with helpful sales people.

We have every intention to maintain our already strong position as a major supplier to the new home, commercial, and industrial markets. We plan system changes to increase efficiency and market penetration. Anticipated improvement in new construction activity will be welcomed and will enable us to utilize our diverse capabilities of providing lumber and other building material products to large tract contractors as well as

Exhibit 2-2 continued

single-family homebuilders. Our prefabricated building components and contract millwork plants are prime examples of our ability to tailor products to meet the needs of our customers.

The do-it-yourself industry is one of the most highly regarded segments of specialty retailing and offers us our greatest long-term opportunity. Because of its exceptional growth in recent years, the do-it-yourself business has been assigned a high priority within our company. Last year's sales in this segment increased by 14%, and we look to continued improvement in 19Y3.

Our success in retailing will be constantly measured against our objectives. As the company prepares for the future, we anticipate that improved new construction activity will help spread operating costs as the less cyclical consumer business builds momentum.

Management Systems

An integrated company of distribution centers, carload trading, and specialty retailing requires proper systems and informed people to achieve success. Instant access to information is imperative, and we intend to develop a data base by expanding our computer capabilities through the company. Financial reporting must be timely to be meaningful and useful to management. Systems to maximize the efficient transportation of product to customer will continue to play a critical role in our business.

Intense competition exists in wholesaling and retailing. Advantageous sourcing of products and reasonable prices contingent on service and investment will play an increasingly important role in our new company. Last year's decision to consolidate our marketing efforts into a single entity has served us well. Under the umbrella of our Marketing Department, we have positioned ourselves to capture a greater share of the available business.

South Wood Corporation

Our company owns 34.5% of the common stock of South Wood Corporation, which owns 117,688 net mineral acres under 261,265 surface acres in southern Mississippi. In 19Y1 significant gas reserves were found on a portion of these mineral rights situated under two deep wells in the Catahoula Creek Field in Hancock County. Commercial production from these wells began in late 19Y2. Our equity in the earnings of South Wood, however, decreased from $333,000 in 19Y1 to $111,000 in 19Y2, primarily due to lower lease bonus income. The South Wood Corporation Annual Report is available to stockholders of Ernest Hanes Lumber Co. upon request.

Financial

The last three years have taken a heavy toll on the company. We will continue to operate our businesses with the balance sheet disciplines

Exhibit 2-2 continued

mandated by the recent economic conditions. Income from the sales of our sawmill properties will be first used to reduce corporate debt and return the company to a position of financial strength.

Management is acutely aware of its obligations to shareholders. Its primary objective is to provide a satisfactory return on invested capital. We will restore our dividend payments at the earliest possible time contingent on a responsible assessment of business conditions.

To Build on Our Heritage

As our company enters into a new and exciting period, we would be remiss not to acknowledge the contributions of our Board of Directors during the past year. Charting a new path for a company is never easy, but we can meet the challenges that coexist with opportunity. We are not disregarding our heritage; rather, we are building upon it as we embark on new business directions fully confident of our growth and promise for the future.

ERNEST HANES
President and Chief Executive Officer

March 18, 19Y3

Exhibit 2-2 continued

Hanes Lumber Co.

CAPITALIZATION (Dec. 31 'Y5)

LONG TERM DEBT—None.

STOCK—	Auth. Shs.	Outstg. Shs.
Common $10 par	2,500,000	1,470,028

IN LIQUIDATION—Oct. 23, 19Y5, stockholders adopted a plan of complete liquidation of Co. within a 3-yr. period. See Dividend, below, for liquidating distributions.

CORPORATE BACKGROUND

Company engaged in the wholesale and retail sale of lumber and other building material products. Dec. 31, 19Y5, Co.'s remaining operational locations included 4 wholesale distribution centers in Fla., Iowa, N.M. and Wis.; 9 retail stores in Wis.; and 3 manufacturing facilities in Wis. (2) and Ill.

In early 19Y6, Co. sold certain assets of its manufacturing facility in Ill.; and the wholesale distribution centers in N.M. and Wis.

Apr. 11, 19Y6, Co. reached an agreement to sell the assets (excluding accounts receivable) of Kid Corp. (9 retail stores and 2 manufacturing facilities were operated under the Kid Corp. name) to Wickes Cos., Inc. Transaction was expected to close in early May, 19Y6.

EMPLOYEES—Dec. 31, 19Y5, 175.

SUBSIDIARIES—wholly owned——Kid Corp.; and several others with the name Ernest Hanes in their titles.

INCORPORATED in Del. July 20, 1933, as Hanes Land & Timber Co. Present title adopted Oct. 31, 1937.

CHAIRMAN & CHIEF EXEC OFFICER, H.H. Hover; PRES, CHIEF OPER OFFICER & TREAS, Frank Rodel; SR V-P, W.M. Abald; V-P & SECY, N.H. Good; CONTR. P.D. Bumkas.

DIRECTORS—C.J. Strauss, Frank Rodel, H.H. Hover.

OFFICE—400 South Wisconsin Ave., Chicago, IL 60604 (Tel.: 312-555-2000). ANNUAL MEETING—In May.

STOCK DATA

STOCKHOLDERS—Dec. 31, 19Y5, 771 (of record). Mar. 21, 19Y6, descendants of Edward Hanes, their families and related trusts owned or controlled 35.6% of the Com.

TRANSFER AGENT—Continental Illinois Natl. Bank & Tr. Co., Chicago.

PRICE RANGE—OTC bid (NASDAQ: HINE):

19Y5	42½	22¼	19Y4	43¾	32½
19Y3	39	14½	19Y2	19¾	13
19Y1	23	15½	19Y0	21½	15½
a19X9	25	18	19X8	48½	37
19X7	41½	33	19X6	37	23½

aAft. 100% stk. divd. June 20; bef., 52½-40½.

RECENT DIVIDENDS: Com. $10 par—$

19Y6 (to June 12)................ †14.00 19Y5........ *20.75
19Y4.......... 0.90 19Y3.......... 0.30 19Y2.............. Nil
19Y1.......... 0.60 19Y0.......... 0.90 19X9............ 0.25
(Bef. 100% stk. June 20, 19X9)
19X9.......... 1.50 1978.......... 2.00 19X7............ 2.50
19X6.......... 1.25

*Incl. $20 init. liq. distrib. paid Nov. 26.

†Consists of $5 liq. distrib. paid Feb. 4 and $9 liq. distrib. paid June 12; an additional liq. distrib. of 1.27 Com. shs. of South Wood Corp. for each Com. share of Co. held of record Feb. 28, was paid Mar. 17.

Cash dividends have been paid each year for the past 40 years, except 19Y2.

EARNINGS AND FINANCES

AUDITORS—Arthur Andersen & Co., Chicago, Ill.

CONSOL. EARNS. (Pr. to Plan of liquidation) Y-E Dec. 31: Thou. $

	Net Sales	Oper. Inc.	Depr. & Depl.
19Y4	280,833	6,523	2,547
19Y3	249,652	4,133	2,115
19Y2	180,533	d1,528	2,279
19Y1	264,946	1,108	12,150
19Y0	270,574	11,445	12,152
19X9	348,516	16,585	9,625
19X8	339,181	28,269	8,729
19X7	288,870	23,262	8,526
19X6	234,834	17,494	7,892

	Inc. Taxes	*Net Inc.	*Sh. Earns.
19Y4	1,725	11,128	6.31
19Y3	1,500	7,329	4.14
19Y2	cr581	d31,611	d17.87
19Y1	cr5,020	d5,836	d3.30
19Y0	cr3,600	d1,714	d0.98
19X9	670	2,757	1.58
19X8	7,280	10,786	12.34
19X7	6,675	3,764	10.04
19X6	3,590	4,817	5.52

dDeficit.

*Incls. net results from discontd. opers. (Thou. $): 19X2, d27,737 or $15.68; 19Y3, 5,500 or $3.11; 19Y4, 8,600 or $4.88.

Also, bef. extraord. items. (Thou. $): 19Y3, cr1,500 or $0.85; 19Y4, cr1,725 or $0.98.

Sh. earns. are as reported by Co.

ADJUSTED EARNS. for June 'X9 100% stk. divid.: $

19X8	19X7	19X6
6.17	5.02	2.76

RESTATED EARNS., Y-E Dec. 31: Thou. $
(Reflects discontd. opers.)

		—Net Income—			
	Sales fr. Contng. Opers.	Contng. Opers. Amt.	*Per Sh.	Discontd. Opers. Amt.	*Per Sh.
19Y1......	195,726	d1,190	d$0.67	d4,646	d$2.63
19Y0......	200,791	483	0.28	d2,197	d1.24
19X9......	253,734	3,470	1.98	d713	d0.40
19X8......	244,287	4,484	2.56	6,302	3.61

dDeficit.

*As reported by Co. adjtd. thru June 'X9 100% stk. divd.

Annual Report—Consol. Inc. Acct., Yr. End. Dec. 31 'Y5: Thou. $

Net sales	244,413
Cost of sales	190,536
Sell., gen. & adm. exps	43,503
Taxes excl. inc.	3,868
Oper. income	6,506

Exhibit 2-2 continued

Gain on sale of fixed assets	1,195
Invstmt. inc	1,242
Equity in earns. of sub	384
Total income	9,327
Depreciation	2,607
Restructuring exps	1,091
Int. exp	481
Income taxes	2,650
Inc. fr. contng. opers	2,498
Discontd. opers	†3,950
Inc. bef. extraord. item	6,448
Extraord. item	acr11,016
Net income	17,464
Cash divds	880
Liquidating cash distr	29,401
Bal. aft. divds	d12,817
*Sh. earns.:	
Fr. contng. opers	$1.46
Discontd. opers	2.31
Bef. extraord. item	3.77
Extraord. item	cr6.43
Net income	10.20

dDeficit.

*Avge. shs.: 1,712,268.

†Represents reduction of estimated loss on disposal of discontd. opers.

aIncls. gains of $1,895,000 or $1.10 a sh. fr. tax loss carryfwd. & $9,121,411 or $5.33 a sh. fr. carrying value adjmts.

Note A: On Oct. 23 'Y5 the Co's. stockholders adopted a Plan of Liquidation & Dissolution (the "Plan"). As a result of the Plan & in accordance with GAAP, the financial statements as of Dec. 31 'Y5 were prepared on a liquidating basis.

Note B: Reduction of certain LIFO inventories in 19Y5 resulted in liquidation of inventory quantities, which increased net income by $3,424,000.

Consol. Bal. Sheet, Dec. 31 'Y5: Thou. $

Assets—	
Cash & equivs	10,915
Accts. rec., net	8,760
Inventories	12,227
Tot. curr. assets	31,902
Retire. plan reversion	8,100
Net property	9,545
Oth. assets	1,140
Invest. in South Wood	8,856
Net realizable value of discontd. opers	7,850
Total assets	67,393
Liabilities—	
Curr. debt mat	454
Accts. pay	2,571
Accruals	10,503
Income taxes	6,282
Curr. reserve for discontd. opers	3,542
Tot. curr. liab	23,352
Defr. compensation	207
Res. for contingent liabs. of discontd. mfg. opers	8,500
†Com. stk. p. $10	14,700
Retain. earns	20,634
Total liabs	67,393
Net wkg. cap	8,550
†Shs.:	1,470,028

Note: See note A above.

Closed-end Funds and Small Business Investment Companies

Closed-end funds and small business investment companies represent another source of potential asset plays.

In recent years mutual funds (also referred to as open-ended investment companies) have provided a medium for the individual investor to participate in the stock market allowing such investors to commit small amounts of money to the stock or bonds markets over extended periods of time. While mutual funds have grown and expanded, closed-end funds and small business investment companies have been relegated to an obscure corner of the investment world. Because of this lack of interest the stocks of many of these investment companies represent potential asset plays.

Closed-end investment companies and small business investment companies have a number of things in common. Unlike mutual funds, which are continually selling new shares to the investing public, closed-end and small business investment companies raise a specific amount of money via an initial public offering. Many such investment companies came into existence in the late 1920s and only recently have any new closed-end investment companies been formed and offered to the public. Also, it is typical for the shares of closed-end and small business investment companies to sell at a discount of 20% or more from the net asset value behind each share. Where such an investment company may have $10 in liquid assets (stocks, bonds, real estate, and so forth) behind each share of its stock, the stock may be selling in the marketplace at a price of $8 representing a discount of $2 or 20% from its underlying assets.

Some recent changes in the marketplace make closed-end investment companies and small business investment companies attractive areas to look for potential asset plays. More and more individual and institutional investors have come to question why such investment companies sell at such a discount from their underlying assets. As a consequence, a number of closed-end and small business investment companies have been acquired by individual investors and liquidated at a premium, or acquired by mutual funds and converted to a mutual or open-ended fund. For the individual investor willing to spend the time and effort, it is still possible to find such companies that offer buying opportunities for the asset-play investor.

Example:

Fischer Corporation ("Fischer") represents a typical closed-end, small business investment company. As Exhibit 2-3 shows, Fischer is licensed under the Small Business Investment Act of 1958. The company provides equity capital and makes long-term loans to small business concerns that possess potential for investment appreciation, and furnishes them with technical assistance, advisory, and counseling services. Trading between $13 and $15 per share in 19Y5,

Fischer had an equity of $18.24 per share as of March 31, 19Y5.

What are some of the factors indicating that Fischer represents an asset play? The company had investments on March 31, 19Y6 consisting of $10,194,702 debt securities and $1,258,361 common and preferred stocks—*all at cost or less*. Directors' valuation was $12,607,005. The first question that should come to your mind as an asset-play investor is this: What are the common and preferred stocks carried on Fischer's books at cost? If you were to examine Fischer's 10K, you would determine that these investments represent holdings in a number of companies that have either recently gone public or are on the verge of going public. Carrying these securities at cost might fail to reflect their true value. At least one professional investor seems to believe that this is the case, as shown by the fact that ESL Services, Inc., a unit of the privately held S.T. Green & Co., purchased 38% of Fischer's common stock.

There are some dangers attached to investing in closed-end, small business investment companies. One of the dangers is that management of these companies can be extremely inbred. As in the case of Fischer, the management owns substantial blocks of company stock. Thus, there is always the danger that the interest of outside stockholders will be shunted aside and management will take care of itself at the expense of the minority holders. Attending an annual meeting of shareholders and asking pointed questions and, in particular, determining how the funds' expense ratio compares with that of other funds of a similar size will help you to determine if management is abusing its position.

Bankruptcies

Investing in the stock of selected bankrupt companies represents another area where the techniques of asset-play investing can prove to be both useful and profitable.

Exhibit 2-3.

Fischer Corp.

CAPITALIZATION (Mar. 31 'Y6)

LONG TERM DEBT—	Outstg.
*Subord. Debs.:	
5½%, due $70,000 anly, thru 19Y7	$140,000
10.595%, due Dec. 1, 19Y9	2,000,000
11.255%, due Aug. 1, 19Y0	3,000,000
11.615%, due Sept. 1, 19Y3	3,500,000
TOTAL	$8,640,000

*All payable to or guaranteed by SBA.

STOCK—	Auth. Shs.	Outstg. Shs.
Common $1 par	2,000,000	†1,003,986

†Excl. 67,014 in treas.

CORPORATE BACKGROUND

Company is registered as a closed-end management investment company under the Investment Company Act of 1940, and is licensed under the Small Business Investment Act of 1958.

Company provides equity capital and makes long term loans to small business concerns which possess potentialities for investment appreciation, and furnishes them (and others on a fee basis) with technical assistance, advisory and counseling services.

Company intends to qualify each year as a regulated investment company under the Internal Revenue Code.

INVESTMENTS at Mar. 31, 19Y6, consisted of $10,194,702 debt securities and $1,258,361 Com. and Pfd. stocks—all at cost or less. Directors' valuation was $12,607,005.

PRESIDENT & TREAS, A.L. Fars; SECY & GEN COUNSEL, J.S. Berg; CONTR & ASST SECY, Elliot Grumman.

DIRECTORS—H.H. Kahn, A.L. Fars; Carl Vogel, C.A. Gold.

OFFICE—7400 Avenue of the Americas, New York, NY 10036 (Tel.: 212-555-4844). ANNUAL MEETING—In June.

STOCK DATA

VOTING POWER—One vote per share, cumulative in electing directors.

STOCKHOLDERS—June 28, 19Y6, 2,500 (of record). Oct. 6, 19Y6, ESL Services Inc., a unit of privately held S.T. Green & Co., owned about 38% of the Com.

REGISTRAR & TRANSFER AGENT—Fidata Trust Co., of NYC.

PRICE RANGE—OTC bid (NASDAQ: FKLN):

19Y5	15	13	19Y4	15¾	12¼
19Y3	15¾	13	19Y2	15	9½
19Y1	12½	9	19Y0	10¼	7⅛
19X9	9⅛	7¼	19X8	9	7¼
19X7	9	5½	19X6	6⅜	2⅞

RECENT DIVIDENDS (Cal. Yrs.)—19X6, $0.55; 19X7, $0.60; 19X8, $0.75; 19X9-Y0, $1.05; 19Y1, $1.10; 19Y2, $1.65; 19Y3, $1.55; 19Y4, $1.35; 19Y5, $1.20, June 30, 19Y6, $1.00.

EARNINGS AND FINANCES

AUDITORS—KMG Main Hurdman, NYC.

EARNINGS, Y-E Mar. 31: Thou. $

	Gross Inc.	Inc. Taxes	*Net Inc.	*Sh. Earns.
19Y6	2,654	cr124	598	0.60
19Y5	2,872	7	569	0.57
19Y4	3,004	77	1,514	1.51
19Y3	3,458	8	1,669	1.66
19Y2	4,006	782	3,424	3.41
19Y1	3,289	52	1,455	1.45
19Y0	2,612	101	1,095	1.09
19X9	2,469	108	987	0.98
19X8	1,999	1,670	3,825	3.82
19X7	1,998	131	641	0.64

dDeficit.

*Aft. the following items: Thou. $

	Net gain on invests.		Net gain on invest.
19Y6	d544	19Y5	d683
19Y4	301	19Y3	186
19Y2	2,233	19Y1	32
19Y0	d49	19X9	d50
19X8	4,787	19X7	53

Sh. earns. are as reported by Co.

Annual report—Inc. Acct., Yrs. End. Mar. 31: Thou. $

	19Y6	†19Y5
Interest income	2,572	2,725
Consult. & advis. fees inc.	58	117
Inc. fr. assets acqd. in liquid	17	8
Divds. inc.	7	13
Gross income	2,654	2,863
Salaries exp.	329	318
Interest exp.	966	971
Oth. exps.	341	316
Net realiz. gain on invest	d544	d683
Income tax	cr124	7
Net income	598	569
Dividends	1,205	1,355
Bal. aft. divds	d607	d786
*Sh. Earns.	$0.60	$0.57

dDeficit

*Avge. shs.: 1,003,986.

†Reclassified.

Bal. Sheet, Mar. 31: Thou. $

Assets—	19Y6	19Y5
bInvests at direct. val	12,607	13,954
cUS Govt. secs	3,836	3,758
Cash & equivs	7,499	8,372
Notes rec	1,125	1,315
Accrd. int. & recbls. net	468	503
Assets acqd. on liquid. of secs	120	400
Other assets	18	22
Total assets	25,673	28,324
Liabilities—		
Accts. pay.& accr	436	468
Income taxes	5	59
Defr. taxes	—	772
Long term debt	8,640	8,710
†Com. stk. p. $1	1,071	1,071
aTreas. stk	dr395	dr395
Paid-in cap.	9,327	9,327
Unrealiz. apprec. of invests	871	1,967
Undistrib. realiz. earns	5,718	6,325
Total liabs	25,673	28,324
Equity per sh	$16.53	$18.24
†Shs.	1,071,000	1,071,000
aShs.	67,014	67,014
bCost	11,453	10,996
cCost	3,832	3,844

In an average year as many as 20,000 or more companies file for protection under the various bankruptcy statutes. Companies filing for bankruptcy range in size from the corner candy store to industrial giants having thousands of employees. Out of these thousands of companies filing bankruptcy there are some that will "come back to life" and go on to become profitable and viable companies.

Whole books have been devoted to the bankruptcy statutes, and it is not the purpose of this book to make the individual investor a bankruptcy specialist. However, before you invest in any bankrupt company there are certain facts of which you should be aware. First, many companies are forced into bankruptcy as a result of the losses incurred in one division or subsidiary. It is frequently the case that a single division will bring down the whole company. Second, poor management is the single biggest contributing factor to a company being forced into bankruptcy. Third, many companies having substantial assets are forced to file bankruptcy to protect their assets from costly suits brought by customers, employees, and other parties.

What is the relevancy of the foregoing in selecting what bankrupt companies to invest in? Again, it means that an asset-play investor should concentrate his or her attention on analyzing the company's balance sheet for "real" or "hard" assets which the company can utilize to bring itself "back to life." The bankruptcy process itself should help the company if indeed it has any substantial assets. This is because the bankruptcy process will allow the company to reorganize and/or dispose of that division or subsidiary which might have triggered the company's bankruptcy. Also, the bankruptcy process will allow for the bringing in of more competent management if such was the major factor behind the company's failure. Thus, the ability to analyze and evaluate assets—the basis of asset-play investing—is a crucial component the decision-making process involved in selecting what bankrupt stocks to invest in.

Example:

> While major bankruptcies such as those of the Johns Manville Co. and A.H. Robbins Co. make financial headlines, the bankruptcies of a number of second tier companies receive only passing mention in the financial press. Reston Metal Co. ("Reston") is an example of just such a company.

Exhibit 2-4 gives detailed information as to its history both as an operating company and as a bankrupt. Reston was incorporated in the 1920s although segments of the company can trace their origins to Colonial America. The company is one of the largest units in the nonferrous metal-fabricating industry. Although listed for many years on the New York Stock Exchange, Reston's stock by 19Y2 had fallen to a low of $4 per share. On October 27, 19Y2, the company filed a voluntary petition with the U.S. Bankruptcy Court for the Southern District of New York seeking reorganization under Chapter XI of the Federal Bankruptcy Code.

The *Wall Street Journal* and other financial papers carried stories as to the circumstances leading to Reston's bankruptcy filing. But within days, all but Reston's shareholders and creditors had lost interest in the company. This was when asset-play analysts (both professional and individual) became interested in Reston.

Why did asset-play analysts become interested in Reston? First, Reston had a "consumer franchise," meaning that the public was well acquainted with the name and the quality of certain of its products. Second, one particular segment of its business had forced Reston into bankruptcy. The company's balance sheet was strong and under the protection of the Bankruptcy Court Reston was able to put its house in order by doing such things as selling off unprofitable divisions, consolidating operations, and bringing in new management. As in previous examples, the fact that Reston represented an opportunity to buy assets at a discount was confirmed by the fact that professional asset-play investors wound up owning better than 50% of Reston's common stock. In May, 19Y6, Reston was taken private and shareholders received $23 per share for the same stock that sold at $4 per share in 19Y2.

While this is an example of a company which successfully came out of bankruptcy, it does not mean that you should blindly invest in every company that goes bankrupt. Many individual investors wait and see if the professional asset-

Exhibit 2-4.

Reston Metal Co.

CAPITALIZATION (Dec. 31 'Y5)

LONG TERM DEBT—	Outstg.
14% Notes, due thru 19Z2	$28,723,000
14% Notes, due 19Z6-2005	20,404,000
12% Subord. Notes, due 2004	*6,818,000
12% Conv. Subord. Debs., due 2004	†19,123,000
6% Indus. Rev. Bonds, due 19Z0	36,010,000
Other	5,028,000
TOTAL (incl. $10,938,000 curr.)	$116,106,000

*Int. is payable in Com. stock valued at 125% of the avg. mkt. price thereof, until pymt. in full of the 14% Notes, due 19Z2.

†Int. is payable in Com. stock valued at 125% of the avg. mkt. price thereof until pymt. in full of the 14% Notes, due 19Z1. After pymt. of the Notes, Debs. are convertible into Com. at $17.50 per share until Dec. 31, 19Z5 and at $18.67 per share thereafter.

STOCK—	Auth. Shs.	Outstg. Shs.
Common $2.50 par	*15,000,000	†7,602,022

*Incl. 1,092,714 for conversion of Debs.; and 73,216 optioned to employees, with 599,633 for future grants.

†Exc. 565 in treas.

MERGER PROPOSED—In May, 19Y6, Co. entered into a definitive agreement whereby it would be acquired by a concern controlled by Smith Management Co. Inc. Under terms of the agreement, Co.'s stockholders would receive $23 cash for each Com. share surrendered. Completion of the transaction was subject to, among other things, approval of Co.'s stockholders.

CORPORATE BACKGROUND

Company, one of the largest units in the nonferrous metal fabricating industry, makes a varied line of nonferrous metal products, including primary aluminum and fabricated aluminum products; fabricated copper, brass, bronze, nickel-silver and cupro-nickel products; and metal stampings. Products include aluminum foil, foil laminations, and extruded aluminum shapes in various specifications, coatings and finishes; copper and brass sheets, rolls, rods and bars, strips, plates, extruded shapes and welded tubes; and metal stampings, including Reston utensils made of copper and stainless steel, and teakettles. Other products include lead and tin foil, copper, zinc and magnesium engravers' plates, and data based management systems.

Main markets include the transportation, building and construction, electrical, capital goods, packaging, and consume durable goods industries. Principal markets for primary aluminum produced by 34% owned Ormet Corp. are extruders, foundries and secondary smelters. In 19Y5, Co. announced that it would attempt to sell its interest in Ormet.

In 19Y5, primary aluminum provided 23.5% of net sales before eliminations (19.4% in 19Y4); fabricated aluminum 38.5% (47.1%); fabricated copper and brass 21.5% (20.9%); metal stampings 13.9% (10.3%); and other 2.6% (2.3%).

ACTIVE SUBSIDIARIES—wholly owned—

Reston Extruders, Inc.
Reston Foil Containers, Inc.
Wells Aluminum Corp.
  Wells Aluminum, Inc.
  Wells Aluminum Southeast, Inc.
  Wells Aluminum Moultrie, Inc.
N.A. Extrusions Corp.
  North American Aluminum Corp.
Reston Courtesy Stores, Inc.
Reston Jamaica Alumina, Ltd.
Reston Copper Products, Inc.
Reston Technology & Consulting Co., Inc.

AFFILIATE—Ormet Corp. (34% owned).

PROPERTY—Principal plants are owned in Ark., Cal., Ill., Ky., Mass. (2), and N.Y. (3); and leased in Ga., Cal. (2), Ill., Ind., Mass., Mich., Mo. (2), Ohio and S.C.

CAPITAL EXPENDITURES, Yrs. End. Dec. 31: Thou. $
19Y5.......9,363 19Y4.......7,199 19Y3.......4,337

EMPLOYEES—Avge. in 19Y5, 3,897.

BANKRUPTCY PLAN CONFIRMED—Oct. 27, 19Y2, Co. filed a voluntary petition with the U.S. Bankruptcy Court for the Southern District of N.Y., seeking reorganization under Chapter 11 of the Federal Bankruptcy Code. Following approval by Co.'s stockholders and creditors and a hearing on confirmation of a plan of reorganization, an order of the court confirming the plan was entered on July 30, 19Y5. Plan became effective Aug. 12, 19Y5.

In 19Y5, in settlement of claims pursuant to the plan or reorganization, Co. made cash payments and offset receivables aggregating $112,000,000, issued or assumed indebtedness of $115,000,000 and issued Com. stock valued at $25,600,000. At Dec. 31, 19Y5, Co. had provided an additional $15,000,000 in current liabilities for settlement of claims. Included in the distributions to creditors was the issuance of $6,820,000 of 12% Subord. Notes, due 2004; $19,125,000 of 12% Conv. Subord. Debs., due 204; and shares of Co.'s Com. stock in settlement of the claims of holders of Co.'s 5½% Conv. Subord. Debs., due 19Z2.

In Aug., 19X5, wholly owned Reston Jamaica Alumina, Ltd. (RJA) suspended its mining and alumina operations and placed its plant on a standby status. In 19X6, Co. made claim under the insurance of its equity investment in RJA issued by the Overseas Private Investment Corp. (OPIC), a U.S Govt. agency. Co's. claim was denied by OPIC, and the dispute was submitted to arbitration as required by OPIC's contract. Aug. 25, 19X8, the arbitration panel awarded Co. $1,131,144. Judicial proceedings instituted by Co. to vacate the compensation portion of the award were not successful. At Dec. 31, 19X5, Co. had provided a reserve of $31,277,000 as a charge against operations representing the difference between the then $95,477,000 carrying value of its investment in RJA and the $64,200,000 insured value of its equity investment in RJA at June 30, 19X4, for which claim had been made against OPIC. In 19X8, Co. increased the reserve against its investment in RJA to eliminate any net carrying value, resulting in an extraordinary charge for the year of $40,227,000 (net of related tax benefit of $27,214,000). In Apr., 19X9, Co. obtained a $2,200,000 refund for insurance premiums paid to OPIC from June 30, 19X4. In June, 19Y0, Co. received a $1,180,000 payment from OPIC, discharging the arbitration award and related expenses. In 19Y1 and 19Y2, Co. recorded gains from reduction of the reserve for ongoing costs of RJA totaling $3,209,000 and $1,184,000, respectively.

In 19Y2, provided reserves totaling $99,813,000 in connection with several suspended or closed operations. Provision included $88,302,000 applicable to Co's. Scottsboro aluminum reduction plant, which in June, 19Y2, suspended operations for an indeterminate period.

Exhibit 2-4 continued

CHAIRMAN & PRES, H.H. Warmel, III; SR V-P & TREAS, R.L. Veale; GROUP V-P, R.M. Pane; ASSOCIATE COUNSEL & SECY, S.H. Kalian; CONTR & ASST TREAS, D.R. Messer.

—V-Ps—

J.J. Bell	B.W. Madeson
F.X. Cavany	Rudy Renta
J.H. Croman	J.W. Wickmann
F.E. Hess	

—DIRECTORS—

P.E. Assay	D.D. Graymann
D.W. Laker	J.H. Groegermann

OFFICE—High Ridge Pk., P.O. Box 10327, Danbury, CT 06904-2327 (Tel.: 203-555-5300).

STOCK DATA

STOCKHOLDERS—Jan. 31, 19Y6, 3,413 (of record). Mar. 15, 19Y6, Reston Ltd. Partnership and Bur-Strand & Co. Inc. owned 2,343,479 Com. shs. (30.8%); Smyth-Veslow Management Co. Inc. and Smyth-Veslow Special Situations Fund, L.P. 400,056 (5.3%); Equal Life Assurance Society of the U.S. 376,900 (5.0%); family holding companies for Sherman, Wes, and Harry Berg 442,400 (5.8%); MRF Corp. 461,300 (6.1%); and Oland Financial Group 1,014,900 (13.3%; 5-12-86).

TRANSFER AGENT & REGISTRAR—Fidata Securities Management Inc., Bentley, N.J.

LISTED—NYSE (Symbol RST); also traded Midwest SE:

19Y5	17¾	10⅛	19Y4	13½	9¾
19Y3	14⅞	6¼	19Y2	14⅞	4¾
19Y1	25⅜	13	19Y0	21¾	10⅞
19X9	17⅜	11½	19X8	19⅛	10½
19X7	21¾	9¾	19X6	12¼	7⅞

RECENT DIVIDENDS—Com. $2.50 par: $
19Y5-Y2 .... Nil 19Y1 .... 0.30 19Y0-X6.......... Nil

6% Cum. Ser. A. Pfd. $100 par paid regularly thru redemption Dec. 15, 19Y0.

DIVIDEND RESTRICTIONS—No dividends may be paid on Com. until the earlier of Jan. 1, 19Y8 or the pymt. in full of Co.'s 14% Notes, due to 19Z2. After Jan. 1, 19Y8 until pymt. of the 14% Notes, dividends are limited to 25% of net income after Jan. 1, 19Y8 plus the cash proceeds after Jan. 1, 19Y5 from sale of, or conversion of debt into, Com. stock. After pymt. of the 14% Notes, due 19Z2, dividends are limited to $17,000,000 plus net earnings after Jan. 1, 19Y5.

EARNINGS AND FINANCES

AUDITORS—Coopers & Lybrand, NYC.

CONSOL. EARNS., Y-E Dec. 31: Thou. $

	Net Sales	Oper. Inc.	Depr.	Fxd. Chgs.	■Tms. Earn.
19Y5	459,008	14,630	5,014	5,380	3.55
19Y4	601,120	61,891	8,027	711	d4.72
19Y3	508,326	22,245	8,120	726	22.72
19Y2	561,574	d53,380	13,559	13,344	—
19Y1	820,851	32,984	13,309	14,675	—
19Y0	748,079	59,218	12,733	13,885	—
19X9	788,121	65,492	12,220	17,546	—
19X8	680,767	67,919	13,647	16,863	—
19X7	597,604	46,617	13,406	15,731	—
19X6	498,418	33,743	13,312	15,933	—

	Inc. Taxes	*Net Inc.	—*Sh. Earns.— Prim.	Dltd.
19Y5	1,625	†12,406	†1.93	1.71
19Y4	421	d4,488	d0.79	a
19Y3	1,801	13,965	2.45	2.02
19Y2	cr27,682	d157,108	d27.61	a
19Y1	5,376	†9,356	†1.64	1.52
19Y0	14,968	†21,865	†2.82	3.24
19X9	13,608	25,713	4.50	3.76
19X8	17,267	21,184	3.71	3.11
19X7	6,670	10,160	1.77	1.60
19X6	769	1,662	0.28	—

dDeficit.

*Bef. extraord. items (Thou. $): 19X6, cr549 or $0.10; 19X7, cr4,717 or $0.83 ($0.64 dltd.); 19X8, dr40,227 or $7.07; 19Y3, cr1,077 or $0.19. ($0.16 dltd); 19Y5, cr420 or $0.07 ($0.06 dltd.).

Sh. earns. are as reported by Co.

†Liquidation of LIFO invtry. quantities increased net inc. by $7,480,000 or $1.17 in 19Y5 & $1,772,000 or $0.31 in 19Y0 & $5,665,000 or $0.99 in 19Y1. This was greatly offset by the expansion of the LIFO method of invtry. acctg. which reduced net inc. by $2,804,000 or $0.49 in 19Y0 &$4,637,000 or $0.81 in 19Y1.

■For 19Y3 & aft. on a pre-tax basis; calculation for prior years eliminated as not comparable.

aAnti-dilutive.

Annual Report—Consol. Inc. Acct., Yrs. End. Dec. 31: Thou. $

	19Y5	19Y4	19Y3
Net sales	459,008	601,120	508,326
Cost of sales	408,702	505,262	425,781
Sell & adm. exp.	35,676	33,967	33,210
Oper. income	14,630	61,891	22,245
Other income, net	6,694	7,568	4,515
Total income	21,324	69,459	26,760
Depreciation	5,014	8,027	8,120
Gain on sale of Scottsboro Aluminum Sheet Mill Assets	12,839	—	—
Settle. of Chapt. 11 claims	—	61,270	—
Prov. for plant closings	10,071	3,518	2,148
Interest	5,380	711	726
Int. capitalized	cr333	—	—
Inc. taxes	686	421	868
Defr. Fed. inc. tax	939	—	933
Inc. bef. extraord. item	12,406	d4,488	13,965
Extraord. item	ccr420	—	bcr1,077
Net income	12,826	d4,488	15,042
Com. earns. bef. extraord. item:			
*Primary	$1.93	d$0.79	$2.45
†Fully diluted	1.71	a	2.02
Extraord. item per sh.:			
*Primary	cr0.07	—	cr0.19
†Fully diluted	cr0.06	—	cr0.16
Net inc. per sh.:			
*Primary	2.00	d0.79	2.64
†Fully diluted	1.77	a	2.18

Exhibit 2-4 continued

Fixed Charges coverage:			
Avail. for Fxd. Chgs	19,078	d3,356	16,492
Gross Fxd. Chgs	5,380	711	726
F.C. Tms. Earn	3.55	d4.72	22.72

dDeficit.

*Avge. com. & com. equiv. shs.: 19Y5—6,419,747; 19Y4—5,705,818; 19Y3—5,703,375.

†Assumes convers. of 12% & 5½% subord. debs., pfd. stk. & exercise of options.

aAnti-dilutive.

bFr. tax-loss carryfwd.

cFr. tax loss carryfwds. of $700,000 & fr. a loss on settlement of liabs. under plan of reorganization of $280,000.

Note A: Reduction of certain LIFO inventories in 19Y5 resulted in liquidation of inventory quantities, which increased net inc. by $7,480,000, or $1.17 per sh., in 19Y5 by $2,114,000, or $0.37 per sh., in 19Y4 & by $7,519,000, or $1.32 per sh., in 19Y3.

Note B: On Dec. 31 'Y5, Co. had avail. net oper. loss & invest. tax credits carryfwds. of apx. $97,088,000 & 3,128,000, respectively, for financial purposes, & $56,566,000 & $11,875,000, for tax purposes.

Consol. Ba. Sheet, Dec. 31: Thou. $		
Assets—	19Y5	19Y4
Cash & equiv	52,000	108,504
Receivables, net	56,180	73,014
Inventories	77,925	96,899
Prepayments	2,142	1,872
Tot. curr. assets	188,247	280,289
Invests. & advs	28,674	28,092
*Net property	54,478	69,313
Other assets & defr. chgs	2,241	6,952
Total assets	273,640	384,646
Liabilities—		
Curr. debt. mat	10,938	857
Accts. & notes pay	35,081	19,517
Accruals	10,686	10,918
Taxes pay	5,212	2,215
Tot. curr. liabs	61,917	33,507
Long term debt	105,168	2,230
Oth. lg.-term liabs	—	289,486
†Com. stk. p. $2.50	77,570	50,742
Retain. earns	4,447	d8,379
Total liabs	273,640	384,646
Net wkg. cap	126,330	246,782
Equity per sh	$10.79	$7.42
dDeficit.		
*Depr. res	122.150	177,755

†Shs.: 19Y5—7,602,022; 19Y4—5,712,922; (excluding 565 treas. shs. in both yrs.)

play investors take a position before they go into a bankrupt stock. If you are willing to spend the time and effort to evaluate a bankrupt company, you can in a number of instances find gold among the casualties of the financial world.

Companies Operating in Depressed Industries– "Bottom Fishing"

Another source for potential asset plays is among those companies operating in depressed industries.

At any given point in time, some industries and companies within such industries are at the high point of their business cycle while others are at the low point. Those industries and companies at the high point of the business cycle are in the financial "spotlight." Typically, the financial press, brokerage community, and so forth will recommend that investors commit all their money to those particular industries and companies that are "booming." Likewise, institutional investors, adhering to the "herd instinct," will heavily invest in those industries and companies that are considered fashionable. History has shown that investing in industries and companies at the peak of their business cycle has proven to be financial suicide.

Adherents of asset-play investing argue that you should spend your time and energy sifting through depressed industries and the companies operating in these industries, seeking to identify which of these companies will be the survivors. This involves identifying and investing in those companies that have the ability because of the strength of their balance sheet to withstand the current downturn and to prosper and grow when the industry in which they operate in takes a more profitable turn. "Contrarian investing" is the term professional investors apply to such an investing technique. "Bottom fishing" is another term used to describe this investment approach. Whatever term is used, this investing technique still has as its cornerstone the concept that this book describes: the buying of assets at a discount. Analyzing a company's balance sheet and deciding whether it has the hard assets to weather a downturn in the particular industry it operates in is the asset-play approach to investing.

Example:

Rather than cite a particular company as was done for other categories of asset plays, it might be more appropriate to single out the oil service industry, which presently provides fertile ground for "bottom fishing."

Beginning with the premise that the oil service industry is at the bottom of its cycle, what are some of the factors to be considered in bottom fishing? Bottom fishing involves identifying those particular companies that have the financial strength to survive the severe downturn the oil service industry is encountering. A strong balance sheet with little debt as well as a management that moves rapidly to consolidate operations and reduce overhead, even if it means laying off personnel and selling idle assets, are some of the signs of a company that will be a survivor. Likewise, those companies in the oil service business that have a positive cash flow (net income + depreciation + depletion + amortization)—which is discussed in detail in later sections of this book—have a far greater chance of being survivors.

Finally, bottom fishing requires that the investor be both patient and have faith in the judgments made by an investor who is not following the crowd. However, the rewards of such a contrarian approach to investing can be substantial as the industry survivors may increase 200%, 300%, or more in value once the industry turns around.

Companies with a Consumer Franchise

Up to this point in describing the categories into which asset plays fit, emphasis has been placed on the hard assets that a company owns and which are reflected on the company's balance sheet. However, there is another aspect to asset-play investing which does not lend itself easily to simply analyzing the numbers, or the "number crunching" approach. This is the aspect concerned with identifying and valuing the worth of a company's "consumer franchise."

What is meant by the term "consumer franchise"? In reality, consumer franchise and name recognition are the same. Certain companies and the products they manufacture and/or sell are household names. When you think of a particular product or service the name of one or a handful of companies comes to mind. In such cases, the company's name or logo is a registered trademark and represents a real asset of the company.

In the past, investors assigned little value to the worth of such trademarks or consumer franchises. Such items were carried on the balance sheet at a negligible value (typically $1) and were given little weight in arriving at a value for the company. All this has changed in recent years as more and more companies have been acquired at what appears to be substantial premiums over the hard assets carried on their balance sheets. However, such premiums do not appear to be out of line or outrageous when one factors into the equation the worth of the company's consumer franchise or name recognition value.

How does asset-play investing assist you in identifying a company with a valuable consumer franchise? For one thing, asset-play investing serves to focus your attention on a company's balance sheet. As you master the techniques and tools of such an approach to investing you will learn to place greater emphasis on valuing all of a particular company's assets—both its hard assets (cash, cash equivalents, marketable securities, real estate, and so forth) and its soft assets (such as consumer franchises and patents)—in arriving at a value for the particular company.

Example:

The concept of consumer franchising is easy to apply since it relies more on name recognition than number crunching. In the past, both professional and individual investors assigned little value to a company's name, but in recent years this has started to change. However, there are still a number of companies selling at prices that do not reflect the value of their consumer franchise.

An example of a name recognition factor is the Coleman Co. ("Coleman"). When one thinks of quality outdoor recreational equipment, the name Coleman comes to mind. Referring to Exhibit 2-5, you can see that the company was

Exhibit 2-5.

Coleman Co., Inc.

CAPITALIZATION (Dec. 31 '85)

LONG TERM DEBT—$44,418,000, excl. $3,786,000 curr. portion.

STOCK—	Auth. Shs.	Outstg. Shs.
Pfd. $1 par	2,000,000	None
Common $1 par	*20,000,000	6,876,828

*Incl. 423,308 for employee stock purchase plan; and 299,305 optioned to employees, with 306,220 for future grants.

LINES OF CREDIT provided up to $55,340,000 on a short term basis, with interest at the prime rate—$31,573,000 taken down at Dec. 31, 1985.

CORPORATE BACKGROUND

Company and subsidiaries make and market outdoor recreational products, including camping products such as lanterns, camp stoves, sleeping bags, catalytic heaters, fuel, camping accessories, air inflators, tents and backpack equipment; patio grills; sailboats, water skis, sailboards, fishing boats, spas and hot tubs, scuba equipment, catamarans, life vests and canoes; portable beverage jugs and cooler chests; recreational air and target guns, archery bows, and accessories; and camping and utility trailers. Co. also makes heating and air conditioning equipment.

Company has facilities in N.Y., Kan. (5), Ont., Ca. (5), Pa., Wash. (2), Tex. (4), Tenn. (2), Ore., Utah, Ariz., S.C., Colo. (2), Australia, W. Ger., Austria, and France (2).

EMPLOYEES—Dec. 31, 1985, 4,800.

SUBSIDIARIES—wholly owned—
Coast Catamaran Corp.
Coast Catamaran France, S.A.
O'Brien Intl., Inc.
Alpha Verwaltungsund Mgmt. GmbH
Alpha Intl. GmbH
Master Craft Skis, Inc.
Master Craft Boat Co.
California Cooperage
Western Cutlery Co.
SoniForm Inc.
Skeeter Products, Inc.
Collins Dynamics, Inc.

Company has several other subsidiaries with the name Coleman in their titles.

INCORPORATED in Kan. Apr. 11, 1928, as The Coleman Lamp & Stove Co., to succeed company of same name founded in 1901. Present title adopted June 12, 1945.

In 1976, acquired Coast Catamaran Corp., maker of sailing catamarans, for $3,250,000, and O'Brien International, Inc., producer of water skis, for $2,750,000.

Exhibit 2-5 continued

OFFICERS—
Sheldon Coleman, Chrm
Clarence Coleman, Vice Chrm
L. M. Jones, Chrm Exec Committee
D. V. Berchtold, Exec. V-P
Frank Shaw, Exec V-P
R. A. Curry, Sr. V-P
J. M. Reiff, Sr V-P
Clair E. McCurdy, Sr V-P
Mary L. Williams, Secy
R. L. Schmidt, Contr & Treas

V-Ps—I.D. Campbell, R.R. Cooper, S.C. Coleman, M.E. Epling, M.L. Adams, T.W. Talbott, C.B. Mcliwaine, J.C. Dell'Antonia, J.C. Minson.

DIRECTORS—W.B. Armstrong, D.V. Berchtold, Clarence Coleman, Sheldon Coleman, R.A. Curry, A.R. Dykes, Christopher Gill, R.D. Harrison, L.M. Jones, P.J. McDonough, Frank Shaw, R.D. Smith, W.H. Sowers, Carolyn C. Vickers, D.L. Wallace.

OFFICE—250 North St. Francis Ave., Wichita, KS 67202 (Tel.: 316-261-3211). ANNUAL MEETING—In May.

STOCK DATA

VOTING POWER—One vote per share, cumulative in election of directors.

STOCKHOLDERS—Dec. 31, 1985, 4,800 (of record). Mar. 24, 1986, officers and directors owned or controlled 28.6% of the Com., including 21.4% by the Coleman family. Wisconsin Investment Board owned 6.9% (475,200 shs.).

COMMON REPURCHASED—Under tender offer expired May 4, 1979, Co. purchased 1,100,000 of its Com. shs. (14.8%) at $20 a share.

TRANSFER AGENTS—Manufacturers Hanover Trust Co., NYC, and Bank IV, Wichita, Kan. REGISTRARS—Manufacturers Hanover Trust Co., NYC, and Union Natl. Bank, Wichita.

LISTED—NYSE (Symbol CLN) Oct. 22, 1981; American SE prior thereto; also listed Midwest SE and traded Phila. and Boston SEs:

1985	32⅜	25½	1984	37¾	25¼
1983	45¾	28	1982	31	19½
1981	29	15⅜	1980	20	13⅞
1979	20	13⅞	1978	22⅝	13½
1977	18⅛	13⅛	1976	19½	12⅜

RECENT DIVIDENDS—Com. $1 par: $:

1986 (to Sept. 12) .... 0.90 1985-83 ....1.20
1982 .... 1.50 1981 .... 0.75 1980 .... 1.00
1979 .... 0.94 1978 .... 0.83 1977 .... 0.71
1976 .... 0.56

Cash dividends have been paid in each year since 1929, except in 1931-33 and 1958.

DIVIDEND RESTRICTIONS—Under terms of debt agreements, $43,866,000 of retained earnings at Dec. 31, 1985, was available for payments on or for Co's. stock. Co. is required to maintain consol. net working capital of at least $60,000,000.

EARNINGS AND FINANCES

AUDITORS—Ernst & Whinney, Kansas City, Mo.

CONSOL. EARNS., Y-E Dec. 31: Thou. $

	Net Sales	Inc. Taxes	Net Inc.	*Sh. Earns.
1985	442,710	9,388	10,019	1.46
1984	454,489	17,164	16,180	2.37
1983	382,282	16,602	17,635	2.61
1982	347,609	12,466	14,475	2.18
1981	359,111	17,026	20,198	3.08
1980	300,481	11,737	b14,090	b2.19
1979	314,252	15,460	17,243	2.54
1978	283,623	18,350	18,209	2.47
1977	256,991	15,088	15,120	2.06
1976	235,384	14,045	14,133	1.95

*Sh. earns. are as reported by Co.

†Change to LIFO method of invtry. valuation reduced 1974 net inc. by $4,405,000 or $0.60 a sh.

bLiquid of LIFO invtry. & change in the useful life of tooling acqd. aft. Jan. 1 '80 incr. net inc. $1,800,000 or $0.28.

Annual Report—Consol. Inc. Acct., Yrs. End. Dec. 31: Thou. $

	1985	1984	1983
Net sales	442,710	454,489	382,282
Cost & exps	400,790	401,812	330,998
Oper. Income	41,920	52,677	51,284
Oth. income, net	dr1,041	dr791	dr129
Total income	40,879	51,886	51,155
Depr. & amort	13,602	12,487	11,310
Interest	7,870	6,055	5,608
Income taxes	9,388	17,164	16,602
Net income	10,019	16,180	17,635
Cash divds	8,241	8,198	8,124
Bal. after divds	1,778	7,982	9,511
*Sh. earns	$1.46	$2.37	$2.61
*Avge. shs	6,866,000	6,828,000	6,761,000

Note A: As prescribed by FASB #33, Co. reported the following supplemental information to disclose the effects of changing prices.

	1985	1984	1983
Current Cost Basis:			
Net inc. (thous. $)	5,599	10,020	13,641
Sh. earns	$0.82	$1.47	$2.02

Consol. Bal. Sheet, Dec. 31: Thou. $

	1985	1984
Assets—		
Cash	6,721	6,898
Receivables, net	85,920	88,254
Inventories	92,360	98,535
Prepayments, etc	8,064	5,683
Tot. curr. assets	193,065	199,370
*Net property	99,030	94,173
Oth. assets	21,849	20,450
Total assets	313,944	313,993
Liabilities—		
Notes pay	31,573	32,418
Curr. debt. mat	3,786	3,586
Accts. pay	27,277	31,354
Accruals	18,646	20,418
Income taxes	314	2,150
Defr. inc. taxes	2,684	2,798
Tot. curr. liab	84,280	92,724
Long term debt	44,418	41,378
Oth. non-curr. liabs	7,218	7,512
Defr. inc. tax	19,080	14,549
†Com. stk. p. $1	6,877	6,854
Paid-in surp	30,680	30,140
Retain. earns	126,248	124,470
Curr. transl. adjt	dr4,857	dr3,634
Total liabs	313,944	313,993
Net wkg. cap	108,785	106,646
Equity per sh	$23.11	$23.03
*Depr. res	92,134	83,816
†Shs	6,876,828	6,853,682

founded in 1928 as the Coleman Lamp & Stove Co. Over the years, the company and its subsidiaries have become synonymous with outdoor recreational products with an ever-expanding product line to meet growing and changing consumer demand. The same source indicates that 29% of the company's stock is held by the Coleman family and family members hold positions of Chairman and Vice Chairman of the company. As of December 31, 1985, Coleman had equity of $23.11 per share versus a market price of $30 per share. To the asset-play investor, this means that the market was placing a value of only $7 on the Coleman name.

But this judgment on the part of the market is probably based on its failure to comprehend the true worth of the Coleman name. Franchising the Coleman name would almost certainly make the company worth more to anyone interested in acquiring the company. Expressed another way, the $7 premium appears low when compared with the value of consumers' recognition of Coleman as a manufacturer of quality products. Also, such things as the age of management and whether the family would be in favor of selling the company would be of importance to an asset-play analyst.

Companies with a Substantial Cash Flow

As in the case of companies with valuable consumer franchises, only in recent years have investors taken a hard look at the concept of cash flow and how it affects the value of a company. The recent wave of merger and acquisition activity has provided the driving force to focus investor attention on cash flow analysis. If one considers a company's cash flow, the prices paid by acquiring companies make sense and, for that matter, may make certain acquisitions appear to be inexpensive.

Chapter 4 deals with the number-crunching aspect to asset plays and has a more detailed description of the alternative approaches to calculating a company's cash flow. For purposes of this discussion it is sufficient to define cash flow as equaling net income + depreciation + amortization + depletion. Alternatively, cash flow represents the amount of money which flows through the business during a particular period of time.

Why is cash flow an important factor in determining the value of a company? Cash flow represents the amount of money a particular company has to work with during a given period of time. A company can put its cash flow to a variety of uses ranging from short-term investments to reduction of outstanding credit lines, and so forth. A positive cash flow means that the company has money to work with and can make the company attractive to merger and acquisition specialists who feel that they can utilize and successfully invest the cash the company is throwing off. It is for this reason that there is some justification for the high prices some companies with poor or nonexistent earnings have commanded in recent years.

Conclusion

The techniques involved in asset-play investing can be put to a wide variety of uses. Asset plays come in a variety of sizes and shapes ranging from the New York and American Stock Exchanges to companies whose shares are traded exclusively in the Pink Sheets. Likewise, asset plays range from companies having extremely strong balance sheets to companies operating under the bankruptcy code.

Two common threads run through all asset-play investing. First, time and attention are directed at analyzing the balance sheet of the company in question. Second, at the heart of all asset-play investing is the desire to locate and purchase assets at a discount. Knowing these two factors, you are ready to learn some of the mathematical techniques which can be used to identify potential asset plays.

How to Locate Asset Plays

CHAPTER 3

This chapter tells how to identify and locate potential asset plays before such stocks are discovered by other investors.

There are a variety of sources you can utilize in locating potential asset plays. They include financial publications such as the *Wall Street Journal, Barron's,* and *Investors Daily*; 13D filings which must be made with the U.S. Securities & Exchange Commission (SEC) by all purchasers of 5% or more of a public company's outstanding stock; quarterly and other periodic reports of those mutual funds which concentrate their efforts and assets in the area of asset-play investing; and also the Pink Sheets. Let's take a closer look at each of these sources.

Financial Publications and Investment Letters

While there are many publications that are helpful when looking for potential asset-play stocks (the *Wall Street Journal, Investors Daily, Forbes,* and *Barron's* to name just a few), for the most part your attention should be directed at the company's balance sheet rather than its income statement. In the past, financial publications tended to highlight currently popular industries and stocks and devote most of their pages to describing how rapid a particular favorite was growing in terms of sales and earnings. Likewise, most financial publications described in great detail the growth stock picks of a few favorite investment managers.

However, in recent years many publications have increased their coverage of companies with significant assets rather than concentrating on growth situations alone. During recent upward trends in the market, particularly with blue chips, many financial publications have had to look far afield for recommendations and investment ideas. For this reason many financial publications are featuring articles about smaller asset-rich companies. The stocks of these companies are traded over the counter and fit into one or more of the categories that encompass asset plays. It's becoming common to find articles in financial publications dealing with closely held companies, bankrupt companies, companies operating in depressed industries, spinoffs, and restructuring situations. Thus, financial publications can provide you with a wealth of potential asset-play stocks.

One drawback to utilizing the ideas contained in financial publications is that by the time a potential asset play is discussed in such a publication it may have already gone up in price and no longer represent an opportunity to buy assets at a discount. For this reason, it is important to determine that you are not investing in an asset-play situation that has already been discovered. Price per share versus the assets behind each share is usually the ultimate test in determining whether the particular stock is overpriced or represents a buying opportunity.

13D Filings

More so than financial publications, 13D filings can provide useful leads in your search for potential asset plays. If interpreted properly, the information contained in a 13D filing can alert an individual investor to those companies which have begun to attract the attention of professional investors.

What is a 13D filing? Under what circumstances must a 13D filing be made? Who is required to make such a filing? These are just a few of the questions that probably have come to your mind. A 13D filing must be made with the SEC by any officer or director of a public company as well as any institution or individual who owns 5% or more of a public company's common stock. The filing must be made within ten days of the acquisition of the 5% position. Also, any changes in such positions (increases or decreases) must be reported to the SEC. Officers and directors of public companies are required to keep the SEC informed of all transactions in their company's stock.

In requiring the filing of a 13D, the drafters of the federal securities laws intended to put all investors on an equal footing with one another. The idea was to prevent large investors from secretly buying up the stock of a public company and at the last minute revealing their activities. Many of the Congressional hearings leading to the enactment of the federal securities laws brought out the abuses that the so-called "pools" worked on the investing public because they were under no requirement to disclose their activities, even in those instances where they owned the bulk of a public company's outstanding stock. While the requirement that all officers, directors, and 5% stockholders report all securities transactions was to prevent such abuses, such filings also aid the individual investor in identifying potential asset plays.

There are a number of ways of keeping track of the 13D filings made with the SEC. One source is the *SEC News Digest,* which is published daily and includes all 13D filings and changes in such positions as they are received by the SEC. Also, the *SEC Monthly Summary of Insider Transactions* lists in alphabetical order all those companies in which there have been purchases or sales of the company's stock by officers, directors, or 5% stockholders. Both of these publications can be obtained via a paid subscription from the publication office of the SEC in Washington, D.C. and are also available at a number of public libraries. In addition, a number of advisory services and newsletters have come into existence to meet this need for tracking 13D filings. Such publications report to their subscribers all 13D filings made with the SEC and provide an analysis of the significance of such filings.

There are a number of reasons why professional investors follow the 13D filings made by individuals and institutions and why these filings can be useful to an asset-play investor. Obviously, the significance of a 13D filing varies from situation to situation, but there are certain guidelines which generally apply. First, the importance that should be accorded to a 13D filing varies according to the individual or entity making the filing. As you become familiar with the names of the major "players" (i.e., individuals and institutions), the filing of a 13D by any of these players will be a signal to look further into the particular company in which the stock was bought. Looking further would entail such things as obtaining a copy of the company's annual report and applying the various analytical tools learned from this book to determine what the particular investor saw in the company to warrant buying its stock.

Second, as you become more familiar with the methods, techniques, and goals of particular players you will be better able to guess what will follow the filing of a 13D. Is the player a "greenmailer," that is, an individual who seeks to get the particular company to buy the position out at a price above the prevailing market? Or is the player an active and successful acquirer of companies? Is the investor an asset player who buys into companies selling at a discount from their liquidation value? As you become more familiar with asset-play investors, you will learn whether their goals fit your own.

Finally, you can learn about a company from the size of the position taken, as indicated in the 13D filing. A position of 5 to 10% indicates an initial interest on the part of the particular investor. Also, such a small position may mean that it is difficult to acquire any of the particular stock. In any event, the acquisition of a position of 5 to 10% means that the individual investor has time to look into the company and reach a decision as to whether the purchase of the particular stock is warranted. A large initial position in most cases means that the stock is no longer undiscovered and the stock is fully priced versus the underlying assets of the particular company.

Tracking Mutual Funds and Investment Advisers Specializing in Asset Plays

Tracking what professional asset-play investors are doing is another means for the individual investor to use in locating asset plays. In many cases, because the individual investor is under no pressure to produce instantaneous results, he or she is better able to hold a particular stock for a longer period of time until its value is recognized. Likewise, as discussed in Chapter 7 dealing with the trading aspects of asset plays, the individual investor has an advantage over the institutional investor in that the individual investor is looking only to acquire a small number of shares. The individual investor also does not have to be concerned with how easy or difficult it is to dispose of such shares.

Table 3-1 is a listing of the names and addresses of mutual funds whose investment objective is to identify and invest in companies representing asset plays. Requesting a copy of their prospectus and the latest annual and quarterly reports to shareholders is the first step to take in tracking their investment stocks. After you receive the information you requested, spend some time reading the material and, in particular, the section of the prospectus describing the fund's investment objectives and approach it utilizes to identify potential asset plays.

The second step is to spend some time reviewing what stocks are held in the portfolios of the funds. A fund's prospectus, annual report, and quarterly report will contain a description of the particular fund's portfolio. How detailed the description is varies from fund to fund, but there are certain observations you will probably reach from scanning such asset-play mutual funds. For the most part, you will not be familiar with the names of the companies in which asset-play funds invest. Few of them will represent companies whose names are household words. It is for just this reason that the stocks of such companies sell below the value of the assets they represent. Also, you will find that the stocks of certain companies will appear in almost all of the portfolios of the asset-play mutual funds listed previously. This is because the managers of many of these funds reached the same conclusion: that the stock of these companies represented an opportunity to buy assets at a discount.

Table 3-1. Names and addresses of asset-play mutual funds, partnerships, and investment advisers.

Name	*Address*
Marc Boyar Associates	202 West 40th Street (8th fl.) New York, NY 10018 (212) 719-1014
Baron Capital Management, Inc.	450 Park Avenue New York, NY 10022 (212) 759-1500
Charter Oak Partners	P.O. Box 5147 Westport, CT 06881 (203) 226-7591
Evergreen Total Return Fund	550 Mamaroneck Avenue Harrison, NY 10528 (800) 235-0064
Gabelli Fund	655 Third Avenue (14th fl.) New York, NY 10017 (212) 490-3670
Industrial Equities, Ltd.	New Zealand
Lindner Fund, Inc.	P.O. Box 11208 200 South Bemiston St. Louis, MO 63105 (314) 727-5305
Mutual Shares/Mutual Beacon/ Mutual Qualified Fund	c/o Herzog, Heine, Geduld, Inc. 26 Broadway New York, NY 10004 (212) 908-4000
OTC-Securities Fund, Inc.	P.O. Box 1537 Fort Washington, PA 19034-1537 (215) 643-2510

Table 3-1 continued

Name	*Address*
Odyssey Partners	437 Madison Avenue New York, NY 10022 (212) 715-8600
Royce Value Trust, Inc.	1414 Avenue of the Americas (9th fl.) New York, NY 10019 (212) 355-7311
Ruane Cunniff, Inc./ RCS Management Co., Inc.	1370 Avenue of the Americas New York, NY 10019 (212) 245-4500
Tweedy, Browne & Co.	52 Vanderbilt Avenue (7th fl.) New York, NY 10017 (212) 916-0600
TBK Partners	Same as above
Windsor Funds, Inc./ Vanguard Group	1300 Morris Drive P.O. Box 2600 Valley Forge, PA 19482 (215) 648-6000
Zweig Fund	900 Third Avenue New York, NY 10022 (212) 486-7110

Once you have familiarized yourself with the investment policies and portfolios of a number of the funds listed in Table 3-1, you are ready to make use of the information gleamed from this source. By scanning a number of such asset plays you should be able to come up with a list of favorite stocks common to many of these portfolios. It would be worth your time and effort to send for the annual and quarterly statements of such companies and, once you receive them, to determine what factors about these companies make them asset plays. Also, it is important to identify those companies in which such asset-play funds have recently taken positions. The fact that such funds have just discovered a particular asset play may mean that the stock still represents a buying opportunity for the individual investor.

Spectrum is an advisory service published by CDA Investment Technologies (115-01 Georgia Ave., Silver Springs, MD 20902). It lists on a quarterly basis the positions of mutual funds as well as the holdings of a number of hedge funds, limited partnerships, and investment advisers. Figure 3-1 is an example of a page drawn from *Spectrum* with the asterisk indicating those positions that were established by the particular fund since the last quarterly report. You can use *Spectrum* to obtain the names of those companies that have been recently identified and had stock bought by professional asset-play investors.

Identifying Asset-Play Stocks Through Professional, Business, and Social Contacts

Your business and social contacts can furnish you with a number of leads to potential asset plays. Whether you work as a secretary, a schoolteacher, an engineer, a homemaker, or any number of other jobs, on a day-to-day basis you come into contact with goods and services provided by hundreds of different companies. If you spend a little time and effort you will find that a number of these companies represent real buying opportunities.

For example, let's assume that you are employed as a chemical engineer with a large semiconductor manufacturer. Like the company for which you work, most of the companies in this industry are large, well known, and followed closely by the investment community. Thus, few, if any of them represent

Figure 3-1.

Continued SHERIFF SECURITIES CORP

KNE	K N ENERGY INC	-13	0	0
KVU	KLEER VU INDS INC DEL	0	16	20
LANE	LANE CO	13	13*	679
LSI	LEAR SIEGLER INC	118	118*	10799
LTC	LEASEWAY TRANSN CORP	15	39	1872
MTZ	MARANTZ CO DEL	124	124*	711
MA	MAY DEPT STORES CO	-1	123	4366
NATH	NATHANS FAMOUS INC	59	59*	461
NLPI	NATIONAL LAMPOON INC	31	31*	207
NELR	NELSON RESH & DEV CO	149	149*	828
OFC	OXFORD 1ST CORP PA	-12	33	565
PZA	PIZZA INN INC	13	13*	132
RNI	RANCO INC	73	73*	2813
SM	SOUTHMARK CORP	0	78	654
SNLA	SUN CHEMICAL CORP CL A	8	16	1066
TVLA	TACO VILLA INC	14	28	96
TPLP	TEECO PPTYS L P	0	152	134
TEX	TEXAS AIR CORP	-1	0	0
TRX	TIMBER REALIZATION CO	-10	0	0
MORW	11 MORROW INC	22	22*	204
UNV	UNITEL VIDEO INC	159	159*	1235
VIA	VIACOM INTL INC	-3	66	2627
WANB	WANG LABS INC CL B	-73	206	2391
	Total of 39 holdings			73458

***** SHUFRO ROSE & EHRMAN

AMT	ACME CLEVELAND CORP	-272	0	0
ACU	ACME UNITED CORP	6	131	1078
ADB	ADOBE RES	116	565	3748
AET	AETNA LIFE & CAS CO	13	13*	739
ALN	ALLEN GROUP INC	-2	971	15291
ALD	ALLIED SIGNAL INC	-3	144	5790
AMB	AMERICAN BRANDS INC	-16	16	681
AFSL	AMERN F S L A COLO PUEBLO	-168	49	369
AHP	AMERICAN HOME PRODS CORP	-11	0	0
AIT	AMERICAN INFO TECH CORP	0	7	895
AMMG	AMERICAN MAGNETICS CORP	108	123	644
T	AMERICAN TEL&TELEG CO	-1	69	1737
AWK	AMERICAN WTR WKS INC	0	8	311
AMKG	AMOSKEAG BK SHS INC	-38	326	7017
AN	AMOCO CORP	-1	39	2565
APA	APACHE CORP	-128	724	6518
APPL	APPLE BK FOR SVGS N Y	29	70	1800
ADCC	APPLIED DATA COMMUNICATIONS	79	835	3759
ASTR	ASTROSYSTEMS INC	0	26	247
ARC	ATLANTIC RICHFIELD CO	3	41	2474
ATTC	AUTO TROL TECHNOLOGY CORP	0	75	298
BRHF	BR COMMUNICATIONS	130	1528	10696
BKO	BAKER INTL CORP	41	41*	488
BOKC	BANCOKLAHOMA CORP	-13	111	306
BK	BANK NEW YORK INC	13	21	806
BCW	BECOR WESTN INC	66	974	10963
BEL	BELL ATLANTIC CORP	-0	13	857
BLS	BELLSOUTH CORP	-0	23	1332
BN	BORDEN INC	0	18	844
CMX	CMI CORP	-17	0	0
CT	CALIFORNIA REAL EST INVT TR	2	473	5388
CPH	CAPITAL HLDG CORP DEL	-0	20	613
CSR	CENTRAL & SOUTH WEST CORP	-3	179	6138
CRT	CERTAIN TEED CORP	23	23*	734
CHV	CHEVRON CORP	-5	34	1530
CFB	CITIZENS FIRST BANCORP N J	4	38	894
CBCO	COBANCO INC	56	56*	647
CBSH	COMMERCE BANCSHARES INC	27	586	20234
CWE	COMMONWEALTH EDISON CO	18	18*	613
CRI	CORE INDS INC	61	61*	765
DPT	DATAPOINT CORP	-1234	575	3668
DTSI	DATRON SYS INC CALIF	79	295	2066
DVL	DEL VAL FINANCIAL CORP	17	203	3899
DSO	DESOTO INC	85	447	17044
DIA	DIAMOND SHAMROCK CORP	0	80	985
DNA	DIANA CORP	127	592	6515
DCI	DONALDSON INC	-1	64	2168
DD	DU PONT E I DE NEMOURS & CO	-1	144	12098
DYR	DYR LIQUIDATING CORP	-4	574	935
EK	EASTMAN KODAK CO	19	311	21329

Continued SHUFRO ROSE & EHRMAN

EBS	EDISON BROS STORES INC	106	806	27292
EMR	EMERSON ELEC CO	0	12	1047
EPSC	EPSCO INC	-3	126	1213
ESL	ESTERLINE CORP	-4	183	2764
ESCC	EVANS&SUTHERLAND COMPUTER CP	-4	96	2424
XON	EXXON CORP	[illegible]	235	16452
FPL	FPL GROUP INC	[illegible]	22*	700
FCA	FABRI CTRS AMER INC	-7	821	9653
FFCI	FFB CORP	[illegible]	115	1604
FALB	FALSTAFF BREWING CORP	0	61	418
FHFC	FARM HOUSE FOODS CORP	136	1083	5014
FMO	FEDERAL MOGUL CORP	58	652	26090
FABC	FIRST ALA BANCSHARES INC	7	43	928
FAMB	1ST AMERN BK FOR SVGS	565	565*	5582
FFMY	FIRST F S L A FORT MYERS FLA	-20	210	6028
FWB	FIRST WIS CORP	205	1063	25511
FRST	FIRSTIER INC	1	479	11845
FPC	FLORIDA PROGRESS CORP	-1	23	915
FRK	FLORIDA ROCK INDS INC	92	211	5268
GTE	GTE CORP	[illegible]	4	218
GE	GENERAL ELEC CO	[illegible]	267	22930
GMW	GENERAL MICROWAVE CORP	[illegible]	148	1937
GM	GENERAL MTRS CORP	[illegible]	186	12257
GFSA	GIANT FOODS INC	[illegible]	74	1842
GPO	GIANT GROUP LTD	[illegible]	59	1411
GILB	GILBERT ASSOC INC	[illegible]	168	5897
GLT	GLATFELTER P H CO	[illegible]	767	18707
GBCA	GREIF BROS CORP	[illegible]	38	0
HRE	H R E PPTYS	[illegible]	195	5211
HAL	HALLIBURTON CO	[illegible]	30	744
HENG	HENLEY GROUP INC	-33	0	0
HSY	HERSHEY FOODS CORP	[illegible]	21	519
HON	HONEYWELL INC	15	69	4103
HOU	HOUSTON INDS INC	15	15*	521
IT	INTELOGIC TRACE INC	858	1585	10506
IFC	INTERFIRST CORP	10	112	521
IBM	INTERNATIONAL BUSINESS MACHS	21	206	24731
KSU	KANSAS CITY SOUTHN INDS INC	30	48	2263
KWN	KENWIN SHOPS INC	-2	98	1460
KMG	KERR MCGEE CORP	-1	46	1296
KNLA	KNOLL INTL INC	-12	305	3506
KGR	KOGER CO	1	37	1096
KOG	KOGER PPTYS INC	19	19*	596
TLAM	LAMA TONY INC	-1	162	1541
LANC	LANCASTER COLONY CORP	85	85*	1614
LDL	LYDALL INC	2	15	218
MCA	MCA INC	186	223	8543
MCMC	MCM CORP	2	16	181
MSCO	MASSTOR SYS CORP	-7	561	1757
MLP	MESA LTD PARTNERSHIP	5	1918	32374
MSA	MESA PETE CO	-548	1016	3809
MAM	MID AMER INDS INC	39	80	601
MMM	MINNESOTA MNG & MFG CO	-1	9	1024
MOB	MOBIL CORP	-1	131	5254
MFGI	MOORE FINL GROUP INC IDAHO	-6	29	655
MMR	MOORE MCCORMACK RES INC	25	25*	508
MRN	MORRISON KNUDSEN CORP	90	319	13485
MRS	MORSE SHOE INC	-128	1441	44680
MYE	MYERS INDS INC	-3	109	1230
NCR	NCR CORP	33	98	4322
NESB	NEW ENGLAND SVGS BK CT	53	252	3813
NYN	NYNEX CORP	-0	13	825
OLP	ONE LIBERTY PPTYS INC	12	22	366
PPG	PPG INDS INC	-0	57	4123
PSX	PACIFIC SCIENTIFIC CO	168	1001	14012
PAC	PACIFIC TELESIS GROUP	-1	10	527
PI	PANDICK INC	-146	0	0
PVIR	PENN VIRGINIA CORP	22	71	3292
PDS	PERRY DRUG STORES INC	368	653	7995
PAE	PIONEER SYS INC	-65	0	0
PSR	PUBLIC SVC CO COLO	37	975	18277
RTE	R T E CORP	26	233	6767
RGO	RANGER OIL LTD	31	66	305
RICH	RICHMOND HILL SVGS BK	191	412	5453
RHR	ROHR INDS INC	71	71*	2056
SAG	SAGE ENERGY CO	14	97	606
SFX	SANTA FE SOUTHN PAC CORP	57	764	22637

Continued SHUFRO ROSE & EHRMAN

SLB	SCHLUMBERGER LTD	-0	53	1676
SMN	SEAMENS CORP	10	10*	74
SMCA	SMITH A O CORP CL A	2	219	4599
SMCB	SMITH A O CORP CL B	25	265	5424
SBC	SOUTHWESTERN BELL CORP	6	12	1325
SOVR	SOVEREIGN CORP	-16	0	0
TERM	TERMINAL DATA INC	-11	120	240
TXU	TEXAS UTILS CO	-169	299	9433
TIX	TIMEPLEX INC	-11	89	2078
TIC	TRAVELERS CORP	10	10*	450
TNV	TRINOVA CORP	24	146	6867
TUCK	TUCKER DRILLING INC	-2	129	677
X	USX CORP	3	995	21394
UNC	UNC RES INC	24	24*	213
USG	USG CORP	-2	155	5849
UJB	UNITED JERSEY BKS HACKENSACK	16	68	1611
USBI	UNITED SAVERS BANCORP	-7	0	0
USL	U S LEASING INTL INC DEL	19	73	3063
USR	UNITED STATES SHOE CORP	-5	130	2692
USW	U S WEST INC	-0	10	544
VBND	VELOB ND INC	0	71	869
WLA	WARNER LAMBERT CO	-2	5	285
WNT	WASHINGTON NATL CORP	204	237	7589
WVTK	WAVETEK CORP	112	2028	14195
WOLA	WOLVERINE TECHNOLOGIES INC	13	13*	122
WRIT	WRIGHT WM E CO	2	58	773
WN	WYNNS INTL INC	-13	399	7933
	Total of 146 holdings			776360

***** SIMMS CAPITAL MGMT. LTD.

AEAG	AGNICO EAGLE MINES LTD	0	91	1738
AC	AMERICAN CAN CO	0	73	6125
AXP	AMERICAN EXPRESS CO	0	108	6133
DIET	AMERICAN HEALTH COS	0	79	1165
AAPL	APPLE COMPUTER INC	0	89	3588
BMGC	BATTLE MTN GOLD CO	0	23	425
BN	BORDEN INC	0	20	938
BRDL	BRENDLES INC	0	52	647
CVC	CABLEVISION SYS CORP	0	59	1121
CRK	CAMPBELL RED LAKE MINES LTD	0	70	1374
CTLN	CENTRAL NORSEMAN CORP N L	0	67	0
CC	CIRCUIT CITY STORES INC	0	121	3700
CMI	CLUB MED INC	0	11	278
CPQ	COMPAQ COMPUTER CORP	0	151	2901
CYPM	CYPRUS MINERALS CORP	0	50	812
DH	DAYTON HUDSON CORP	0	104	4441
DEC	DIGITAL EQUIP CORP	0	71	7406
DRV	DRAVO CORP	0	58	1075
ECO	ECHO BAY MINES LTD	0	70	1610
ENUC	ELECTRO-NUCLEONICS INC	0	118	1331
FFF	FEDERAL CO	0	111	4452
FLD	FIELDCREST CANNON INC	0	198	6646
FFSB	1ST FED SVGS BK CALIF	0	22	467
FRN	FRANCE FD INC	0	36	406
GE	GENERAL ELEC CO	0	20	1720
GER	GERMANY FD INC	0	25	253
GTA	GREAT AMERN FIRST SVGS BK CA	0	35	612
GNN	GREAT NORTHN NEKOOSA CORP	0	45	2909
HAN	HANSON TR PLC SPON ADR	0	54	777
HBE	HONEYBEE INC	0	29	207
ICH	I C H CORP	0	257	5084
KNBW	KIRIN BREWERY	0	3	288
LLY	LILLY ELI & CO	0	96	7135
MCD	MCDONALDS CORP	0	94	5729
NBSI	NATIONAL BUSINESS SYS INC	0	21	251
NWSY	NEWS LTD	0	7	338
NORK	NORSK DATA A S	0	67	1760
NGX	NORTHGATE EXPL LTD	0	42	194
MO	PHILIP MORRIS COS INC	0	42	2997
PLC	PLACER DEV LTD	0	42	940
RAL	RALSTON PURINA CO	0	60	4252
RTN	RAYTHEON CO	0	92	6160
SFCD	SAFECARD SVCS INC	0	55	1666
SPP	SCOTT PAPER CO	0	71	4430
SGAT	SEAGATE TECHNOLOGY	0	171	3264
SLC	SOUTHLAND CORP	0	108	5062

undiscovered asset plays. In your job you deal with companies that supply a variety of products and services to the company for which you work. Among such suppliers you may find a number who stand out above the rest in the way they do business. You will probably find that many of these "star performers" are regional companies as opposed to national in scope and have been in business for a number of years. Also, such a company in many cases might have been successful in carving out for itself a specialized market niche within the industry while its stock remained "undiscovered." Your next step is to determine if the stock of the company is publicly traded (even if only on a regional basis) and send for a copy of the company's annual and quarterly reports.

Work is not the only place that might lead you to discover a potential asset play. Your daily experience as a consumer may also furnish you with leads. A toy you buy for a child may prove particularly sturdy or creative in design. You should look into the company that manufactured the toy to see if it is publicly traded and what the company's financial state is. At the heart of this whole approach to locating potential asset plays is the idea that you have to be constantly aware of the goods and services you see and consume on a daily basis and identify those companies that provide a superior product or service and whose stock price does not reflect this fact.

Perhaps as a consumer you may identify a change in the way in which a particular type of good or service is marketed. It is not enough simply to notice the change; you have to carry the process one step further and determine which companies originated this shift in marketing of the particular good or service. An example of this is those investors who discovered in the 1970s that the marketing of toys was changing. No longer being sold through "mom and pop operations" or department stores, toy warehouses were coming to dominate the marketplace. For those investors who looked behind this shift in marketing approach and discovered the subsidiary of a bankrupt discounter at the center of this "revolution," the returns for every dollar invested have been extremely high. For such were the beginnings of Toys R Us.

Personal contacts are particularly important in locating local or regional stocks that represent potential asset plays. Until recent years, brokerage firms concentrated their research efforts exclusively on following the activities of the large, well-capitalized companies listed on the New York or American Stock Exchanges. While this has changed somewhat in recent years, for the most part little or no attention is paid to the many thousands of local and regional companies. Outside of the community or region in which the particular company is located, in most instances there are few investors who are aware of the fact that the company is public and that shares of its stock are available in the marketplace. The only way you can learn of the existence of many of these local or regional companies is through personal contact. Thus, by keeping alert to the existence and activities of those companies located in your particular community or region, you will be surprised at the number of potential asset plays you will discover. By investing in a company before it has gained national recognition, many astute investors have been able to reap substantial profits on small initial investments.

Personal Contact with Company Management

Personal contact with company management is a source of potential asset plays frequently overlooked by individual investors.

Number crunching is an important tool in determining whether a certain situation represents an opportunity to buy assets at a discount. It is for this reason that a substantial part of this book is devoted to teaching you this necessary skill. But there is another aspect to identifying potential asset plays, and that is evaluating a company's management. Just as it is important to reach a conclusion as to the quality of a company's numbers, so it is important to reach a conclusion as to the quality of its management. Only then can you decide whether or not you have uncovered an asset play in which you should invest your money.

What are some of the ways you as an individual investor

can establish a relationship with a company's management? Who should you contact at a company? What questions should you ask a company's management? Requesting a copy of the company's annual report and 10K is perhaps the best way to initiate contact. With few exceptions, companies are only too happy to supply individual investors with copies of such documents. After all, it is to the company's benefit to foster public interest in the company. Many companies today have whole departments whose only purpose is to handle investors relations.

Figure 3-2 is a sample of a letter you might utilize in requesting information from a company. Once you receive the information you requested, the first step is to review the various annual and quarterly reports to see which ones can be immediately rejected as potential asset plays. The second step is to apply the number-crunching techniques (see Chapter 4) learned from this book to further narrow down your list of potential asset plays. Typically out of a number of annual reports you might be

Figure 3-2.

____
____

____
____

Re: Request for financial information

Dear ______________:

I am an individual investor. My particular area of interest is ________ ______. I would therefore appreciate it if you could send me the following information about your company:

1. Current Annual Report
2. Current 10K
3. Current Proxy
4. Current Quarterly Report

I would appreciate it if you could place my name on the mailing list to receive quarterly and other financial reports as they become available.

Thank you in advance for your consideration of this request.

Sincerely,

____

left with very few that warrant you personally contacting the company's management. Thus, you can see that identifying asset plays involves a large measure of research, but returns can be very high.

Many individual investors hesitate to call a company's management, believing that management will be unfriendly or unwilling to speak to an individual investor. While undoubtedly this is true in some cases, for the most part corporate officers are receptive to a telephone call from an individual investor. Individual investors are also concerned with to whom they should speak when they call a company. The answer to this question varies from company to company. Investors may find that senior management is eager to talk to them in some companies, while in other cases the call may be shifted to someone in the finance or public relations department. While it is more desirable to speak to senior management, the most important objective is to make the initial contact with management at whatever level.

In dealing with a company's management, it is important to distinguish between hesitancy and hostility. For example, the management of many closely held companies appear to be hesitant in dealing with outside investors. Some of this might come from the fact that they are seldom approached by members of the investing public. But once approached they are willing to supply the information and discuss the company's present and future prospects. It is among these companies that are seldom if ever contacted by either individual or institutional investors that you are likely to find the best buying opportunities. This is because their story is not known by every Wall Street analyst and followed daily in all the financial publications.

If management is unwilling to supply you with the information you have requested and appears hostile to answering any questions, you would be wise to look elsewhere to invest your money. Likewise, if a company's management seems to be more interested in the performance of its stock than in the selling of the company's products, think long and hard before you invest in such a company. Companies whose managements meet regularly with security analysts and are always available to "tell the company's story" can potentially represent poor investments.

Before you make the initial call to a company's management you should prepare a detailed list of questions that you wish to pose to management. The following is a listing of some of the kinds of questions you might wish to ask.

1. After reviewing the reports you recently sent me, I see that the company's sales have shown a continuing pattern of growth. How do you account for this pattern, and do you see it continuing in the future?
2. Earnings have been growing at a very rapid rate. Do you see this continuing in the future? Has the company been able to maintain and/or expand its profit margin as its sales have grown? Is the company's product mix shifting toward higher profit margin products?
3. Is the company presently involved in or contemplating in the near future the modernization or expansion of its plant capacity?
4. What means do you see the company using (for example, debt or internally generated funds) to finance plant expansion or modernization?
5. The company is selling at a relatively low P/E ratio. Do you have any feelings why this is so? Any reason this should change in the future?
6. Aside from what was described in the annual report you sent me, has the company developed new products, expanded into new markets, or undergone restructuring of corporate assets?
7. Have any other individual or institutional analysts contacted you recently? If so, do you know if they have written any research reports about the company and if I can obtain copies of those reports?

Obviously, this is far from a complete listing of all of the questions you might wish to pose to a company's management. Your questions would be influenced by the nature of the company's business, management style, and what insights you personally might bring to the questioning process. The important thing to keep in mind is that you are seeking to establish a personal contact with the company's management. Also, you should rely on your reaction to the way management does or does not answer your questions as well as any feeling you may have about management's strengths or weaknesses. Any experienced investor will tell you that you should *invest only in those companies whose managements you respect and believe in.*

Furthermore, whenever possible attend the annual meeting of any company you invest in as another way of getting to know management. By attending a company's annual meeting you will begin to see who are the real managers of the particular company and if any family or business relationships exist within management. Frequently, after leaving an annual meeting you will reach a conclusion as to whether you wish to buy more of the company's stock or sell whatever shares you presently own.

Pink Sheets

Companies that have their stock listed in the Pink Sheets range from mature, well-known companies to small start-up ventures. While some of the companies listed in the Pink Sheets may have millions of shares outstanding and thousands of their shares traded on a daily basis, others have a few hundred thousand shares outstanding and trade on an irregular basis. It is the latter rather than the former category that offers the greatest potential for buying assets at a discount. The rationale behind this conclusion is that because a company has a few shares outstanding and is not actively traded, it is unlikely that a large number of analysts will follow the company or that the company will be an institutional favorite.

How can you identify those companies that represent potential asset plays by simply scanning the Pink Sheets? As an individual investor, you can utilize the same technique that professional investors use, namely, identify those stocks which certain brokers make a market in (that is, have their name listed in the Pink Sheets as interested in buying or selling the particular stock). Table 3-2 is a listing of those brokerage firms that are identified as market makers in asset plays. A simple exercise is to go through the Pink Sheets periodically and see what stocks these brokers are making a market in, especially those stocks

Table 3-2. Asset-play market makers.

Hill Thompson Magid, Inc.	First Manhattan Co.
Robotti & Eng, Inc.	Gruntal & Co.
Chicago Corp.	Herzog Heine Geduld, Inc.
S.D. Wolf & Co.	Carret & Co.
William C. Rooney & Co.	Tweedy, Browne & Co.
Brooks Weinger R & L, Inc.	Carr & Thompson, Inc.
Cantor Fitzgerald & Co.	Hoppin, Soliday & Co.

that they have just started to quote. Once you have identified the stocks these asset-play market makers are interested in, you are ready to take the next step. That consists of sending for the annual report, quarterly statement, and proxy statement of those companies in which these brokers have shown interest. Reviewing the financial information when you receive it should give you some possible answers as to why these asset-play market makers are trading these particular stocks.

Conclusion

This chapter has concentrated on the key techniques for identifying potential asset plays. At this point, it would be useful to summarize these techniques as well as describing their weaknesses and strengths.

1. *Financial publications and investment letters.* These are useful as a starting point, but you must be careful that you are not buying a stock that has already been "discovered."
2. *13D filings.* These are also useful, but with one limitation: you have to develop a knowledge of the operating characteristics of the various "players" (merger and acquisition specialists, hedge funds, limited partnerships, and arbitrageurs).
3. *Tracking mutual funds and investment advisers specializing in asset plays.* This is an effective way of identifying potential asset plays with the same warning as cited in number 1: beware of paying too much for a given stock, because its price may already reflect full valuation of the underlying assets.

4. *Identifying asset plays through professional, business, and social contacts.* This is an approach to finding potential asset plays which most individual investors overlook and which can lead you to some worthwhile investments.
5. *Personal contact with management.* This is another approach which many individual investors do not make use of. It is necessary if you are to be able to determine the true worth of a company's assets, particularly in those cases where you anticipate making a significant dollar investment.
6. *Pink Sheets.* Scanning the Pink Sheets to see which stocks key market makers are investing in is a useful way of locating potential asset plays.

Basic Techniques for Analyzing Asset Plays

CHAPTER 4

This chapter is about the mathematical techniques for identifying asset-play stocks.

The balance sheet is the core element to any asset-play stock. Since by its very definition an asset play represents the opportunity to buy assets at a discount, in some cases for as little as fifty cents on the dollar, in analyzing any potential asset play your attention will be concentrated for the most part on the company's balance sheet. However, during the course of this chapter you will also learn some of the key ratios which can be utilized to evaluate a company's income statement.

While the balance of this chapter will deal with the various ratios and mathematical techniques that are used to identify potential asset plays, the quality and trend of a company's figures are two factors that you should always keep in mind. "Quality of the figures" means how much faith you can put in their accuracy and honesty. The existence of extensive footnotes to a company's annual report, the utilization of every available accounting rule, the frequent replacement of outside accountants, or a very complex accounting procedure should cause you to examine the reported figures more closely. Likewise, in evaluating any company it is necessary to determine the company's financial trends. To do this you should calculate the applicable ratios for a five-year period. You will then be able to determine whether the particular company's balance sheet has improved, stayed the same, or deteriorated, and you will establish some standard to gauge the company's present financial position.

Before we look at the various techniques used to identify asset plays, let's review the Annual Report and Proxy Statement of the Summerfield Production Company (see Exhibit 4-1).

Exhibit 4-1.

Summerfield Production Company

Annual Report 19X3

Exhibit 4-1 continued

PRESIDENT'S MESSAGE

Sales and profits showed a decrease for Summerfield Production Company in 19Y3. Sales were $4,267,259 down from $5,500,545, while net income in 19Y3 was $134,455 down from $293,349 in 19Y2. Our decrease in sales in 19Y3 was 22.4%.

The year of 19Y3 has been another disappointing one for Summerfield due to the continued severe competition in the photocopy industry. The Japanese photocopy manufacturers continue to flood the U.S. market with new model, low-priced, plain paper copiers that have drastically affected the sale of our PMC coated-paper copier. The obsolescence of electrostatic copiers in favor of plain paper copiers has also sharply curtailed our sale of paper and toner for electrostatic machines. At the present time we are negotiating with outstanding Japanese and German manufacturers to distribute their table-top, low-priced, plain paper copiers through our national dealer sales organization.

Summerfield anticipated these problems and has made every effort to reduce our overhead in every possible way and will continue to do so. As part of this program, we are in the process of phasing out the manufacture of our coated-paper copiers. We have always been conservative and our main object is to maintain the highest standard of liquidity in order to protect our stockholders and the net worth of our Company. We have no liens or mortgages on any of our holdings, we have no outstanding bank loans, accounts payable or contingent liabilities. Our current assets over our current liabilities is approximately 1900 to 1. In addition to our current assets, Summerfield has $539,000 in secured first mortgages on the properties we sold. These mortgages are payable monthly with a weighted average interest rate of approximately 11½%.

Our fixed assets have been depreciated to $248,000 which is 3% of our book value and represents a small investment in relation to our sales and total assets. We also have fixed assets that are still in use, such as the 83,000 sq. ft. building we now occupy, which have been fully depreciated on our books.

As a result of the current uncertainty as to the direction of our business, we have decided to defer consideration of the payment of a cash dividend at this time. Should Summerfield be successful in obtaining distribution rights for an outstanding, low-priced, plain paper copier to be distributed through our national dealer sales organization, we feel confident that it would increase our sales and earnings in 19Y4.

Respectfully submitted,

Arthur Sanders
President

March 15, 19Y4

Exhibit 4-1 continued

FINANCIAL HIGHLIGHTS

	19Y3	19Y2	19Y1
Net sales	$4,267,259	$5,500,545	$6,660,572
Income before income taxes	$ 200,455	$ 349,349	$ 547,676
Federal and state income taxes	$ 66,000	$ 56,000	$ 245,000
Net income for the year— Amount	$ 134,455	$ 293,349	$ 302,676
Percent to sales	3.2%	5.3%	4.5%
Percent to shareholders' investment	1.8%	3.9%	4.1%
Per share*	9¢	20¢	21¢
Inventories	$ 975,578	$1,842,863	$2,027,896
Working capital	$6,873,677	$6,790,062	$6,855,910
Current ratio	1,910 to 1	364 to 1	1,063 to 1
Federal, state, and local taxes	$ 192,928	$ 224,887	$ 428,890
Per share*	13¢	15¢	29¢
Number of shares outstanding*	1,456,302	1,456,302	1,456,302
Number of shareholders	1,277	1,358	1,423

*Based on average number of shares oustanding during each year adjusted for stock dividends of 5% in each of 19Y1 and 3% in each of 19Y2 and 19Y3.

Exhibit 4-1 continued

SUMMERFIELD PRODUCTION COMPANY
BALANCE SHEETS
DECEMBER 31, 19Y3 AND 19Y2

ASSETS

	19Y3	19Y2
CURRENT ASSETS:		
Cash	$ 286,978	$ 227,046
Marketable securities, at cost (primarily U.S. Government issues—market value at December 31, 19Y3, $4,241,859)	4,230,775	3,068,468
Accounts and notes receivable, less allowance of $55,000 in 19Y3 and $45,000 in 19Y2 for uncollectibles	1,112,194	1,370,793
Pre-paid income taxes	65,305	137,510
Inventories (Note 1):		
Finished goods and resale items	594,556	781,935
Raw materials and work in process	381,022	1,060,928
Prepaid expenses and other assets	206,446	162,093
Patents, trademarks and goodwill, less accumulated amortization	1	1
Total current assets	$6,877,277	$6,808,774
FIRST MORTGAGE NOTES RECEIVABLE, LESS CURRENT PORTION (Note 5)	$ 529,757	$ 539,858
PROPERTY, PLANT AND EQUIPMENT, AT COST (Note 1):		
Land	$ 119,893	$ 119,893
Buildings and improvements	363,183	363,183
Machinery and equipment	599,684	603,588
	$1,082,760	$1,086,664
Less—Accumulated depreciation	834,418	756,797
	$ 248,342	$ 329,867
	$7,655,376	$7,678,499

The accompanying notes to financial statements are an integral part of these balance sheets.

Exhibit 4-1 continued

LIABILITIES AND SHAREHOLDERS' INVESTMENT

	19Y3	19Y2
CURRENT LIABILITIES:		
Notes payable to banks (Note 3)	$ —	$ —
Accounts payable and accrued expenses	3,600	18,712
Accrued income taxes	—	—
Total current liabilities	$ 3,600	$ 18,712
COMMITMENTS AND CONTINGENT LIABILITIES (Note 4)	$ —	$ —
DEFERRED INCOME TAXES ARISING FROM INSTALLMENT SALES OF PROPERTY (Note 1)	$ 120,242	$ 121,320
SHAREHOLDERS' INVESTMENT:		
Common shares, $1 par value—2,000,000 shares authorized; issued and outstanding—1,456,302 shares in 19Y3 and 1,413,885 shares in 19Y2 (Note 2)	$1,456,302	$1,413,885
Paid-in surplus	4,711,389	4,586,513
Retained earnings	1,363,843	1,538,069
	$7,531,534	$7,538,467
	$7,655,376	$7,678,499

Exhibit 4-1 continued

SUMMERFIELD PRODUCTION COMPANY
STATEMENTS OF INCOME
FOR THE THREE YEARS ENDED DECEMBER 31, 19Y3

	19Y3	19Y2	19Y1
NET SALES	$4,267,259	$5,500,545	$6,660,572
COSTS AND EXPENSES:			
Cost of sales	$3,408,382	$4,722,505	$5,293,655
Selling, general and administrative expenses	1,120,756	1,324,185	1,205,863
	$4,529,138	$6,046,690	$6,499,518
Operating income (loss)	$(261,879)	$(546,145)	$ 161,054
OTHER INCOME:			
Interest income, net	$ 462,334	$ 454,474	$ 384,527
Gain on sale of assets (Note 5)	—	441,020	2,095
	$ 462,334	$ 895,494	$ 386,622
Income before income taxes	$ 200,455	$ 349,349	$ 547,676
PROVISION FOR INCOME TAXES (Note 1):			
Current	$ 72,000	$ (62,000)	$ 245,000
Deferred	(6,000)	118,000	—
	$ 66,000	$ 56,000	$ 245,000
NET INCOME	$ 134,455	$ 293,349	$ 302,676
NET INCOME PER SHARE (Note 1)	$ .09	$ .20	$ .21

The accompanying notes to financial statements are an integral part of these statements.

Exhibit 4-1 continued

SUMMERFIELD PRODUCTION COMPANY
STATEMENTS OF PAID-IN SURPLUS
AND RETAINED EARNINGS
FOR THE THREE YEARS ENDED DECEMBER 31, 19Y3

	19Y3	**19Y2**	**19Y1**
PAID-IN SURPLUS			
BALANCE AT BEGINNING OF YEAR	$4,586,513	$4,475,318	$4,315,168
EXCESS OF MARKET VALUE OVER PAR VALUE OF COMMON SHARES ISSUED AS STOCK DIVIDENDS (transferred from retained earnings)	124,876	111,195	160,150
BALANCE AT END OF YEAR	$4,711,389	$4,586,513	$4,475,318
RETAINED EARNINGS			
BALANCE AT BEGINNING OF YEAR	$1,538,069	$1,534,364	$1,457,204
NET INCOME	134,455	293,349	302,676
DIVIDENDS—			
Stock (3% in 19Y3—42,417 Shares; 3% in 19Y2 41,182 Shares and 5% in 19Y1—65,367 Shares)	(167,292)	(152,374)	(225,516)
Cash ($.10 per share)	(141,389)	(137,270)	—
BALANCE AT END OF YEAR	$1,363,843	$1,538,069	$1,534,364

The accompanying notes to financial statements are an integral part of these statements.

Exhibit 4-1 continued

SUMMERFIELD PRODUCTION COMPANY
STATEMENTS OF CHANGES
IN FINANCIAL POSITION
FOR THE THREE YEARS ENDED DECEMBER 31, 19Y3

	19Y3	19Y2	19Y1
SOURCE OF FUNDS:			
Operations—			
Net income	$ 134,455	$ 293,349	$ 302,676
Items not affecting working capital:			
Depreciation and amortization	81,526	126,448	195,002
Sale of properties—			
Mortgage notes receivable	10,101	(539,858)	—
Book value of property sold	—	277,577	—
Deferred income taxes	(1,078)	121,320	—
Total funds provided	$ 225,004	$ 278,836	$ 497,678
APPLICATION OF FUNDS:			
Property, plant and equipment additions, net	$ —	$ 7,414	$ 38,967
Payment of cash dividends	141,389	137,270	—
Total funds applied	$ 141,389	$ 144,684	$ 38,967
INCREASE (DECREASE) IN WORKING CAPITAL	$ 83,615	$ 134,152	$ 458,711
CHANGES IN WORKING CAPITAL:			
Increase (decrease) in current assets—			
Cash and marketable securities	$1,222,239	$ 345,848	$1,202,041
Accounts and notes receivable, net	(258,599)	(144,302)	184,013
Prepaid income taxes	(96,205)	80,785	(25,782)
Inventories	(867,285)	(185,032)	(1,002,750)
Prepaid expenses and other assets	68,353	49,299	60,409
	$ 68,503	$ 146,598	$ 417,931

Exhibit 4-1 continued

(Increase) decrease in current liabilities—			
Accounts payable and accrued expenses	$ 15,112	$ (12,446)	$ 40,780
Accrued income taxes	—	—	—
	$ 15,112	$ (12,446)	$ 40,780
INCREASE (DECREASE) IN WORKING CAPITAL	$ 83,615	$ 134,152	$ 458,711

The accompanying notes to financial statements are an integral part of these statements.

NOTES TO FINANCIAL STATEMENTS FOR THE THREE YEARS ENDED DECEMBER 31, 19Y3

(1) SUMMARY OF MAJOR ACCOUNTING POLICIES:

Inventories—

Inventories are priced to include the cost of raw materials, labor and manufacturing expenses incurred during the period of production. The lower of first-in, first-our cost or market is used in valuing all inventories. Market is generally determined using replacement cost for raw materials and net realizable value for other inventories.

Property, Plant and Equipment—

The company currently provides for depreciation for both financial reporting and income tax purposes using an accelerated method for tooling and straight-line methods for plant and equipment acquired prior to 19Y1. For depreciable property acquired after 19Y0 the company is providing depreciation for both financial reporting and income tax purposes using the Accelerated Cost Recovery System.

Repair and maintenance costs are charged directly to income. Renewals and betterments of fixed assets are charged to property and equipment. Upon retirement or other disposition of property, the cost and related depreciation or amortization are removed from the accounts. Gains and losses on such retirements are included in income.

Income Taxes—

Except as indicated below, the company had no material differences between book and tax income. In 19Y2, the company accounted for gains on the sale of certain assets using the accrual method for financial reporting purposes and the installment method for tax purposes. This accounting resulted in the deferral of $121,320 of 19Y2 taxes to later years. Investment tax credit is deferred by the company and amortized to income over the estimated useful lives of the applicable assets.

The difference between the statutory tax rate of 46% and the effective tax rate is due primarily to lower tax rates on the first $100,000 of income, state income taxes, the amortization of deferred investment tax credits, and in 19Y2 the benefit of lower tax rates on capital gains (which reduced 19Y2 income taxes by approximately $84,000).

Exhibit 4-1 continued

The Internal Revenue Code permits net operating losses to be carried back three years and forward fifteen years. Taxable income of $729,174 was earned in the years 19Y3, 19Y2 and 19Y1. In the event of future net operating losses, they could be carried back to the extent of taxable income in three years and claims for refund could be filed for earlier taxes paid.

Research and Development—

Research and development costs related to both future and present products are expensed as incurred and are not material.

Net Income Per Share—

Net income per share is computed based on the average number of shares outstanding during each year after retroactive adjustments for stock dividends of 3% in each of 19Y3 and 19Y2 and 5% in 19Y1.

(2) STOCK OPTIONS:

On June 30, 19Y0 the Board of Directors adopted the 19Y0 Summerfield Production Company's Stock Option Plan. The Plan reserved 66,836 shares of the Company's unissued common stock (after adjustment for subsequent stock dividends) for issuance to officers and key employees at option prices not less than 85% of the fair market value on the date of grant. Options are exercisable one year after date of grant and expire five years from date of grant. In 19Y0 the Board granted options for 38,988 shares at a price of $2.575 per share, which was 85% of the fair market value thereof on the date of grant (after adjustment for subsequent stock dividends). In 19Y1, the remaining 27,848 options were granted at a price of $2.804 per share, which was 85% of the fair market value thereof on the date of grant (after adjustment for subsequent stock dividends). As of December 31, 19Y3 all of the aforementioned options were exercisable although none have been exercised.

(3) BANK LINES OF CREDIT:

At December 31, 19Y3, the company had available unused and unsecured lines of credit of $4,500,000 at several banks at their prime rate of interest. In connection with these lines of credit, the company is expected to maintain compensating balances which are not legally restricted and which are not in excess of normal operating balances. The company did not draw upon these lines of credit during 19Y3, 19Y2 or 19Y1.

(4) COMMITMENTS AND CONTINGENT LIABILITIES:

At December 31, 19Y3, the company had no commitments under long-term leases, guarantees or discounted notes. In management's opinion, there were no significant commitments or contingent liabilities at that date.

(5) GAINS ON SALE OF REAL PROPERTY:

During 19Y2 the Company recognized gains on the sale of two buildings which represented excess space for the anticipated level of future manufacturing activity. Both transactions were financed by the Company through the use of notes secured by first mortgages on the properties after adequate down payments were received.

Exhibit 4-1 continued

AUDITORS' REPORT

To the Shareholders of Summerfield Production Company:

We have examined the balance sheets of Summerfield Production Company (an Illinois corporation) as of December 31, 19Y3 and 19Y2, and the related statements of income, paid-in surplus, retained earnings and changes in financial position for each of the three years in the period ended December 31, 19Y3. Our examinations were made in accordance with generally accepted auditing standards and, accordingly, included such tests of the accounting records and such other auditing procedures as we considered necessary in the circumstances.

In our opinion, the financial statements referred to above present fairly the financial position of Summerfield Production Company as of December 31, 19Y3 and 19Y2, and the results of its operations and changes in the financial position for each of the three years in the period ended December 31, 19Y3 all in conformity with generally accepted accounting principles applied on a consistent basis.

ANDREW ARTHURSON & CO.

Denver, Colorado
March 1, 19Y4

DESCRIPTION OF BUSINESS AND MANAGEMENT'S DISCUSSION AND ANALYSIS OF SELECTED FINANCIAL DATA

Description of Business

Summerfield is engaged in a single line of business: the manufacture and distribution of office equipment and related supplies. The Company's principal products are photocopy equipment and related supplies and other items of office equipment. These products are marketed through independent dealers and distributors located throughout the United States.

Selected Financial Data

The following selected financial data for the five years ended December 31, 19Y3 has been adjusted for stock dividends declared during subsequent periods.

	Year Ended December 31				
	19Y3	**19Y2**	**19Y1**	**19Y0**	**19X9**
Net sales	$4,267,259	$5,500,545	$6,660,572	$5,845,566	$8,017,553
Net income	134,455	293,349	302,676	193,488	616,702
Net income per share	.09	.20	.21	.13	.42
Total assets	7,655,376	7,678,499	7,388,651	7,126,754	7,048,186
Long-term debt	—	—	—	—	—
Cash dividends per share	.10	.09	—	.09	.08

Exhibit 4-1 continued

The variations in sales and earnings for the five years covered by the foregoing financial statements and selected financial data are primarily attributable to the stage of product development and introduction and market acceptance of the Company's line of photocopiers. These factors, coupled with the rapid change in photocopy technology resulting in new and improved products and the keenly competitive conditions in the industry, cause the foregoing financial information to not necessarily be indicative of future operations and earnings.

19Y3—Compared to 19Y2, sales decreased $1,233,285, or 22.4%, mainly due to continuing competitive pressure from low-priced plain paper copier imports. In addition, sales of supplies were adversely impacted by the replacement of machines using those supplies with plain paper copiers, which do not. Gross margins increased from 14.1% of sales in 19Y2 to 20.1% of sales in 19Y3 reflecting the benefit of cost reduction programs begun in 19Y2 and a rebound from the obsolescence charges absorbed in 19Y2. Operating expenses decreased $203,429 from 19Y2 because of cost reduction programs, lower level of sales activity and a reduction of bad debt expense after some extraordinary charges incurred in 19Y2.

Interest income remained stable between years, with larger average levels of invested funds offsetting the drop in interest rates from 19Y2 to 19Y3.

The financial position of the company continues to be strong as liquidity was improved in 19Y3 through lower working capital requirements for receivables and inventory.

19Y2—Compared to 19Y1, sales decreased $1,160,027, or 17.4%, due to general economic conditions, technical obsolescence and low-priced plain paper copier imports. Gross margins decreased from 20.5% of sales in 19Y1 to 14.1% of sales in 19Y2 mainly because of obsolescence reserves provided in 19Y2 and the combined impact of fixed costs and lower manufacturing activity. Operating expenses increased $118,322, reflecting increased advertising and sales efforts in the face of tough foreign competition and increased bad debt expenses because of economic conditions.

Net interest income increased from 19Y1 as continuing high interest rates were received on higher average outstanding balances of invested funds throughout the year. In addition, the Company recognized gains on the sale of real property (as described in Note 5) and on U.S. Treasury Notes in 19Y2, so that total non-operating income increased $508,872 from 19Y1 while income before income taxes decreased $196,327 for the same period.

The effective tax rate decreased from 44.7% of income before income taxes in 19Y1 to 16.0% in 19Y2 because of the large portion of capital gain income to total income in 19Y2.

19Y1—Compared to 19Y0, sales increased $815,006, or 13.9%, while income from operations increased $148,003. The increase in sales is related to sales of the Company's PMC Copier, which was introduced late in 19Y0, offset by decreases in sales of other product groups. Gross margins improved slightly between years as increased manufacturing activity in 19Y1 caused a higher level of fixed overhead expense to be absorbed by production, more than offsetting an increase of approximately $46,000 of depreciation related to PMC tooling. Operating expenses increased $93,417 reflecting increased

Exhibit 4-1 continued

marketing efforts required to promote the new copier and the general increase in costs due to inflation.

Larger average cash balances invested at continuing high interest rates throughout 19Y1 caused other income to increase $91,225, so that income before income taxes increased $239,228.

19Y0—Compared to the year before, sales decreased $2,171,987 mainly because of lower revenues from Magnetic Dry Copier (MDC) shipments. The MDC became more difficult to market during 19Y0 because of the introduction of lower-priced plain paper copiers and the overall economic climate. The PMC copier, a lower-priced version of the MDC, was introduced late in 19Y0 and therefore did not have a significant impact on operations. Gross margins decreased from 26% of sales the year before to 19% of sales in 19Y0, reflecting the relatively fixed nature of many of the costs included in overhead. In addition, an increase of $80,242 in depreciation expense was charged to cost of sales in 19Y0 related to tooling for the PMC. This combination of lower sales and margins caused gross profit to decline $951,601 from the previous year. Operating expenses remained stable from the previous year to 19Y0, with the impact of the inflation offsetting the lower level of sales activity in 19Y0. Increased interest income caused by record interest rate levels in 19Y0 narrowed the decrease in income before income taxes to $[illegible]3,254.

MARKET AND DIVIDEND INFORMATION

The following table shows the quarterly per-share sales price ranges of the Company's common stock on the American Stock Exchange and dividends paid for 19Y3 and 19Y2, adjusted for a 3% stock dividend paid in March, 19Y3 (on March 26, 19Y4, there were 1,456,302 shares of common stock outstanding):

	First Quarter	**Second Quarter**	**Third Quarter**	**Fourth Quarter**
19Y3				
High	$5.000	$6.125	$6.000	$5.625
Low	3.398	3.875	4.000	4.750
Dividends:				
Stock	3%	—	—	—
Cash	.10	—	—	—

	First Quarter	**Second Quarter**	**Third Quarter**	**Fourth Quarter**
19Y2				
High	$4.124	$3.519	$3.155	$4.248
Low	2.474	3.034	2.791	3.034
Dividends:				
Stock	—	3%	—	—
Cash	.09	—	—	—

Exhibit 4-1 continued

PROXY STATEMENT OF THE SUMMERFIELD PRODUCTION COMPANY FOR ANNUAL MEETING OF SHAREHOLDERS

The accompanying proxy is solicited by the Board of Directors of Summerfield Production Company for use at the Annual Meeting of Shareholders to be held on April 27, 19Y3, and any adjournment thereof. Anyone giving the proxy may revoke it at any time before it is exercised, but a revocation will not be effective until written notice thereof has been received by the Secretary of the Corporation.

Proxies will be solicited by mail. After the mailing, proxies may be solicited by directors, officers and a small number of regular employees of the Corporation personally or by telephone or telegraph, but such persons will not be specifically compensated for such service. Proxy soliciting material will be furnished to brokerage houses, custodians, nominees and fiduciaries upon request for forwarding to the beneficial owners of Common Shares held of record by such persons. The entire cost of solicitation will be borne by the Corporation.

SHARES OUTSTANDING AND VOTING RIGHTS

The Board of Directors has fixed the close of business on March 14, 19Y3, as the record date for the determination of shareholders entitled to notice of and to vote at the Annual Meeting. On that date 1,456,302 Common Shares of the Corporation (after adjustment for the 3% stock dividend paid March 22, 19Y3) were outstanding and entitled to one vote each. The shareholders have the right to cumulate their votes for the election of directors and there is no condition precedent to the exercise of that right.

Except as hereinafter indicated, the only person known by management to own of record or beneficially more than 5% of the outstanding Common Shares of the Corporation is Mr. Arthur Sanders, President of the Corporation, who on March 1, 19Y3, owned of record and beneficially 375,897 shares, constituting approximately 26% of the shares entitled to vote at the meeting. In addition, as of March 1, 19Y3, an aggregate of 353,572 Common Shares (approximately 24% of the Common Shares outstanding) were owned of record by Messrs. John Z. Bangel, Ernest B. Sanders, and Irving M. Sanders (each of whom is a nephew of Mr. Arthur Sanders) as joint trustees under a Trust Agreement dated October 1, 19X4. The trust was established by Mr. Arthur Sanders for the benefit of his three sisters and 11 nieces and nephews and grants to the trustees the power to determine what portion of the trust corpus is to be allocated from time to time to each of the 14 beneficiaries. The foregoing share amounts have been adjusted for the 3% stock dividend paid March 22, 19Y3.

ELECTION OF DIRECTORS

Six directors are to be elected to serve until the next Annual Meeting of Shareholders or until the election and qualification of their respective successors. Proxies which are returned will be voted for the persons named in the

Exhibit 4-1 continued

following table except as otherwise directed by shareholders in the accompanying form of proxy. If any of them should become unable to accept nomination or election for any unforeseen reason, the persons named in the proxies will have the right to vote for a substitute in each such case. The persons named in the proxies will have the right to vote cumulatively for any or all of the named nominees or their substitutes, as they deem best. Unless otherwise indicated, each nominee has served in the position set forth for more than five years. All share amounts have been adjusted for the 3% stock dividend paid March 22, 19Y3.

Name and Principal Occupation	Year First Elected as Director	Age	Shares Beneficially Owned as of March 1, 19Y3	% of Class
ARTHUR SANDERS.................. President of the Corporation	1935	79	375,897(1)	26%
ERNEST B. SANDERS.............. Secretary of the Corporation	19X4	56	1,118(2)	(6)
BOB TIDDE............................... Vice President and Sales Director of the Corporation	19W5	80	1,262	(6)
JONATHAN INCH Treasurer of the Corporation since June 24, 19Y0; previously audit manager in the accounting firm of Andrew Arthurson & Co.	19Y1	36	— (3)	—
IRVING M. SANDERS............... Sole practitioner in the practice of law since January 1, 19Y2; previously partner in law firm of Sanders, Schwartz, and Kraft, Denver, Colorado, since January 1, 19X9; previously partner in law firm of Sanders and Winer, Denver, Colorado.	19X6	38	104(4)	(6)
JOHN Z. BANGEL.................... Director, Colorado Department of Law Enforcement since August 15, 19Y0; previously Director, Department of Revenue, State of Colorado, since February 1, 19X9; previously Executive Director, Colorado Law Enforcement Commission.	19X7	42	3,823(5)	(6)

Exhibit 4-1 continued

(1) Mr. Sanders disclaims any beneficial interest in the 353,572 shares owned of record by his nephews as trustees. See "Shares Outstanding and Voting Rights."
(2) Excluding 133 shares owned by Mr. Sanders as custodian for his minor children. Mr. Sanders disclaims any interest in such shares. In addition, Mr. Sanders has a beneficial interest in 353,572 shares owned of record by him and two relatives as trustees. See "Shares Outstanding and Voting Rights."
(3) Excluding 244 shares owned by Mr. Inch's wife as custodian for their minor children. Mr. Inch disclaims any interest in such shares.
(4) Mr. Sanders has a beneficial interest in 353,572 shares owned of record by him and two relatives as trustees. See "Shares Outstanding and Voting Rights."
(5) Mr. Bangel has a beneficial interest in 353,572 shares owned of record by him and two relatives as trustees. See "Shares Outstanding and Voting Rights."
(6) Less than 1%.

Directors and officers as a group owned 382,204 Common Shares of the Corporation, representing 26% of the total shares outstanding.

Remuneration of Directors and Officers

The following table sets forth the aggregate remuneration during the year ended December 31, 19Y2 of (1) the executive officers of the Corporation whose aggregate cash and cash-equivalent remuneration exceeded $50,000 and (2) all directors and officers of the Corporation as a whole:

		Cash and Cash-equivalent Forms of Remuneration		
Name of Individual or Persons in Group	**Capacity in Which Served**	**Salaries, Directors' Fees, and Deferred Compensation**	**Noncash Compensation**	**Aggregate of Contingent Forms of Remuneration***
ARTHUR SANDERS	President	$122,998	$ —	$9,141
JONATHAN INCH...	Treasurer	52,755	—	—
All directors and officers as a group consisting of 6 persons, of whom 2 received no direct remuneration		235,199	—	9,141

*Represents excess of market value over option price of common shares at the date of grant of stock options under the 19Y0 Stock Option Plan.

Mr. Arthur Sanders is employed as chief executive officer of the Corporation under an employment agreement, as amended, terminating in 19Y9, at an annual salary of not less than $98,000. Mr. Sanders may terminate the agreement prior to December 31, 19Y9, upon ninety days prior written notice. Upon cessation of Mr. Sanders' active employment by the Corporation (whether resulting from expiration of the term of the agreement or from termination of the agreement), he shall be entitled under its terms to a lifetime retirement benefit equal to 80% of the compensation being paid to him immediately prior to his retirement, adjusted annually to reflect changes in the consumer price index, provided that he renders such consulting and advisory services as the Corporation may request.

Exhibit 4-1 continued

Stock Options

No options under the Corporation's 19Y0 Stock Option Plan were exercised or granted during 19Y2. The following table sets forth option information as to certain officers of the Corporation and all directors and officers of the Corporation as a group (after adjustment for the 3% stock dividend paid March 22, 19Y3):

	Arthur Sanders	Jonathan Inch	Directors and Officers as a Group
Outstanding as of 12/31/Y2:			
Number of optioned shares	51,453	5,569	62,590(1)
Potential (unrealized) value	$59,907	$7,286	$76,477

(1) Options were granted at 85% of market price at date of grant at an average option price of $2.66.

APPOINTMENT OF INDEPENDENT PUBLIC ACCOUNTANTS

The accounting firm of Andrew Arthurson & Co. has been selected by the Board of Directors to serve as the Corporation's independent public accountants for several years, including the year ended December 31, 19Y2. It is intended that Andrew Arthurson & Co. will serve as the Corporation's accountants for 19Y3. It is not expected that representatives of Andrew Arthurson & Co. will be present at the Annual Meeting.

OTHER MATTERS

The Corporation's Board of Directors held eight meetings during the year 19Y2. The Corporation does not have audit, nominating or compensation committees.

The management does not intend to present any item of business at the Annual Meeting other than those specifically set forth in the notice of the meeting. However, if other matters are presented for a vote, the proxies will be voted for such matters in accordance with the judgment of the persons acting under the proxies.

Shareholder Proposals

Proposals of shareholders intended to be presented at the Company's 19Y4 annual meeting of shareholders must be received by the Company not later than January 3, 19Y4, for inclusion in the issuer's proxy statement and form of proxy relating to that meeting. Any such proposal must relate to a matter which is proper for consideration at such a meeting and not of the type which the Company is specifically permitted to omit by the regulations of the Securities and Exchange Commission.

By Order of the Board of Directors,

ERNEST B. SANDERS
Secretary

If you're like most investors, the judgments you reach regarding a public company are based on the information presented at the front of an annual report, namely, management's description of the company's business and how it did during the past year. Let us examine some of the possible conclusions you could reach from reading management's description of Summerfield's business and the results it achieved over the past year.

The President's Message contains the first clue that Summerfield represents an asset play. The president states that "we have always been conservative and our main object is to maintain the highest standard of liquidity in order to protect our stockholders and the net worth of our company. We have no liens or mortgages on any of our holdings, we have no outstanding bank loans, accounts payable, or contingent liabilities. Our current assets over our current liabilities is approximately 1900 to 1." The citing of a ratio of 1900 to 1 introduces the first ratio an "asset-play" analyst turns to, namely, the "current ratio." There are a number of ratios that fall into the category of "cash ratios"; they are discussed next.

Cash Ratios

Current Ratios

By definition, the current ratio is equal to current assets divided by current liabilities. In mathematical format, current ratio (CR) is expressed as follows:

$$\text{Current ratio} = \frac{\text{Current assets}}{\text{Current liabilities}}$$

In the case of Summerfield, CR is calculated as follows:

$$\text{CR} = \frac{\text{Current assets}}{\text{Current liabilities}} = \frac{\$6,877,277}{\$3,600} = 1900 \text{ to } 1$$

Obviously, a current ratio of 1900 to 1 is atypical, but a current ratio above 10 to 1 should be considered a signal that a particular company warrants further examination.

Quick Ratios

Typically the next step an asset-play analyst takes is to determine the company's "quick ratio." The quick ratio (QR) serves to identify how much of the company's current assets is represented by cash and cash equivalents. By definition, the QR is equal to cash plus marketable securities plus receivables divided by current liabilities. In mathematical format, QR is expressed as follows:

$$\text{Quick ratio} = \frac{\text{Cash} + \text{Marketable securities} + \text{Receivables}}{\text{Current liabilities}}$$

In the case of Summerfield, the QR is calculated as follows:

$$\text{QR} = \frac{\$286{,}978 + \$4{,}230{,}775 + \$1{,}112{,}194}{\$3{,}600} = \frac{\$5{,}629{,}947}{\$3{,}600}$$

$$= 1564 \text{ to } 1$$

The quick ratio highlights the percentage of current assets versus current liabilities as shown by cash and items that easily can be converted into cash. Again, with a quick ratio of 1564 to 1 Summerfield is atypical, but a quick ratio of 8 to 1 or above should signal that the company represents a potential asset play.

By zeroing in on current and quick ratios, an asset-play analyst is able to spot rapidly those companies that represent pure cash plays. As a result of the recent wave of merger and acquisition activity, many of these financial dinosaurs have been either taken over or liquidated. Some, however, still remain and offer interesting investment possibilities. Figure 4-1 is a page drawn from a recent edition of the Graham Rea Report. By utilizing a screening process in conjunction with a data base of many thousands of companies, the Graham Rea Report identifies those companies that are "cash rich" and hence is a useful tool to spotlight potential asset-play companies.

Figure 4-1.

GRAHAM-REA FUNDAMENTAL VALUES

(BASED ON BENJAMIN GRAHAM'S CRITERIA FOR COMMON STOCK INVESTMENTS)

SUBSCRIPTION RATES FOR NET-CURRENT-ASSET COMPANIES: $300 PER YEAR $180 PER SIX MONTHS $40 PER ISSUE

DATE: 01 - 29 - 88

FOR NET-CURRENT-ASSET COMPANIES: (ISSUED MONTHLY - NO SAMPLES)

AVE. AAA INDUSTRIAL BOND RATE: 9.493

Buy Price ≤ NCA & P/E ≤ 250/AAA (not a loss company)

RESEARCH HAS SHOWN THAT BUYING AT OR BELOW NCA VALUE IS BETTER THAN BUYING AT OR BELOW 2/3 NCA VALUE.

NOTE: THE MAXIMUM BUY LEVEL ≤ NCA, BUT NOT GREATER THAN 2/3 BOOK VALUE.

BUYS	COMPANY SIC/TIC	EXCH	NOTE	TOT TANG BOOK & DEBT $MIL	DEBT TO BOOK	12 MO PRICE HIGH & LOW	MONTH VOL (100) & SHRS OUT (MIL)	BOOK P/S	NCA P/S	INV TO CUR AST	CSH TO CUR LIB	(Y) CUR YLD	P/E	RISK RATING	$ PER SHARE: MONTH END PRICE	$ PER SHARE: MAX BUY PRICE	$ PER SHARE: (+50%) SELL PRICE
001)	ASA LTD 6795 ASA	NYS	F	795 4.0	0.0	73.4 39.4	11897 9.60	82.84	82.84	0.0	3.4	** 8.7	PG 12.5	1.1	45.7	55.1	82.6
002)	AMPAL AMER 6150 AIS.A	ASE	W F	93.1 1129	12.1	3.4 1.5	600.0 16.8	5.54	2.51	NR	NR	3.7	PG 5.6	1.0	1.5	2.4	3.6
003)	COUNTRYWIDE 6798 CWM	NYS	W F	87.9 1627	18.5	17.7 5.2	4778 7.75	11.35	11.35	NR	NR	** 23.4	5.1 DE	1.0	6.5	7.4	11.2
004)	ELGIN NATL 1600 ENW	NYS		56.1 42.5	0.8	15.3 8.1	708.0 3.04	18.47	9.06	0.2	0.6	0.0	(42.9)	1.0	9.0	9.0	13.4
005)	FAR WEST FN 6120 FWF	NYS	W F	161 2888	18.0	17.1 6.6	1862 8.35	19.26	17.91	NR	NR	3.6	3.6	1.1	11.1	12.6	19.2
006)	GUILD MTG 6798 GUM	ASE	W F	27.1 157.1	5.8	12.6 3.3	1261 3.10	8.73	8.73	NR	NR	** 22.0	4.6	1.0	5.0	5.6	8.5
007)	HOMESTD-CLA 6120 HFL	NYS	W F	136 5374	39.5	13.3 4.1	2367 12.9	10.56	8.71	NR	NR	3.6	3.5 DE	1.1	6.7	7.0	10.4
008)	KEY CO 6552 KC.B	ASE	W	10.2 14.5	1.4	5.7 1.6	108.0 2.26	4.51	3.04	0.8	0.3	** 14.3	(+100)DE	1.0	1.6	3.0	4.4
009)	LAMA (TONY) 3140 TLAM	OTC		28.9 29.5	1.0	12.4 6.4	356.0 1.93	14.98	8.78	0.6	0.0	0.0	(35.9)	1.1	8.2	8.6	13.1
010)	LINPRO SPEC 6798 LPO	ASE	F	17.1 0.5	0.0	11.0 3.0	739.0 1.86	9.22	9.22	0.0	NR	** 23.8	4.3	1.0	3.5	6.1	9.1
011)	MICHAELS(J) 5712 MICH	OTC		12.3 4.8	0.4	13.0 7.4	24.0 0.876	14.00	12.59	0.1	4.7	4.4	9.2 DE	1.0	8.2	9.2	14.0
012)	PEC ISRAEL 5080 IEC	ASE	F	127 20.7	0.2	13.4 9.2	30.0 7.32	17.32	17.32	NR	0.4	0.0	PG 10.5	1.1	11.0	11.4	17.2
013)	RES MTG INV 6798 RMI	ASE	W F	39.4 51.2	1.3	9.5 3.2	1795 4.22	9.33	9.33	NR	NR	** 20.3	5.0	1.1	6.0	6.1	9.2
014)	STEWART INF 6361 SISC	OTC	F	113 71.7	0.6	25.6 10.6	4586 4.03	28.14	20.05	NR	0.8	5.2	PG 4.2	1.0	14.4	18.6	28.1
015)	THREE D-B 5999 TDD.B	ASE		14.7 4.3	0.3	4.0 2.7	14.0 3.12	4.72	3.35	0.6	1.2	2.0	PG 11.1	1.1	3.0	3.1	4.5

There are a number of other services and techniques that an asset-play analyst can use to identify "cash-rich" companies. To begin with, you should determine the reasons behind the company having such a cash surplus. There could be a number of reasons; for example, management's age and attitude. The management of Summerfield describes itself as being "extremely conservative." If you were to examine the company's Proxy Statement you would discover that the president of the company was eighty years old and that a number of the other officers and directors were in their seventies and eighties. Having lived through the 1929 Crash, many of these managers were concerned with having extremely conservative balance sheets. This explains Summerfield's "cash horde." Alternatively, a large cash position might result from the fact that the company recently has gone public or had a secondary offering. If such were the case, the cash surplus shortly would be invested in the business and disappear from the balance sheet. A third reason might be that the company has recently sold off some divisions or subsidiaries and is merely holding the money pending management's decision as to where to invest the money. A final possibility is that the company is in the process of liquidating itself.

Once you have determined why the company has a cash surplus, you are better able to decide whether or not to invest in the company. If you determine that the company's management is simply holding the cash without a view towards either utilizing it in the business or alternatively liquidating the business itself, it is probably not appropriate to invest in it unless the company is selling at a substantial discount, such as at a price of 50% or less of the cash in back of each share, and then only when you have some hope of constructive action on the part of the company's management. Remember that there is a time value attached to any money you invest and that every investment has to be compared to the returns you could get from alternative investments.

Identifying a "Net" "Net" Asset Play

Professional asset-play investors will frequently refer to a particular company they are interested in as being a "net" "net" situation. For a particular stock to represent a "net" "net" situation, it has to be selling at a price lower than the per share figure obtained by subtracting from the company's current assets all liabilities and dividing by the number of shares outstanding. In a mathematical format, the "net" "net" value is expressed as follows:

$$\text{"Net" "net" value} = \frac{\text{Current assets} - \text{Total liabilities}}{\text{Number of shares outstanding}}$$

Perhaps the best way to familiarize yourself with the "net" "net" concept is with an actual example. Summerfield Company could be described as a "net" "net" situation. The following is the calculation of Summerfield's "net" "net" value:

$$\text{"Net" "net" value} = \frac{\$6,877,277 - \$123,842}{1,456,302}$$

$$= \frac{\$6,753,435}{1,456,302} = \$4.64 \text{ per share}$$

Since Summerfield's principal assets are cash and cash equivalents, a "net" "net" value of $4.64 means that every share has $4.64 behind it. Thus, if you are able to purchase Summerfield's stock for anything less than $4.64, you are in effect buying "pure cash" at a discount and are not paying anything for the company's other assets (plant, equipment, patents, and so forth). The concept of "net" "net" value is simply another way of identifying companies with sizable cash "hordes."

As in the cash of companies having high current and quick ratios, you should not simply invest in such a company because it represents a "net" "net" situation. You should ask some questions of management, such as: is it likely that the company will be sold, liquidated, or restructured, or will it continue as it has in the past. Whatever answer you receive should be evaluated in light of the other information you discover about the company from your own research and reaction to management. Another thing to consider before investing in a particular "net" "net" situation is what price the stock is selling at versus its "net" "net" assets. The greater the discount between the price of the stock and its "net" "net" assets, the greater should be your interest in the situation.

Other Balance Sheet Items–Accounts Receivable, Notes Receivable, Inventory, and Marketable Securities

Up to this point your attention has been directed toward finding and evaluating companies with substantial cash and cash equivalents. While accounts receivable, notes receivable, inventory, and marketable securities are included in the calculation described previously, no time has been spent advising how to view such elements of a company's balance sheet. Let's therefore spend some time reviewing under what circumstances current asset items represent either "hidden risks" or "hidden assets."

Typically, accounts receivable, notes receivable, and inventory represent more of a risk than an opportunity. This is because it is in such figures that problems are frequently hidden from the investor's view. For example, the inventory figure may have buried in it goods which cannot be sold at any price, accounts receivable may represent uncollectible debts, and notes receivable may be of doubtful value.

However, there are a number of "red flags" that should alert you to potential dangers in this area. First, inventories and receivables should track sales figures—increasing or decreasing as sales expand or decline. Likewise, inventory and receivables should over time represent approximately the same portion of a company's current assets and not grow dramatically as cash declines and sales remain stagnant. This is particularly true in the case of a company operating in a mature industry. Also, special attention should be paid to notes receivable, in particular, if the notes represent loans made to corporate officers. Being aware of these factors should help prevent you from making a mistake in the investments you select.

On the other hand, the presence of marketable securities on a balance sheet might represent hidden assets. To determine if indeed this is the case, you have to determine the nature of the marketable securities and whether they are being carried at cost or market value.

Perhaps the best way to understand this concept is through an example (see Exhibit 4-2). The first page of the Winston 19Y6 Annual Report is a balance sheet for this publicly held company. On its balance sheet, Winston carries marketable securities at a value of $3.9 million. However, if you were to examine this same company's latest 10K filing you will find these same marketable securities carried at a value of $19.5 million. The reason for this apparent discrepancy is because the balance sheet figure represents the cost basis for these securities purchased some 75 years ago, whereas the figure listed in the 10K represents current market value. Therefore, you can see how important it is to determine on what basis marketable securities are carried, as their true value may represent a hidden asset.

Book Value

In the beginning of this chapter you learned the mathematical techniques that would help you to identify companies with substantial cash assets. Cash and cash equivalents are frequently referred to as above-the-line balance sheet items. But for every company with substantial above-the-line assets there are many more whose assets are carried below the line, that is, in the noncurrent category. Such noncash assets as real estate (both developed and undeveloped), plant and equipment, patents and trade names, holdings in other companies and valuable subsidiaries fall below the line.

Calculating a company's book value is the starting point in seeking to determine if the particular company you are analyzing has such hidden assets. By definition, the book value of a share of common stock is obtained by adding up all of the company's assets (generally excluding such intangibles as goodwill), subtracting all liabilities and stock issues ahead of the common, and then dividing by the number of shares outstanding. Alternatively, book value per share can be determined by dividing shareholders' equity by the number of shares outstanding.

Exhibit 4-2.

Winston

19Y6 Annual Report

Exhibit 4-2 continued

THE WINSTON OIL COMPANY
Balance Sheet
December 31, 19Y6, 19Y5, and 19Y4

	19Y6	19Y5	19Y4
Assets			
Current Assets:			
Cash and short-term investments..	$ 22,168,623	$ 16,379,097	$ 15,585,314
Accounts receivable	3,844,783	6,487,051	6,265,983
Due from Federal government	66,144	600,343	674,583
Inventories	1,507,952	1,667,846	1,752,720
Prepaid expenses	114,302	70,062	63,608
Total current assets	27,701,804	25,204,399	24,342,208
Marketable Securities	3,905,068	2,798,760	2,934,803
Property, Plant and Equipment, at cost:			
Oil and gas properties (successful efforts method)	159,790,156	176,357,061	163,755,662
Transportation, office and other properties	6,535,659	6,534,034	6,267,437
	166,325,815	182,891,095	170,023,099
Less—accumulated depreciation, depletion and amortization.	88,529,354	95,896,068	85,928,874
Net property, plant and equipment...	77,796,461	86,995,027	84,094,225
Deferred Charges and Other Assets	356,189	767,644	923,290
	$109,759,522	$115,765,830	$112,294,526

Exhibit 4-2 continued

	19Y6	19Y5	19Y4
Liabilities and Stockholders' Investment			
Current Liabilities:			
Accounts payable	$ 2,048,979	$ 2,741,923	$ 2,754,307
Accrued income taxes	697,025	329,594	369,236
Accrued liabilities	1,105,711	1,235,123	1,236,336
Current portion of purchase payment obligation	405,130	386,123	183,502
Total current liabilities	4,256,845	4,692,763	4,543,381
Purchase Payment Obligation	1,085,124	1,403,041	738,998
Deferred Income Taxes	12,742,015	15,511,275	15,014,175
Stockholder's Investment:			
Common Stock—$3 par value; 20,000,000 shares authorized; 9,115,572 shares issued	27,346,716	27,346,716	27,346,716
Preferred stock—$10 par value; 300,000 shares authorized; none issued	—	—	—
Paid-in capital	3,079,502	3,079,502	3,079,502
Retained earnings	61,994,622	64,477,835	62,166,868
Less: Treasury stock 46,854, 46,854 and 37,354 shares, at cost	745,302	745,302	595,114
Total Stockholders' Investment	91,675,538	94,158,751	91,997,972
	$109,759,522	$115,765,830	$112,294,526

The accompanying notes are an integral part of these financial statements.

Exhibit 4-2 continued

THE WINSTON OIL COMPANY
Notes to Financial Statements
December 31, 19Y6, 19Y5 and 19Y4

1. Summary of Significant Accounting Policies

a. Principles of Reporting—The financial statements include the accounts of the Winston Oil Company and the Company's proportionate interest in the accounts of a 60% owned partnership. Intercompany accounts and transactions have been eliminated.

b. Oil and Gas Properties—The Company follows the "successful efforts" method of accounting for its oil and gas properties. Under this method of accounting, all costs of property acquisitions and exploratory wells are initially capitalized. If a well is unsuccessful, the capitalized costs of drilling the well, net of any salvage value, are charged to expense. The capitalized costs of unproved properties are periodically assessed to determine whether their value has been impaired below the capitalized cost, and if such impairment is indicated (usually as a result of unsuccessful exploration in the area of the property or a lack of plans to continue evaluation of the property), a loss is recognized. Geological and geophysical costs and the costs of retaining undeveloped properties are expensed as incurred. Expenditures for maintenance and repairs are charged to expense, and renewals and betterments are capitalized. Upon disposal, the asset and related accumulated depreciation are removed from the accounts and any resulting gain or loss is reflected currently in income.

c. Depreciation, Depletion and Amortization—Depreciation, depletion and amortization of the costs of producing oil and gas properties is computed for individual properties using the units-of-production method based on estimated proved reserves. Depreciation of transportation, office and other properties is computed using the straight line method over the estimated useful lives of these assets.

d. Income Taxes—The Company provides deferred income taxes for timing differences in the recognition of revenues and expenses for tax and financial reporting purposes. Investment tax credits are used to reduce the provision for income taxes in the year they are utilized for tax purposes. Investment tax credits utilized were $393,000 and $376,000 in 19Y5 and 19Y4 respectively. The Tax Reform Act eliminated the investment tax credit in 19Y6.

The provisions for income taxes for the three years ended December 31, 19Y6 are as follows (in thousands):

	19Y6	19Y5	19Y4
Current:			
Federal	$2,178	$3,894	$5,763
State	215	489	757
	2,393	4,383	6,520
Deferred*:			
Federal	(2,654)	469	(1,818)
State	(115)	28	(79)
	(2,769)	497	(1,897)
Total provision (credit) for income taxes	$ (376)	$4,880	$4,623

*The only significant timing difference relates to intangible drilling and development costs.

Exhibit 4-2 continued

A reconciliation of the statutory Federal income tax rate to the Company's effective tax rate follows:

	19Y6	19Y5	19Y4
Tax provision at the statutory rate	46%	46%	46%
Statutory depletion in excess of cost basis on certain properties	(32.0)	(4.0)	(4.3)
State income taxes, net of Federal income tax benefit	4.4	2.1	2.9
Investment tax credits	—	(3.0)	(2.9)
Dividends received credit	(30.3)	(3.5)	(3.3)
Capital gain on the sale of securities	(15.2)	(0.6)	(1.6)
Other, net	(3.7)	(0.2)	(0.4)
	(30.8%)	36.8%	36.4%

e. Short-Term Investments—Short-term investments of $22,460,000 in 19Y6, $16,608,000 in 19Y5 and $16,130,000 in 19Y4 are recorded at cost plus accrued interest, which approximates market.

f. Marketable Securities—Marketable securities are recorded at cost and have year end market values of $19,560,000 in 19Y6, $18,347,000 in 19Y5 and $14,588,000 in 19Y4. Capital gains recognized on the sale of marketable securities were $1,033,000 in 19Y6, $456,000 in 19Y5 and $1,157,000 in 19Y4.

g. Inventories—Oil and gas product inventories are recorded at the average cost of production. Materials and supplies are recorded at the lower of average cost or market.

h. Accrued Liabilities—Accrued liabilities include accrued vacation and payroll of $324,000 in 19Y6, $379,000 in 19Y5 and $387,000 in 19Y4 and property taxes of $493,000 in 19Y6, $453,000 in 19Y5 and $407,000 in 19Y4.

2. Tertiary Oil Recovery Project

In December 19Y0, the Company began a tertiary oil recovery project on a 170 acre tract representing a portion of the B. Shride Field of Lee County, Kentucky. The Company had in the past produced oil from this field using primary and secondary recovery techniques. The tertiary recovery project involved chemical injection into the oil producing formation to enable additional recovery of oil reserves. Due to the decline of oil prices during 19Y6 and poor oil recovery from the project, the operation of this project has been terminated. The total expense of this project incurred in 19Y6, including depreciation and depletion, was less than $700,000. In 19Y4 the capitalized cost of this project was written-down by $6.2 million.

3. Oil and Gas Producing Activities

Set forth below is certain information regarding the aggregate capitalized costs of oil and gas properties and costs incurred in oil and gas property acquisitions, exploration and development activities (in thousands):

	19Y6	19Y5	19Y4
Capitalized Costs:			
Proved properties	$145,492	$160,916	$147,195
Unproved properties	14,298	15,441	16,561
	159,790	176,357	163,756

Exhibit 4-2 continued

	19Y6	19Y5	19Y4
Accumulated depreciation, depletion and amortization	84,406	92,506	83,181
Net capitalized costs	$ 75,384	$ 83,851	$ 80,575
Costs Incurred:			
Property acquisition	$ 2,331	$ 3,727	$ 7,699
Exploration	4,238	5,678	7,529
Development	3,384	12,877	10,784

4. Stock Bonus Plan

In 19Y3, the Company established the 19Y3 Restricted Non-Qualified Stock Bonus Plan in order to attract, retain and motivate skilled and competent key employees. Under this plan, the Board of Directors may grant to full-time key employees shares of the Company's common stock, 4,646 were granted to key employees in 19Y3. The grant has certain restrictions related to employment and performance by each employee receiving a grant. The employees will receive, without restrictions, one-fifth of the shares granted annually over the five year period beginning in 19Y4, if the employee has not violated any of the restrictions of the grant. Treasury shares were issued in 19Y3 for the 4,646 shares which have been granted under this plan. An additional 35,354 shares may be granted by the Board of Directors under this plan.

OMB APPROVAL
OMB Number: 3235-0063
Expires: February 28, 1989

Securities and Exchange Commission
Washington, D.C.
20549

Form 10-K

Annual Report Pursuant to Section 13 or 15(d) of
The Securities Exchange Act of 1934

For the fiscal year ended December 31, 19Y6 Commission file number 0-4562

The Winston Oil Company
(Exact name of registrant as specified in its charter)

Delaware	55-5021282
(State or other jurisdiction of incorporation or organization)	(I.R.S. Employer Identification No.)
Sistersville, West Virginia	26175
(Address of principal executive offices)	(Zip Code)

Registrant's telephone number, including area code 1-403-562-8316

Securities registered pursuant to Section 12(b) of the Act: None

Title of each class	Name of each exchange on which registered

Securities registered pursuant to section 12(g) of the Act:

Capital Stock--Par Value, $3.00 Per Share
(Title of class)

Exhibit 4-2 continued

SCHEDULE I

THE WINSTON OIL COMPANY
MARKETABLE SECURITIES
DECEMBER 31, 19Y6

December 31, 19Y6	Units Owned	Cost	Market Value
Colonial Royalties	3,024	$ 9,072	$ 9,072(1)
Consolidated Natural Gas	22,952	116,050	748,809
E. I. DuPont	31,452	665,128	2,641,968
Diamond Shamrock Corp.	1,914	1,793	23,447
Mobil Corporation	44,000	504,609	1,765,500
Union Exploration Ptnrs. Ltd.	91	1,572	1,463
Cypress Minerals	3,968	6,300	64,480
Chevron	55,196	574,002	2,504,519
Amoco	39,680	319,435	2,589,120
Union Oil of California	3,185	5,934	84,801
Exxon Corporation	129,166	1,632,173	9,057,766
Ward Williston Drilling Co.	20,000	69,000	69,000(1)
		$3,905,068	$19,559,945

(1) Market value quotations are not available.

Book Value Ratio

Here is the ratio for calculating book value:

$$\text{Book value (BV)} = \frac{\text{Assets} - \text{Liabilities} - \frac{\text{Stock issues}}{\text{prior to common}}}{\text{Number of shares outstanding}}$$

The best way to understand how to calculate a company's book value is by an example. Referring back to Summerfield's financials, let's calculate its book value:

$$\text{BV} = \frac{\$7{,}655{,}376 - \$123{,}842}{1{,}456{,}302}$$

$$= \frac{\$7{,}531{,}534}{1{,}456{,}302} = \$5.17$$

Thus, Summerfield has a book value of $5.17, which compares with a "net" "net" figure of $4.64. This confirms our starting observation that Summerfield represents a "pure cash" play.

What is the significance of book value in identifying asset plays? Should you automatically buy a stock selling at below its book value?

The first thing you should learn about book value is not to accept the figure blindly. If you find a company whose stock is selling substantially below book value, it should cause you to ask some questions and do some research. For example, the stocks of many steel companies sell well below their respective book value. But there is a valid reason for this situation because the book value of such companies consists principally of steel plants and facilities that are valuable only to the companies owning them. Likewise, within certain industries such as the life insurance industry, or during certain periods of time, companies have sold at or below book value. The fact that a particular company is selling below its book value should be compared to other companies within the same industry to see if this is the norm or if the situation represents a potential asset play.

Now that you have been alerted to the dangers of automatically buying a stock because it is selling below book, what are some of the ways book value can be used to identify asset plays? For one thing, you will find that the majority of asset-play stocks are selling below book. Once you determine that the particular stock is not selling below book because of the industry it is in, or because of the nature of what the book value represents, you are ready to determine if buried in its book value are any hidden assets.

Hidden Assets

Real Estate (Developed and Undeveloped)

The concept of asset-play investing rests on the belief that the individual investor should be able to identify companies whose assets are not properly valued in the marketplace. While many asset-play stocks are out of the investment mainstream, undervalued assets tend to fall into certain distinct categories. Real estate represents the most important source of such hidden assets.

Let's again turn our attention to the Summerfield Company. In the President's Message to Shareholders, the following statement appears:

> "Our fixed assets have depreciated to $248,000, which is *3% of our book value* and represents a small investment in relation to our sales and total assets. We also have fixed assets which are still in use, such as the 83,000 square foot building we now occupy, which have been *fully depreciated* on our books."

The above paragraph contains certain key points which should signal the existence of hidden assets in two areas: real estate and plant and equipment. The fact that the company owns an 83,000 square foot building free and clear should signal you to look at Summerfield Company's 10K and determine the location of the building. If you were to check with the real estate people in that area, you might discover that the building is worth a substantial amount of money, even though it is fully depreciated on Summerfield Company's balance sheet. The same might be the case with regard to the company's fully depreciated plant and equipment. As an asset-play analyst, you should always look into fully depreciated assets carried on a company's balance sheet.

The preceding example based on the Summerfield Company highlighted the fact that developed real estate and plant and equipment represent an important source of hidden assets. Likewise, undeveloped land can be a valuable and sometimes hidden asset. This is one of the reasons an increasing number of professional analysts price out a company's land holdings whenever they evaluate a public company. Forest product companies, water utilities, sewerage companies, real estate holding companies, and companies involved in the recreational and resort industry (for example, theme parks and race tracks) frequently carry at cost on their books raw land that has substantially increased in value. Also, in many instances undervalued real estate can be found on the balance sheets of companies which have "wound down" their major business and moved into the status of a holding company.

Exhibit 4-3, the Greenfield Company's 19Y5 Annual Report, gives an example of the balance sheet and relevant footnotes of a company having substantial holdings in undeveloped land.

If you were to look behind the balance sheet and relevant footnotes and speak to real estate people in the area where the property is located, as a professional asset-play analyst would, you would find that such property goes for substantially more than the $750 per acre carried on the company's books.

Exhibit 4-3.

GREENFIELD COMPANY

ANNUAL REPORT 19Y5

Exhibit 4-3 continued

To the Stockholders:

Results from operations, after taxes and before a non-recurring deferred tax adjustment, were $1.18 per share for the period ended April 30, 19Y5, versus $.89 per share for the prior period. The effective tax rate for Fiscal Year 19Y5 before taking credit for a non-recurring deferred tax adjustment was 18%, compared to 35% for the previous reporting period (Fiscal Year 19Y4). At the end of the 19Y5 Fiscal Year, the Company recalculated its deferred tax requirements resulting from various timing differences in the handling of tax and book income and expenses. The computed credit adjustment was $365,635, which reduced the Retained Earnings Deficit and was equivalent to additional earnings of $.66 per share.

Except for the information contained in the Proxy Statement, mailed separately with this report, the balance of the "Form 10K" filed with the Securities and Exchange Commission for the year ended April 30, 19Y5 is incorporated with this letter to form this year's annual report.

In summary, the main components of income were as follows:

Rental Operating Income	$195,837
Oil & Gas Operating Income	157,809
Grove Investment Income	736,254
Interest Income and Money Market Dividends	79,836
Other Miscellaneous Income	5,000
Provision for Doubtful Accounts and other Adjustments	(14,876)
General and Administrative Expense	(361,759)
Income before Income Tax Expense	$798,101

As stated earlier, you will find detailed information in the following pages which has been reprinted from the "Form 10K."

It is anticipated that rental and oil and gas operating incomes for Fiscal Year 19Y6 will be about the same as those for Fiscal 19Y5. Because of the cyclical nature of the citrus industry, it is estimated that earnings of the Grove will be one-half those for Fiscal Year 19Y5. Interest income will be lower because of lower prevailing interest rates and a reduction in funds invested. It is forecast that the Company's income, before income tax expense for Fiscal Year 19Y6, will be approximately $400,000.

As of September 28, 19Y4, Super Oil Company was merged into Monument Oil Corporation. Monument thereby became the operator of the oil and gas interests that our wholly-owned subsidiary Greenfield Petroleum, Inc., owns. Due to the management transition, a number of delays have been experienced in obtaining from Monument certain accounting information, including that

Exhibit 4-3 continued

pertaining to oil and gas reserve figures and net cash flows. We have been promised that such information will be forthcoming, but it has not been provided as of this date. Nevertheless, we are in a position to advise you that the present oil and gas monthly income hovers at about $40,000 and that the monthly operating expenses are about $30,000. There appears to be a glut of gas and oil at the moment, and any further softening of the prices and/or sales will make the petroleum operation marginal.

The Company does not anticipate that compliance with federal, state and local provisions that have been enacted or adopted regulating the discharge of materials into the environment will have a material effect upon capital expenditures, earnings or the competitive position of the company and its subsidiaries.

During Fiscal Year ended April 30, 19Y5, the Company purchased 20,175 shares of Common Stock $1 Par Value; of these shares, 175 shares were purchased directly from non-affiliated stockholders, and 20,000 shares were purchased from the Greenfield Pension Fund. These shares are included in the Treasury Stock Account in the accompanying Balance Sheet. As a result of these purchases, the number of Common Shares outstanding decreased from 563,325 on April 30, 19Y4 to 543,150 on April 30, 19Y5.

The Directors and Officers wish to express their appreciation for the effort of all the people associated with Greenfield.

Sincerely,

Paul Potankis
President

October 16, 19Y5

Exhibit 4-3 continued

PART I

Item 1—Business

(a) General Development of Business

Incorporated in New York, Greenfield, for twenty-five years, was primarily engaged in the design, testing, development and production of coaxial helicopters. Substantially all work was conducted for the U.S. Navy, with a small procurement by the Japanese Navy.

Following the sharp reduction of its helicopter business and eventually the total elimination of it (except for providing spare parts to the Japanese Maritime Self-Defense Force), the Company began subdividing its idle facilities in order to derive rental income. The Company is not currently planning to actively return to the production of helicopters, however, continuing efforts are being made to market technical information, hardware and tooling which, in the opinion of Management, still have value because of their unique character.

Greenfield Petroleum, Inc. was incorporated in Delaware with the primary purpose of diversifying away from total dependency on aerospace. Farfield Properties, Inc. was incorporated in New York to manage investments in marketable securities and to participate in a limited partnership of a citrus grove in Florida. Two additional subsidiaries, Greenfield Research Laboratories, Inc. and Clay Helicopter Systems, Inc. were created to pursue areas of technology. However both of these subsidiaries have since become inactive.

(b) Financial Information Relating to Business Segment

	Year Ended April 30, 19Y5	19Y4	19Y3
Rental Income	$ 727,655	$ 691,594	$ 609,474
Less: Rental Costs and Expenses	531,818	548,963	710,734
Rental Operating Income	$ 195,837	$ 142,631	$−101,260
Oil and Gas Sales	$ 554,551	$ 579,329	$ 679,220
Less: Oil and Gas Operating Expenses	396,742	136,458	583,791
Oil and Gas Operating Income	$ 157,809	$ 442,871	$ 95,429
Identifiable Assets at Net Carrying Value			
Real Estate Fixed Assets	$ 436,759	$ 444,394	$ 459,269
Oil and Gas Assets	1,599,708	1,106,194	$ 192,204

Note 1—All inter-company transactions have been eliminated.

Note 2—All company activity was within the United States of America.

Exhibit 4-3 continued

Note 3—For additional detail, see Greenfield Company of America, Inc. Consolidated Statement of Income.

(c) Business Segments

The Business Segments represented in the financial statements reflect the activities of Greenfield Company of America, Inc. (unconsolidated)—real estate and Greenfield Petroleum, Inc.—oil and gas activity. Farfield Properties, Inc.'s Grove income is carried as investment income on the consolidated statements of income under the heading "Other Income."

(c)(1) Real Estate

The company owns approximately 321 acres of land at St. James, New York, which, for the most part, is zoned for light industry. The property is located on the North Shore of Long Island approximately 40 miles east of New York City. The property is surrounded by residential areas and is located adjacent to the State University of New York at Stony Brook campus. Seven miles northeast of the Long Island Expressway, the property is not located near the transportation hub.

Almost all of the approximately 207,000 square feet of buildings are suitable for renovation as office, engineering, manufacturing and warehouse space. There are approximately five miles of improved roads and approximately 10 acres of paved parking areas. Rental unit sizes range from 500 square feet to 18,000 square feet, with the small units being most numerous. Where practical, separate utilities have been provided for each suite. Given the location and size of rental units, the industrial park attracts small start-up companies that are not dependent on extensive material/product handling. The complex has no nearby competition for tenants; however, it is limited as specified above.

The average age of all facilities is twenty years, and the property is entering a major maintenance cycle for roofs, road and parking lot repairs and exterior building maintenance. Almost all available space has been subdivided, except for 25,000 square feet which has been reserved for Company use. Of the 182,000 gross square footage available for rent, approximately 20,000 square feet comprise common areas such as hallways, foyers and restrooms. The average occupancy rate for the 162,000 net square feet during the last three years has fluctuated between 85% and 92%, reflecting economic conditions which affect business start-ups and small business in general.

(c)(2) Oil and Gas

Greenfield Petroleum, Inc. was established primarily to manage oil and gas interests through joint ventures. The initial major partners were Apache Oil and Austral Oil Company. All Apache Oil joint venture working interests were later disposed of. Austral Oil Company, Inc. sold its assets to the Super Oil Company. Super Oil Company was merged into Monument Oil Company. Monument thereby became the managing partner of the following fields in which this subsidiary has a net working interest as indicated below.

Exhibit 4-3 continued

Field (1)	Location County/State Gross Acreage	% Avg. Net Working Int. in Income	GPI Proven Reserves (1)
Ackerly	Dawson Texas 6540 Acres	4.5%	
Rulison	Garfield and Mesa Colorado 14,360 Acres	19.0%	
Basin Dakota	San Juan Co. New Mexico 2,880 Acres	2.75%	

Note (1) Actual number of producing wells, proven reserves, and the discounted net future cash flows relating to proven reserves are not available at this time, but will be provided by amendment shortly.

(c)(3) Citrus Grove

The Company, through its wholly-owned subsidiary, Farfield Properties, Inc. holds a 20% interest in the Citrus Grove (a limited partnership) located 16 miles west of Palm Beach, Florida. This limited partnership was formed in 19W4 and maintains its books and records on a calendar year basis and by Partnership Agreement on the cash basis. However, Grove was required for federal income tax reporting purposes to change the reporting of taxable income from the previously used cash basis to the accrual method of accounting for 19Y1 and subsequent years.

In 19Y1, the Grove reached "payout," i.e., cumulative realized revenues equaled and exceeded cumulative expenses, at which time, under the Partnership terms, the General Partners commenced receiving one-eighth of the cash basis net the Limited Partners were allocated seven-eighths of the net revenue.

As reported previously in the form 10Q for the period ended January 31, 19Y5, the cash distribution for the fourth quarter of FY19Y5 was expected to be $115,000. Actual receipts were $91,000 for the fourth quarter and $726,100 for the Fiscal Year ended April 30, 19Y5. The lower than expected earnings were a direct result of poor sales of grapefruits and a higher than normal incidence of fruit dropping from trees. A spotty blossoming for grapefruits during the 19Y4–Y5 blossom season resulted in a cautious forecast for the 19Y5 crop. The actual crop came in with a low number of oversized fruit and therefore a reduced yield per acre. A large portion of the grapefruit crop had to be sold for concentrate which brought a much lower price than is available from fresh fruit. Additional pressure on revenues was attributable to the severe freeze of January 21 and 22, 19Y5, the ultimate effects of which were not fully accessible until the latter part of March 19Y5.

The Grove Manager has advised that there will be continuing pressure on

Exhibit 4-3 continued

revenues and profits during calendar year 19Y5. The cyclical nature of the tree blossoms and the following fruit harvests indicates that although calendar 19Y5 will be a poor year, the prospects for calendar year 19Y6 seem, based on early blossoms, very promising. Estimated results for calendar year 19Y5 were revised downward on June 20th, 19Y5 to approximately $285,000 for the year. No income estimate has been received for the calendar 19Y6 year.

Two caveats for calendar 19Y6 seem to be possible marketing difficulties associated with white grapefruit sales which are contingent on the Japanese import market. Demand by the Japanese has been hurt by the sharp rise in the dollar. Also as of the end of the 19Y5 shipping season, Japan will no longer accept fruit that has been fumigated with ethyl dibromide (EDB), which is currently in widespread use throughout Florida. On the basis of a changing grapefruit market and increased competition from the other Indian River area groves, Grove has undertaken a program to reduce the acreage of grapefruit from 40% of the total grove to 30%. The replacement trees will be Murcott oranges, which the Grove Manager advises enjoy an excellent economic outlook. The other intangible is the price of concentrate which, in one year, has plummeted from $1.90 to $1.45 in response to the flood of supply from Brazil.

The Grove presently consists of 3,665 acres with approximately 350,000 citrus trees of various varieties. There are more than fifteen buildings consisting of residences, administrative offices, equipment sheds, machine shops, storage sheds, etc., on the property.

The Company's investment in this property totaled $1,621,395 at April 30, 19Y4. The Company is committed to an additional investment of $110,000 on demand as provided by the original partnership agreement. However, the Grove Manager has advised that no cash calls are presently contemplated.

Based in part upon an independent appraisal by Timothy H. Peter, MAI, SRPA, Realtor, President of Timothy H. Peter Appraisal Co., Inc. of Orlando, Florida, made as of December 31, 19Y4, the Grove Manager had estimated Farfield Properties, Inc. 20% interest in the net asset value of the citrus grove as a whole to be worth approximately $5,016,000, an increase of approximately $858,000 (20.6%) over the prior year's appraisal. This is approximately $3,394,600 more than the cost of the Grove.

One of the major factors in the continuing rise in the asset value of the grove is that Florida has experienced severe freezes in four of the last five years with the December 19Y3 freeze being the most devastating of the century, especially to groves in northern Florida. This has resulted in an increase in value of those groves which survived the freezes, particularly those groves lying in the southeast and southwest coasts of the state. Estimates by the Grove Manager of the Net Asset Value of the Grove are based on the Grove as a complete unit with the highest and best use of the property as a citrus grove.

As of December 31, 19Y2, 19Y3 and 19Y4, the Grove Manager estimated the Net Asset Value of the Citrus Grove to be as follows:

Exhibit 4-3 continued

	19Y2	December 31, 19Y3 (in Thousands)	19Y4
Land and Citrus Trees	$17,592	$19,036	$24,071
Buildings & Domestic Water Systems	330	340	432
Equipment and Supplies	2,478	2,396	3,341
Total Appraisal (1)	$20,400	$21,772	$27,844
Cash & Other Assets (2)	811	446	1,193
Value of Fruit Trees (3)	2,449	4,235	3,536
Total	$23,660	$26,473	$32,573
Less:			
Notes Payable	2,949	2,401	3,598
Other Liabilities	329	311	315
	3,278	2,712	3,913
Net Asset Value	$20,382	$23,761	$28,660
Net Asset Value Allocable to General Partners	2,548	2,970	3,582
Net Asset Value Allocable to Limited Partners	$17,834	$20,791	$25,078

	FARFIELD PROPERTIES, INC. Value of 20% Interest in Grove		
Net Asset Value	$ 3,567	$ 4,158	$ 5,016
Less:			
Approximate Deferred Income Tax Cost (4)	120	110	90
Value After Present Worth of Tax Liability Re 1/1/Y1 Accrual Adjustment	$ 3,447	$ 4,048	$ 4,926

(1) Appraisal prepared by Timothy H. Peter, MAI, SRPA, Realtor, President of Timothy H. Peter Appraisal Co., Inc. of Orlando, Florida.

(2) Amounts for 19Y3 and 19Y4 reflect a write-down of the book value of advances to cooperatives. No value is attributed to organization and deferred debt expense.

(3) The value of fruit on trees and the amounts receivable from fruit delivered, but not paid for, are not included in the appraised assets. This figure is equal to 75% of the estimated future revenue from fruit delivered, but not paid for, plus 66⅔% of estimated net on-tree revenue from the unpicked current season crop at the year-end.

(4) Based on 12% annual discount, compounded quarterly, and a 50% income tax rate.

Exhibit 4-3 continued

Item 2—Properties

(1) Real Estate Properties

Greenfield Company of America, Inc. (Unconsolidated) owns approximately 321 acres in the North Shore area of Suffolk County just to the west and north of the State University at Stony Brook, New York, on which it presently has approximately 207,000 square feet of building space. The buildings and approximately 139 acres are located at St. James, New York, in the Township of Smithtown, and the contiguous balance of approximately 182 acres are located at Stony Brook, New York, in the Township of Brookhaven.

The approximate 321 acres of land are zoned for use as shown below.

	Approximate Acreage		
Township	**Total**	**Light Industry**	**Residential and/or Buffer**
Smithtown	139	120	19
Brookhaven	182	173	9
Total	321	293	28

All of the land is contiguous. However, the Port Jefferson Branch of the Long Island Railroad runs through the property with 73.5 acres lying to the north of the railroad and the balance south of the railroad.

The approximately 321 acres of land are carried on the Company's books at cost in the amount of $166,490, while the 207,000 square feet of space are carried at a depreciated cost of $228,113. The property and buildings which are used by the Real Estate segment of the business are entirely without financial encumbrances.

Item 3—Legal Proceedings

Neither the Company nor its subsidiaries are party to, nor is any of their property subject to any material pending legal proceedings.

Item 4—Submission of Matters to a Vote of Security Holders

No matters were submitted to the vote of security holders during the fourth quarter of Fiscal Year 19Y5.

Exhibit 4-3 continued

PART II

Item 5—Market for Registrant's Common Stock and Related Stockholder Matters

(a) Price Range of Common Stock

The Company's Common Stock $1 P.V. is traded on the Over-the-Counter Market under the NASDAQ symbol "GRNF." The following are the reported low and high bid and ask prices of the stock for the period indicated as reported by NASDAQ market quotations.

Fiscal Year Ended April 30,	Bid Price Low	Bid Price High	Ask Price Low	Ask Price High
19Y4				
1st Quarter	6½	8	7¼	8¼
2nd Quarter	5½	7¼	6¼	7¾
3rd Quarter	6¼	7	6¾	7¾
4th Quarter	5¾	6½	6¼	6¾
19Y5				
1st Quarter	4½	6	5¾	6½
2nd Quarter	4⅝	7½	6	8½
3rd Quarter	6⅛	7	7½	8
4th Quarter	6¼	6½	7½	7¾

(b) Approximate Number of Equity Security Holders

Title of Class	Number of Record Holders as of July 29, 19Y5
Common Stock, $1.00 Par Value	2,484

(c) No dividends were paid during the last two fiscal years.

(d) In view of the approximate $1,598,292 Consolidated Deficit as of April 30, 19Y5, there is no near-term prospect of dividends being paid.

Item 6—Selected Financial Data (in Thousands except for per Share Data)

	19Y5	19Y4	19Y3	19Y2	19Y1
Net Operating Revenues	$1,284	$1,274	$1,289	$1,205	$1,123
Continuing Operations	657	502	208	601	556
Deferred Tax Adjustment	366	0	0	0	0
Retained Earnings (Deficit)	−1,598	−2,621	−3,123	−3,331	−3,932

Exhibit 4-3 continued

Income per Share from:					
Continuing Operations	$ 1.18	$ .89	$ .36	$ .99	$ .82
Deferred Tax Adjustment	.66	0	0	0	0
Total Assets	4,865	4,223	2,917	3,384	3,400
Cash Dividends					
Declared per Share	0	0	0	0	0

Item 7—Management's Discussion and Analysis of Financial Condition and Results of Operation

Total revenue for the Fiscal Year ended April 30, 19Y5, rose slightly over the previous period to $1,284,100. A steady trend of improvement has been recorded in rental income over the last six report periods.

Fiscal Year	Revenue
19Y0	$500,800
19Y1	569,500
19Y2	586,000
19Y3	609,500
19Y4	691,600
19Y5	727,700

The cost of maintaining rental property for Fiscal Year 19Y5 was slightly lower than in the prior year. Due to inclement weather, major facilities' repairs, although scheduled, were not undertaken during the 19Y5 year. It is the opinion of management that Fiscal 19Y6 will show a substantial increase in operating expense. The primary maintenance projects include parking lot sealing, road resurfacing, and roof repairs.

Sales from Oil and Gas operations were marginally lower during the year reflecting a continued weakness in prices. The comparison of expenses for Oil and Gas operations for the periods ended April 30, 19Y5 and April 30, 19Y4 is $396,800 and $136,500 respectively. However, FY19Y4 costs were affected by a credit adjustment of $381,000 to expenses due to the capitalization of prior years' intangible drilling costs. The unadjusted FY19Y4 expenses would have been $517,624 versus $396,742 or $120,712 higher than the current period. Substantially lower costs were recorded in Operating Production Expense, $120,745 for FY19Y5 for a $198,680 decrease from the prior period. This was partially offset by an increase in FY19Y5 Depreciation Expense of $85,103 to $178,459.

As detailed in Form 10K for Fiscal Year 19Y4, a reduction of accruals for franchise taxes and interest thereon was made in that year. The interest adjust-

Exhibit 4-3 continued

ment resulted in a credit to General and Administrative expense in the amount of $55,000. The unadjusted result for Fiscal Year 19Y4 would have been $339,425 which compares with $361,759 for Fiscal Year 19Y5 and $346,121 for Fiscal Year 19Y3.

Income from the Grove was exceptionally high during Fiscal Year 19Y5 as had been anticipated in the three 10Q reports filed for the current year. A particularly favorable set of circumstances contributed to the record results. A record harvest at the Grove was complimented by unusually high prices, which were created by supply shortages, due to two severe freezes and repeated embargos imposed on Florida citrus because of the citrus canker infestation.

The Grove maintains its books on a calendar year basis, therefore income estimates received from the Grove Manager at this time project through December 31, 19Y5. Actual earnings for Calendar Year 19Y4 were $885,654 of which $736,254 were recorded during the 19Y5 Fiscal Year ended April 30, 19Y5 with the balance recorded in Fiscal 19Y4. Estimated earnings by the Grove Manager for Calendar Year 19Y5 have been revised downward to $285,000 which will translate into much lower earnings for Fiscal Year 19Y6. It is the Grove Management's opinion that based on preliminary marketing and economic data, Calendar Year 19Y6 should compare favorably with CY19Y5, however this improvement will not yield the record results attained in CY19Y4. A more detailed discussion of the economic outlook of the Grove is presented in Item (c)(3) of this report.

As a result of very high interest rates at the beginning of the 19Y5 Fiscal Year and an increase in monies invested in interest bearing accounts, the Company recorded an increase of $33,436 in Interest Income and Money Market Dividends over the previous year ended April 30, 19Y4. The lower prevailing interest rates during the first half of Calendar Year 19Y5 and a continued soft economic picture indicate that interest rates will tend to remain lower for the 19Y6 Fiscal Year than were available for much of Fiscal 19Y5.

Earnings from operations before taxes for the current year ended April 30, 19Y5 were $798,101 or approximately $30,000 higher than the prior period. Major income and expense swings were recorded in: 1) the gross operating margin for real estate operations which recorded a $50,000 increase during the current period, 2) an approximate $285,000 drop in the operating margin of Oil and Gas operations, 3) an increase of approximately $320,000 in income from the Grove, 4) an increase of approximately $33,000 in Interest Income, and 5) an approximate $22,000 net increase in G&A expense in FY 19Y5 was coupled with a $55,000 credit in FY19Y4 G&A which affected year-to-year comparisons.

Results from operations after taxes and before a nonrecurring tax adjustment were $1.18 for the period ended April 30, 19Y5 versus $.89 for the prior period. The effective tax rate for Fiscal Year 19Y5 before taking credit for the nonrecur-

Exhibit 4-3 continued

ring deferred tax adjustment was 18% compared to 35% for the previous reporting period. At the end of the 19Y5 Fiscal Year, the Company recalculated its deferred tax requirements which were a result of various timing differences in the handling of tax and book income and expenses. The resultant credit adjustment was $365,635 or $.66 per share and raised the earnings to $1.84 per share.

Liquidity and Capital Reserves

A modest decrease in the current ratio from .987 to 1 to .964 to 1 was experienced during the current Fiscal Year ended April 30, 19Y5. However, a substantial improvement was recorded in the quick ratio which rose to .774 to 1 from .554 to 1. A portion of the increase in the cash position was due to the receipt of approximately $100,000 in Federal Income Tax Refund Claims filed by the company. Additionally, a reduction in Accounts Receivable reflected primarily payments received against Grove income that had been previously booked.

A $155,600 increase in Accounts Payable is attributable to the drilling program commitments of Greenfield Petroleum which will wind down during FY19Y6. A decrease of $202,248 in Accrued Salaries and Wages reflected the payment of deferred wages from the prior period. The Company's Management has and will continue to utilize a cash management system which defers some salaries in order to conserve cash to meet open commitments. A $64,391 reduction in Current Accrued Federal and State Taxes—Deferred was made by the Company reflecting current year's timing differences attributable to the treatment of oil, gas and citrus property investment costs.

Additional planned subdivision of existing buildings into rental units and a pay down of accounts payable and open commitments will be made, as far as possible, out of normal cash flow and current working capital. However, should such sources prove insufficient, either long term or short term bank loans may be necessary. The Registrant anticipates a continuation of the present current ratio through the 19Y6 Fiscal Year.

Effects of Inflation

It has been the Company's policy to have all current leases contain Cost-of-Living, real estate tax, and fuel cost index adjustments, therefore rental income has not been adversely affected by inflation.

The continued oil glut has kept oil prices depressed for almost two years. The Registrant expects low prices to prevail for the coming year, however the effects of low prices may in part be offset by increased production. The new oil and gas wells coming on line in CY19Y5 should offset any reduced production from older wells. Cash flow from the new gas wells in the Rulison Field did not commence in Fiscal Year 19Y5 as anticipated but did start in FY19Y6. The overall result in FY19Y5 was slightly lower revenue. For FY19Y6 preliminary indications are that results should improve.

Exhibit 4-3 continued

Item 8—Financial Statements and Supplementary Data

GREENFIELD COMPANY OF AMERICA, INC.:
CONSOLIDATED BALANCE SHEET April 30

ASSETS	19Y5	19Y4
Current		
Cash—Operating Accounts	$ 41,128	$ 17,087
Cash in Banks—Interest Bearing Accounts	762,112	604,139
Federal Income Tax Refund Claim	0	119,011
Accounts Receivable Net of Allowance	79,276	255,565
Accrued Interest Receivable	4,146	6,942
Prepaid Expenses	113,574	104,216
Total Current Assets	1,000,236	1,106,960
Fixed Assets		
Land	166,490	166,490
Building and Improvements	2,996,592	2,996,592
Machinery, Equipment and Furniture	194,646	182,256
Total	3,357,728	3,345,338
Less: Accumulated Depreciation	2,920,969	2,900,944
	436,759	444,394
Investments		
Investments in Oil and Gas Properties		
Fixed Asset and Capitalized Drilling Costs	2,289,143	1,519,632
Less: Accumulated Depreciation Amortization	689,435	413,438
Net Investment in Oil and Gas	1,599,708	1,106,194
Investment in Citrus Grove	1,621,395	1,491,741
Total	3,221,103	2,597,935
Other Assets		
Deferred Leasing Costs	742,940	742,940
Less: Amortization	718,911	679,029
Net Deferred Leasing Costs	24,029	63,911
Other Assets	2,512	9,678
Total	26,541	73,589
TOTAL ASSETS	$4,684,639	$4,222,878

Exhibit 4-3 continued

LIABILITIES	19Y5	19Y4
Current		
Accounts Payable	$ 747,559	$ 591,959
Accrued Salaries and Wages	120,445	322,693
Accrued Expenses	9,298	5,035
Accrued Real Estate Taxes	82,940	77,939
Accrued Interest Payable	0	3,425
Accrued Fed & State Taxes on Income		
Current	31,726	10,756
Current Deferred	45,209	109,600
Total Current Liabilities	1,037,177	1,121,407
Deferred Income Taxes	575,900	941,535
Total Liabilities	1,613,077	2,062,942
STOCKHOLDERS' EQUITY		
Common Stock P.V. $1 per share		
Authorized—2,000,000 shares		
Issued—1,107,268 shares	1,107,268	1,107,268
Capital in Excess of Par Value	6,806,946	6,806,946
Retained Earnings (deficit) Exhibit	−1,598,292	−2,621,160
	6,315,922	5,293,054
Less: Treasury Stock—at Cost		
19Y4—543,943 shares		−3,133,118
19Y5—564,118 shares	−3,244,360	
Total Stockholders' Equity	3,071,562	2,159,936
Commitments and Contingent Liabilities		
TOTAL LIABILITIES AND STOCKHOLDERS' EQUITY	$4,684,639	$4,222,878

Patents and Trade Names

Patents and trade names are another important type of below-the-line hidden asset. Exhibit 4-4 contains an example of the balance sheet of just such a company. As the balance sheet discloses, the DEF Company had approximately $2.57 in cash behind every share. As such, it represented on the surface a "pure cash" play. For a period of time it sold at a price below that of its cash value. However, the real hidden asset was not in the cash it had, but rather in certain scientific processes it controlled. The asset-play investor who invested in the company based solely on a value approach would have seen the stock increase 500% or more in price once the professional investors "discovered" the value of the scientific processes the company owned. Many analysts are only recently becoming aware of the hidden value represented by a company's consumer franchise—another way of describing the fact that consumers are very aware of the names of the products and services they use on a day-to-day basis.

Exhibit 4-4.

DEF COMPANY

19Y7 FIRST QUARTER REPORT
ENDING MARCH 31, 19Y7

Exhibit 4-4 continued

Dear Fellow Shareholders:

Developments in the Company's blood storage program have highlighted an extremely eventful first quarter. An important success for DEF's unique corporate blood storage program was achieved with the signing in January of a contract with Warren Communications providing for autologous blood storage for its 8,000 employees. This was followed in March with the signing of a contract with IMS International covering 5,000 employees. These contracts, similar to the first such contract signed in 19Y6 with D.H. Blare, represent the beginnings of a national network which will be capable of supplying blood anywhere in the U.S. within 6–8 hours and locally within 2 hours.

DEF became a nationally known Company in the first quarter, as both the general public and the financial community became aware of the implications of the spreading AIDS epidemic. The Company has been featured multiple times in the print and television media, including articles in the *Wall Street Journal, Investor's Daily,* and most recently, *Forbes* magazine. The discovery of the Company by the financial community led to marked fluctuations in the price of the stock. At the time of the signing of the Warren contract, the stock was selling for little more than its cash assets. With the recent trading activity we now have an estimated 5,500 shareholders.

Frozen autologous (self-storage) blood as provided by the Company continues to be the ideal answer to the dangers of the present transfusion system, whether provided as an individual, family, or corporate plan. The incidence of transfusion hepatitis is approximately 10%; the risk of transfusion AIDS is difficult to estimate but may be as high as one chance in 400, considering the fact that the average transfusion consists of multiple blood products each taken from a different donor. There is a three-month window of infectivity using the current antibody screening test for AIDS during which an individual can have an active AIDS infection, donate blood and not be detected. The magnitude of the risk can be approximated from the fact that the N.Y.C. Health Commissioner has stated that there are 500,000 people in N.Y.C. alone already infected with the AIDS virus! The majority of these people do not know that they are already infected. Directed donation using frozen blood can virtually eliminate the risk of AIDS, as stored blood can be quarantined for the period of potential infectivity, and the donor rechecked for antibodies. Directed donation using DEF's program also decreases the risk of hepatitis, because more stringent liver screening tests are applied, but most significantly because donated blood can be taken from a single donor instead of multiple ones. Frozen storage is essential because it enables autologous donations to be spread out over safe intervals, and ensures that patients storing blood prior to surgery will not be blood-depleted at the time of surgery.

In May, the Company signed a contract with its major subcontractor for manufacture of its blood volume analyzer. This contract was essential for

Exhibit 4-4 continued

completion of both the FDA approval and patent application processes.

Income, revenue, and profits for the first quarter were the greatest in the Company's history. Net income for the quarter was $2,108,629 vs. $317,362 in 19Y6. Net income per share was $.40 vs. $.06. A major contributor to earnings was the partial sale of securities in the company portfolio; after-tax profits on the sale were $1,772,167 and pre-tax profits were $2,454,167. At the end of the quarter, the Company still had unrealized gains of $5,325,604, or $1.00 per share, in its securities portfolio. In 19Y7 total assets increased to $24,607,865 from $21,266,535 at December 31, 19Y6. The Company's unrealized capital gains are not reflected in total assets as per accounting principles; the sum of total assets and unrealized capital gains is $29,933,469.

In closing, I most strongly urge stockholders and other readers of this letter within the New York region to contact the company to establish a family blood storage reserve. In the past year, we have had numerous instances of individuals planning to store blood and then unexpectedly needing it before they actually got around to making their donations—these individuals were forced to accept banked blood with all its risks. One of my own relatives was in this situation. I therefore again advise those of you within our service area to provide this protection for yourselves and your families.

Respectfully yours,

John Feinstein, M.D.
President

Exhibit 4-4 continued

DEF CORPORATION
CONSOLIDATED BALANCE SHEETS (UNAUDITED)

	December 31, 19Y6	March 31, 19Y7
ASSETS		
Current assets:		
Cash and short term investments	$ 51,828	$ 5,747,303
Marketable securities at cost (Notes 1 and 2)	20,409,795	17,987,280
Accounts receivable	284,816	303,479
Other current assets	24,871	89,668
Total current assets	20,771,310	24,127,730
Equipment and improvements:		
Storage tanks	96,992	96,992
Leasehold improvements, furniture and equipment	296.666	281,555
Laboratory equipment	155,693	158,622
	549,351	537,169
Less accumulated depreciation and amortization	(329,298)	(342,858)
Net equipment and improvements	220,053	194,311
Other assets	275,172	285,824
Total assets	$21,266,535	$24,607,865
LIABILITIES AND SHAREHOLDERS' EQUITY		
Current liabilities:		
Accounts payable and accrued liabilities	$ 171,023	$ 1,019,022
Loans payable (Notes 1 and 2)	6,951,857	5,500,000
Other liabilities (Note 1)	—	1,597,093
Total current liabilities	7,122,880	8,116,115
Shareholders' equity (Note 3):		
Common stock, par value $.01 per share: authorized 10,000,000 shares; issued and outstanding 5,282,250 shares at March 31, 19Y6 and 5,307,650 at March 31, 19Y7	52,822	53,076
Additional paid-in capital	8,392,998	8,566,061
Retained earnings	5,763,984	7,872,613
Treasury stock	(66,149)	—
Total shareholders' equity	14,143,655	16,491,750
Total liabilities and shareholders' equity	$21,266,535	$24,607,865

See accompanying notes to financial statements

Exhibit 4-4 continued

DEF CORPORATION
CONSOLIDATED STATEMENTS OF OPERATIONS (UNAUDITED)

	March 31, 19Y6	March 31, 19Y7
Revenues:		
Operating revenues	$ 451,712	$ 521,756
Dividend income	389,054	540,832
Gains (losses) on sale of securities	(11,185)	2,454,167
Total revenues	829,581	3,516,755
Costs and expenses:		
Operations of laboratories	184,302	233,856
Selling, general and administrative	140,201	154,692
Interest expense	154,020	131,695
Total costs and expenses	478,523	520,243
Net income before income taxes	351,058	2,996,512
Provision for income taxes	33,696	887,883
Net income	$ 317,362	$2,108,629
Number of shares outstanding	5,282,250	5,307,650
Net income per share	$ .06	$ .40

See accompanying notes to financial statements

DEF CORPORATION
NOTES TO CONSOLIDATED FINANCIAL STATEMENTS (UNAUDITED)
THREE MONTHS ENDED MARCH 31, 19Y6 AND 19Y7

In the opinion of the Company, the accompanying unaudited consolidated financial statements contain all adjustments (consisting of only normal recurring accruals) necessary to present fairly the financial position as of December 31, 19Y6 and March 31, 19Y7, and the results of operations for the three months ended March 31, 19Y6 and 19Y7 and changes in financial position for the three months then ended. The consolidated financial statements include the accounts of the Company and its subsidiary. All significant intercompany transactions and balances have been eliminated in consolidation.

1. Marketable Securities

At December 31, 19Y6, the marketable securities held by the Company had a market value of $26,258,042 and a cost basis of $20,409,795 resulting in a net unrealized gain of $5,848,247 or 28.7% of cost. At March 31, 19Y7, the marketable securities held by the Company had a market value of $23,312,884 and a cost basis of $17,987,280 resulting in a net unrealized gain of $5,325,604 or 29.1% of cost. At December 31, 19Y6 and March 31, 19Y7 marketable securities, primarily consisting of preferred and common stocks of utility companies, were valued at cost.

Exhibit 4-4 continued

At March 31, 19Y7, the Company also maintained a short position in certain stocks. This position was sold for $1,597,093 and had a market value of $1,539,975 as of March 31, 19Y7, resulting in an unrealized gain of $57,118.

2. Loans Payable

At December 31, 19Y6 and March 31, 19Y7, the Company had loans outstanding aggregating $5,500,000 borrowed on a short-term basis from a bank which is secured by certain marketable securities owned by the Company. These loans bear interest at 8%.

Short-term margin debt due to brokers, secured by the Company's marketable securities, totaled $1,451,857 at December 31, 19Y6, and 0 at March 31, 19Y7.

3. Stockholders' Equity

On March 12, 19Y7 an additional 25,400 shares of stock were issued resulting in an increase of $254 in capital stock and an increase of $164,846 in paid-in capital. In addition, the Company sold 12,000 shares of Treasury stock resulting in an increase in paid-in surplus of $8,217.

Holdings in Other Companies

Holdings of 5% or more in other companies represent still another kind of below-the-line hidden asset. Exhibit 4-5 contains the balance sheet of a company falling into this category. As you can see from reviewing its balance sheet, CYCLOMATICS, Inc. had substantial holdings in another public company. For a period of time the price of CYCLOMATICS, Inc. failed to reflect the value of its holdings in the other public company, probably because the company was not followed by professional analysts. By utilizing the numerical techniques described in this chapter, you can identify the company's hidden assets early.

Exhibit 4-5.

CYCLOMATICS, INC.

19Y6 Annual Report

Financial Highlights	**19Y6**	**19Y5**	**19Y4**
Revenues	$12,158,436	$35,964,209	$40,261,200
Net Earnings	$298,669	$1,472,785	$1,256,045
Earnings Per Share	$.21	$1.00	$.77
Stockholders' Equity	$12,319,768	$11,893,298	$11,072,934

Exhibit 4-5 continued

Cover: **An indifferent foot** would be as much a plague to the measurement standards of today as it was to those of the 17th century were it not for Metrology, the science of measurement. Fortunately for our society, the National Bureau of Standards (NBS) has progressed well beyond the anatomy of the random Chancellor (since 19Y3, length is measured by the path of light traveled in a vacuum over a specific time prior thereto certain atomic wavelenghths were used and, even earlier, physical rods were crafted from special metals). Physical standards maintained by the NBS are, in turn, used to check regional standards. These in turn are used to check local standards, and so forth down a contiguous line of measurement ultimately used to check test instruments and end components. Imagine a world in which measurements differed regionally or where the instruments used to test and correct accuracy were themselves inaccurate. Imagine the outcome.

Dedication: The **Metrology Division** of CYCLOMATICS has provided critical technical and operational support to the military services under numerous metrology-related contracts since 19Y3. From the monthly scheduling of thousands of precision test instruments into specialized laboratories for calibration and adjustment, to the maintenance of equipment used to test the purity of aviators breathing oxygen, Metrology Division personnel have contributed significantly over the years both to the success of military metrology/calibration programs and to the success of the Company.

CYCLOMATICS, in addition to dedicating the cover of its 19Y6 Annual Report, is honored to pay special tribute to the dedicated personnel of the Metrology Division who over the years have been responsible for unparalleled success in sustaining their operational and technical efforts on behalf of the Company.

The head of CYCLOMATICS' metrology efforts in Vice President and Metrology Division Manager, Mr. James Lowe, Jr. James joined the Company in April 19Y3 after 20 years of technical experience with the armed forces. Among his other contributions while at CYCLOMATICS, he is the designer and co-author of numerous calibration manuals used by the U.S. Navy. Under his calm hand and able leadership, the programs of the Metrology Division have successfully progressed over the years to become the most sustained efforts in the Company's history.

Management's Report

Material Developments Fiscal 19Y6 was for CYCLOMATICS the story of two inversely dramatic events. On the one hand, the Company suffered the largest decline in revenues in its history (66%), with a concomitant reduction in net earnings (80%), primarily attributable to the loss of two of its principal contracts in the previous year. On the other hand, the stock purchase ($5.2 million) made for diversification in Insituform East, Inc., also in the previous year, underwent a spectacular rise in market price through 19Y6 year-end. Even after significant price resettlement, the stock currently has a market value over three times the

Exhibit 4-5 continued

original purchase investment. In short, during a year of small operating earnings the underlying value of CYCLOMATICS may arguably be assessed to have soared. However, both conservatively and properly, the unrealized market appreciation in the Insituform shares owned by CYCLOMATICS is not reflected in the Company's financial statements. As required by generally accepted accounting principles, only those undistributed net earnings of Insituform allocated to CYCLOMATICS under the equity method, as well as a proportionate participation in certain capital changes, are reflected in the CYCLOMATICS statements. It is necessarily left to shareholders to judge the additional value, if any, to be assigned to the underlying value of CYCLOMATICS from unrealized Insituform market appreciation existing at any point in time.

Operating Results CYCLOMATICS had net earnings in 19Y6 of $299,000 (down 80%) on total revenues of $12.2 million (down 66%). Earnings per share were $.21 (down 79%). The previous year's earnings were $1.5 million ($1.00 per share) on total revenues of $36.0 million. The decreased operating results are primarily attributable to the expected effects of the previous year's loss of two of the Company's principal contracts, known as the "C-9" and the "TC-4C" aircraft material support contracts. During the preceding fiscal year ended June 30, 19Y5, the C-9 and TC-4C contracts together accounted for $24.3 million (68%) of the Company's total contract revenue of $35.4 million. During the year ended June 30, 19Y6, the C-9 and TC-4C contracts did not contribute to the Company's contract revenue of $11.7 million.

Dividends CYCLOMATICS declared semiannual dividends during 19Y6 cumulating to $.12 per share on its Class A Common Stock and $.10 per share on its convertible Class B Common Stock, equaling dividend amounts of the previous year. In anticipation of a decline both in operating results and in cash generation during the forthcoming year, the Company reduced the initial 19Y7 semiannual dividend declaration to $.03 per share on its Class A Common Stock and to $.02 per share on its convertible Class B Common Stock. The amount or payment of the second 19Y7 semiannual dividend, if any, will depend upon financial conditions as they unfold over the course of the 19Y7 year.

Significant Transactions Under terms of an agreement effective March 14, 19Y6, the Company purchased in a cash transaction of approximately $400,000 certain of the business of The Stanwick Corporation of Arlington, Virginia. The major portion of the business acquired included continuation by CYCLOMATICS, as successor in interest under novation agreement, of various Department of Defense contracts. In addition to the contracts, CYCLOMATICS transferred to its employ approximately 40 technical personnel. Contract revenue attributed to the acquisition represented approximately $800,000 (6.9%) of total contract revenue for the fiscal year ended June 30, 19Y6.

On June 13, 19Y6, pursuant to an exchange offer, the Company exchanged 296,141 shares of Insituform Common Stock for an equal number of shares of convertible Insituform Class B Stock. Details about the transaction are included in Note 5 to the financial statements. At June 30, 19Y6, CYCLOMATICS held 1,100,000 shares of Insituform Common Stock and 296,141 shares of convertible Insituform Class B Stock representing approximately 25.9% of the Common

Exhibit 4-5 continued

Stock, 92.5% of the Class B Stock, 30.6% of the total equity and 54.5% of the total voting power of all outstanding classes of Insituform stock. Three members of the Board of Directors of CYCLOMATICS currently serve on the Board of Insituform, and two of the three additionally have been elected senior officers of Insituform and serve part-time as members of its Chief Executive Officer Committee.

Business Developments The Company views the future development of its traditional line of business in defense-related services with some concern. The Competition in Contracting Act (19Y4), formally implemented April 1, 19Y5, has substantially curtailed single or sole source contracts, particularly in the areas where the Company has historically provided its services. As an expedient to mandated competition, the Company believes that there has resulted a change in government emphasis to price over quality. This is viewed to be a significant disadvantage to the Company, which has traditionally built its contract base on the quality of its professional staff and services.

There are of course positive developments and adjustments. First, the Company recently was the successful offeror on a combined recompetition of two of its largest existing contracts. The new contract award alone is anticipated to sustain the majority of the Company's Metrology efforts through September 19Y9. Second, Material Systems efforts have established the Company's initial foothold in commercial activity including meaningful growth during 19Y6. Third, of considerable future potential to the Company is the continuing evolution of the government's renewed interest in the ARAPAHO concept. The ARAPAHO concept and the Company's involvement are detailed in the Advanced Technology section of this annual report. Finally, the Company's diversification effort through its investment in Insituform East, Inc. is anticipated to reap substantial long-term benefits to CYCLOMATICS. The Company intends to investigate other diversified investments as well.

Outlook On overview, CYCLOMATICS anticipates a pause or reversal in near-term results in favor of continued focus on and investment in larger long-term gains. We intend to remain positioned to take advantage of our significant financial strength and flexibility as we assess the changes occurring in our traditional markets.

Respectfully,
The Corporate Executive Committee

Roger Endbin President	Carl M. Mueller Executive Vice President & Chief of Operations	Gerard P. Edwards Executive Vice President & General Counsel

November 7, 19Y6

Exhibit 4-5 continued

The Business Concept

The Need for Technical Services Increased technical sophistication of our world and its machines has demanded increased specialization in the people who keep it all running. In the transition from blacksmith to aircraft mechanic, and from grainkeeper to logistics engineer, both the pounder and the planner have had to revolutionize to keep up. And no entity runs so fast to stay technically abreast, necessarily, as our own Government.

In managing its increasingly complex array of methods and machines to act on the public's behalf, the U.S. Government relies on contracts with commercial sources in the private sector to accomplish a host of its service needs. Such services run the gamut from the most mundane to the most arcane, from the simplest to the most sophisticated, from janitorial functions to state-of-the-art research and development.

Among the various Government agencies, the Department of Defense is the largest single user of contract technical services. While overall management responsibility for any military project or activity resides with the Department of Defense, there are simply neither enough men under arms nor public employees, by intent, to provide all of the rapidly changing, limited-duration specialized technical services necessary to meet the nation's defense needs.

National Policy

"In the process of governing, the Government should not compete with its citizens. The competitive enterprise system, characterized by individual freedom and initiative, is the primary source of national economic strength. In recognition of this principle, it has been and continues to be the general policy of the Government to rely on commercial sources to supply the products and services the Government needs."

Thus, in clear and direct language, the Office of Management and Budget, the business arm of the U.S. Government, has set forth in its Circular A-76 the background to Federal Policy under which goods and services are to be acquired for Government needs.

After recognizing both the role of competitive costing and that certain functions are inherently governmental in nature, requiring performance by Federal employees, Circular A-76 turns to reliance on the commercial sector as the third component of Government policy necessary in determining whether commercial activities should be performed under contract with commercial sources or in-house, using Government facilities and personnel:

"The Federal Government shall rely on commercially available sources to provide commercial products services. In accordance with the provisions of this Circular, the Government shall not start or carry on any activity to provide a commercial product or service if the product or service can be procured more economically from a commercial source."

Exhibit 4-5 continued

CYCLOMATICS' Role CYCLOMATICS, Inc. is a commercial source specializing in the economical provision of engineering, analytical and technical support services to the U.S. Government, with primary emphasis on defense-related requirements. Since its founding, CYCLOMATICS has successfully completed hundreds of service contracts with the U.S. Government, and has earned a reputable position among professional services firms in its field.

CYCLOMATICS, Inc., together with its wholly-owned subsidiary, Systems Research Corporation, comprises a qualified staff of approximately 250 employees, including engineers, military analysts, computer scientists, logisticians, budget and management specialists, technical editors, graphics technicians and skilled support personnel. The CYCLOMATICS family is large enough to be comprehensive, yet concentrated enough to maintain flexibility and capacity for quick response.

As a valuable resource in the private sector, CYCLOMATICS helps to meet the needs of Government for specialized technical services and practical application of up-to-date expertise in:

- *Metrology* and calibration of weaponry and test equipment
- *Logistics* engineering for weapon systems
- *Systems Research* in defense and Government operations
- *Advanced Technology* applications to military systems
- *Material Systems* support for aircraft and related systems

Our democratic free enterprise system has produced the most powerful economic force on earth. From the very beginnings of American history, the Government has tapped this force by relying on and teaming with commercial sources to act on the public's behalf. CYCLOMATICS is proud to be a part of that team.

Exhibit 4-5 continued

CYCLOMATICS, Inc.
Consolidated Balance Sheets

	June 30	
	19Y6	19Y5
Assets		
CURRENT ASSETS:		
Cash and cash equivalents	$ 653,994	$ 2,008,678
Temporary investments at cost (approximates market)	2,286,590	2,616,485
Accounts receivable (Notes 2 and 7)	6,742,009	9,558,756
Prepaid expenses	112,597	116,155
TOTAL CURRENT ASSETS	9,795,190	14,300,074
PROPERTY AND EQUIPMENT—net (Note 3)	1,728,829	1,722,714
OTHER ASSETS:		
Investment in affiliate (Notes 5 and 7)	5,630,078	5,329,864
Capitalized contract rights—net (Note 4)	243,409	—
Marketable securities (Note 6)	62,929	60,334
Deposits and other	33,222	57,980
TOTAL OTHER ASSETS	5,969,638	5,448,178
TOTAL ASSETS	$17,493,657	$21,470,966
Liabilities and Stockholders' Equity		
CURRENT LIABILITIES		
Loans payable (Note 7)	$ 105,000	$ 2,984,564
Accounts payable and accrued liabilities (Note 8)	1,803,033	3,052,879
Deferred income taxes (Note 12)	776,000	931,000
Current portion of long-term liabilities	361,851	273,370
TOTAL CURRENT LIABILITIES	3,045,884	7,241,813
LONG-TERM LIABILITIES (less current portion shown above) (Note 7)	1,875,005	2,236,855
DEFERRED INCOME TAXES (Note 12)	253,000	99,000
TOTAL LIABILITIES	5,173,889	9,577,668
COMMITMENTS AND CONTINGENCIES (Notes 9 and 10)		
STOCKHOLDERS' EQUITY:		
Common stock (Note 11)		
Class A, $.10 par value authorized 3,500,000 shares		
Issued 1,291,454 shares		129,145
Outstanding 1,081,154 shares (at June 30, 19Y5)		
Issued 1,312,430 shares	131,243	
Outstanding 1,114,630 shares (at June 30, 19Y6)		
Class B (convertible), $.10 par value authorized 700,000 shares Issued 413,500 shares		41,350
Outstanding 363,800 shares (at June 30, 19Y5)		
Issued 392,524 shares	39,252	
Outstanding 342,824 shares (at June 30, 19Y6)		
Additional paid-in capital	9,330,523	9,143,523
Retained earnings	4,961,500	4,829,280
Cost of shares of common stock in Treasury (Note 11)	(2,142,750)	(2,250,000)
TOTAL STOCKHOLDERS' EQUITY	12,319,768	11,893,298
TOTAL LIABILITIES AND STOCKHOLDERS' EQUITY	$17,493,657	$21,470,966

See notes to consolidated financial statements.

Exhibit 4-5 continued

Notes to Consolidated Financial Statements

For the Three Years Ended June 30, 19Y6, 19Y5 and 19Y4

1. Summary of Significant Accounting Policies

Principles of Consolidation The consolidated financial statements include the accounts of CYCLOMATICS, Inc. (the "Company") and its wholly-owned subsidiary, Systems Research Corporation ("SRC"). All intercompany balances and transactions have been eliminated in consolidation.

The Company accounts for its investment in its unconsolidated affiliate, Insituform East, Incorporated ("Insituform"), by the equity method.

Contract Revenues Substantially all of the Company's services are performed for the United States Government under various cost-plus-fee, fixed-price and labor-hour contracts in the areas of defense-related engineering, technical and management services. On cost type contracts, revenues are recorded at provisional rates and are adjusted to actual rates at the end of each quarter. On fixed-price contracts, revenues are recorded as a percentage of total contract price in the ratio of contract cost to date compared to the ultimate or estimated cost at completion. To the extent cost at completion exceeds contract price, charges are made to current operations in the period in which it is first determined, with a related reduction of unbilled accounts receivable. On labor-hour contracts, revenues are recorded in relation to fixed hourly rates, as provided under the contract.

Depreciation and Amortization Property and equipment are stated at cost. Depreciation has been provided in the financial statements primarily using the straight-line method at rates which are based upon reasonable estimates of the property's useful lives. These lives range from three to ten years for equipment and furniture, and 30 years for buildings. Leasehold improvements are amortized using the straight-line method over the life of the lease.

Repairs and maintenance are charged directly to expenses as incurred. Betterments or improvements which increase the estimated useful life of an asset are capitalized.

The excess of cost over the fair value of the Insituform net tangible assets acquired (goodwill) is amortized using the straight-line method over 40 years.

Income Taxes The Company provides for federal and state income taxes at the statutory rates in effect on taxable income. Investment tax credits are recognized under the flow-through method.

Deferred income taxes result from recognizing certain items of income and expense in consolidated financial statements in different years from those in income tax returns. These timing differences relate principally to retainages by the U.S. Government until contracts are completed and accepted; use of accelerated depreciation methods for tax purposes; and elections to expense for tax purposes certain capitalized items.

Research and Development Costs Research and development costs are charged to operations as incurred. Approximately $31,623, $48,000 and $53,700 were expensed in fiscal years 19Y6, 19Y5 and 19Y4, respectively.

2. Accounts Receivable

Accounts receivable consist of:

Exhibit 4-5 continued

	19Y6	19Y5
U.S. Government		
Billed	$3,183,824	$4,189,472
Unbilled	3,391,381	4,630,191
	6,575,205	8,819,663
Refundable taxes	156,516	721,554
Miscellaneous	10,288	17,539
	$6,742,009	$9,558,756

No allowance for doubtful accounts is required in 19Y6 and 19Y5.

3. Property and Equipment

Property and equipment consist of:

	19Y6	19Y5
Building	$ 171,187	$ 171,187
Equipment	1,206,907	1,027,379
Furniture and fixtures	379,978	491,232
Leasehold improvements	697,660	711,136
	2,455,732	2,400,934
Less accumulated depreciation and amortization	(726,903)	(678,220)
	$1,728,829	$1,722,714

4. Capitalized Contract Rights

On March 14, 19Y6, the Company purchased for approximately $400,000 in cash selected assets of The Stanwick Corporation, including a value of $286,646 attributable to certain successor contract rights. These capitalized rights are being amortized using the straight-line method over the average of their remaining contractual lives of approximately two years. An amortization expense of $43,237 was charged to operations during fiscal year 19Y6 related to these rights.

5. Investment in Unconsolidated Affiliate

On March 15, 19Y5 the Company purchased in a private transaction for cash a total of 864,094 restricted shares of common stock of Insituform East, Incorporated constituting 32.87% of the then outstanding shares of Insituform common stock. As a result of this transaction, the Company became affiliated with Insituform as its largest stockholder.

On October 15, 19Y5 Insituform issued a 50% stock dividend, increasing the number of shares held by the Company to 1,296,141.

On June 13, 19Y6, pursuant to an exchange offer, the Company exchanged 296,141 shares of Insituform Common Stock. The principal differences between the classes of stock consist of distinctions in voting power, dividend rights and Board representation. Class B Stock has greater voting power but less dividend rights than the Common Stock. Common Stock shares are entitled, for the next three of Insituform's fiscal years in which cash dividends are declared, to a 20% cash dividend preference over shares of Class B Stock. Common Stock has one vote per share on all matters upon which stockholders vote

Exhibit 4-5 continued

together (including mergers, asset sales, dissolution and Certificate and By-law amendments), while the Class B Stock has 10 votes per share. Holders of shares of Common Stock, voting separately as a class, are entitled to elect not less than twenty-five percent (25%) (rounded to the nearest whole number) of the members of the Board of Directors; however, holders of shares of Class B Stock, voting separately as a class, are entitled to elect the remaining members of the Board of Directors. At June 30, 19Y6 CYCLOMATICS held 1,100,000 shares of Insituform Common Stock and 296,141 shares of Insituform Class B Stock representing approximately 25.9% of the Common Stock, 92.5% of the Class B Stock, 30.6% of the total equity and 54.5% of the total voting power of all outstanding classes of Insituform stock.

The Company's equity in the earnings of such unconsolidated affiliate represents its proportionate allocation of the net earnings of Insituform, based upon the amount and duration of its common stock ownership, reduced by amortization of goodwill. Goodwill was estimated to be $3,486,352 at the date of acquisition, of which $87,159 and $25,555 were amortized during fiscal years 19Y6 and 19Y5, respectively.

Since purchase, Insituform has issued additional shares of stock as a result both of stock dividends and of exercised stock options. Changes in capital structure resulting from such additional stock issues decreased the Company's equity ownership to 30.6% and 32.5% as of June 30, 19Y6 and June 30, 19Y5, respectively. The Company's interest in these changes in capital structure was $88,000 and $30,000 during each of the two periods. If all the options and warrants of the affiliate outstanding at June 30, 19Y6 were exercised, the resulting percentage of the Company's equity ownership would be 28.9%.

Summarized financial information relating to Insituform is as follows (in thousands):

Earnings Statement Information
(Insituform)

	Year ended June 30, 19Y6	Year ended June 30, 19Y5
Revenues	$11,973	$9,749
Earnings before income taxes	1,647	2,029
Income taxes	701	840
Net earnings	946	1,189

Balance Sheet Information
(Insituform)

	As of June 30, 19Y6	As of June 30, 19Y5
Current assets	$6,517	$4,077
Other assets	175	—
Property, plant and equipment	4,586	3,879
Current liabilities	2,920	1,485
Other liabilities	698	538
Stockholders' equity	7,660	5,933

Insituform's Common Stock is traded in the over-the-counter market (NMS) under the NASDAQ symbol INEI. Summarized investment information relating to Insituform is set forth below as of year-end on June 30, 19Y6, except for the purchase investment amount which is recorded as of acquisition on March 15, 19Y5:

Exhibit 4-5 continued

Insituform Investment Information:

	Per share	Total
Carrying investment:		
Purchase investment	$ 3.75	$ 5,241,419
Equity in earnings, since purchase	.19	270,659
Interest in capital changes, since purchase	.09	118,000
Total carrying investment	$ 4.03	$ 5,630,078
Market price	$26.00	$36,299,666[1]

[1]During the fourth quarter of fiscal 19Y6 and the first quarter of fiscal 19Y7, the price of Insituform shares experienced large market fluctuations. Between March 19, 19Y6 and September 19, 19Y6, the share price ranged from a high of $27½ to a low of $11. In view of such short-term market price volatility, comparison of market prices at financial statement dates in successive years is not necessarily indicative of the underlying long-term rate of investment appreciation since purchase. At September 19, 19Y6, the market price of the Company's investment was $17.5 million for a gross unrealized gain of $11.8 million.

6. Marketable Securities

Marketable securities consist of Common Stock held for investment and are valued at the lower of cost or market:

	19Y6	19Y5
Marketable securities, at market	$121,654	$105,084
Marketable securities, at cost	62,929	60,334
	$ 58,725	$ 44,750
Gross unrealized gains	$ 60,494	$ 45,959
Gross unrealized losses	(1,769)	(1,209)
	$ 58,725	$ 44,750

There were no realized gains or losses during the fiscal years ended June 30, 19Y6 and 19Y5.

7. Loans Payable and Long-Term Debt

On September 23, 19Y5, the Company renegotiated its Revolving Credit and Term Loan Agreement (the "Agreement") to replace a short-term borrowing arrangement with American Security Bank, N.A., Washington, D.C. (the "Bank"). The Agreement enables the Company to borrow up to $5,500,000 in the form of a $3,000,000 revolving credit loan and a $2,500,000 term loan. Effect was given to this transaction in the financial statements as of June 30, 19Y5.

The Agreement grants a security interest in all accounts receivable as collateral, with the Term Loan further collateralized by the shares of Insituform stock. Under the terms of the Agreement the Company must maintain a stipulated ratio of total debt to tangible net worth and a ratio of current assets to current liabilities. In addition, the Company has agreed that it: (i) will not exceed a stipulated ratio of total indebtedness to the bank to total receivables; (ii) will maintain quick assets equal to or greater than the term loan balance; (iii) will maintain a minimum tangible net worth of not less than $9,000,000, including the goodwill recorded as a result of the purchase of stock in Insituform; and (iv) will not enter

Exhibit 4-5 continued

into certain other major corporate transactions without the prior approval of the Bank.

The revolving credit loan enables the Company to borrow up to $3,000,000 at a rate equal to the Bank's prime rate of which $105,000 and $2,984,564 were outstanding as of June 30, 19Y6 and 19Y5, respectively. In addition, the Company must pay a commitment fee of ½% per annum of the unused portion of the loan. The agreement expires on November 30, 19Y6.

The term loan is at the Bank's prime rate plus ½%, and is payable in quarterly installments with a final balloon payment due on September 30, 19Z0 of $714,300.

The Company's subsidiary, SRC, had a revolving credit loan agreement with a commercial bank whereby they could borrow up to $300,000, at an interest rate equal to the bank's prime lending rate. The agreement was guaranteed by CYCLOMATICS. At June 30, 19Y5, the outstanding balance under the agreement was $300,000, which was paid in full on August 1, 19Y5.

Long-term liabilities consist of:

	19Y6	19Y5
Term loan payable	$2,232,145	$2,500,000
Note payable, interest at 15%, payable monthly to 19Y7	4,711	10,225
Less current maturity, included in current liabilities	(361,851)	(273,370)
	$1,875,005	$2,236,855

Long-term liabilities at June 30, 19Y6 mature as follows:

19Y8	$ 357,140
19Y9	357,140
19Z0	357,140
19Z1	803,585
	$1,875,005

8. Accounts Payable and Accrued Liabilities

Accounts payable and accrued liabilities consist of:

	19Y6	19Y5
Accounts payable	$1,064,065	$2,282,568
Dividends payable	82,489	82,278
Salaries and wages	182,729	145,007
Leave	312,212	394,072
Payroll taxes and taxes withheld from employees	132,583	101,075
Interest	19,283	45,990
Other	9,672	1,889
	$1,803,033	$3,052,879

Exhibit 4-5 continued

9. Commitments

The Company utilizes certain equipment and occupies most of its facilities under operating leases providing for payment of fixed rentals and the pass-through of certain landlord expenses. Rental expense was approximately $874,000, $973,800 and $970,800 for the years ended 19Y6, 19Y5 and 19Y4, respectively. Minimum future rental commitments under long-term leases in effect at June 30, 19Y6, are as follows:

19Y7	$ 677,000
19Y8	468,000
19Y9	179,000
19Z0	144,000
19Z1	131,000
Thereafter	—
	$1,599,000

10. Contingencies

Contract costs for services supplied to the U.S. Government, including indirect expenses, are subject to audit and adjustment as the result of negotiations between the Company and Government representatives. All contract revenues are recorded in amounts which are expected to be realized upon final settlement. The Company has submitted all costs through 19Y5 and settled all costs through 19Y3.

The Company, in the normal conduct of its business, commences work on various projects based upon advice from the customer prior to receipt of a definitive contract from such customer. Any such revenues recognized by the Company are subject to the receipt of an executed contract and it is possible that such revenues will not be realized. As of June 30, 19Y6, approximately $76,000 of revenues were in this category. Although no assurance can be given that the contracts will be received or that all costs incurred will be recovered, the Company expects to recover substantially all such costs. The Company has in the past received in due course substantially all such contracts and recovered substantially all costs incurred prior to receipt of such contracts.

Between July 19X9 and August 19Y2, David A. Jones, a former employee and director, together at times which his subsequently formed company, filed a series of lawsuits against the Company and its three principal executive officers essentially arising out of his termination for cause by the Board of Directors in February 19X9. The cumulative total of monies sought in such suits is approximately $9,000,000. The first suit instituted, which sought $300,000, was dismissed by voluntary nonsuit. Defendants have counterclaimed, intend to seek dismissal, or intend to defend vigorously all other suits. Under the Company's By-Laws and Delaware law, the Company's officers named individually by plaintiffs in the above.

Spinoffs and divestitures are corporate developments that are of special significance to an asset-play investor. An asset-play analyst is especially prepared and capable of understanding the true value of the division or subsidiary being spun off. For this reason, it is important that you keep abreast of divestiture activity and seek to screen the more interesting ones for further analysis. You will find that at some point in time the market may price the stock in line with your valuation.

Cash Flow Analysis

Up to this point, you have learned that asset-play analysis consists of the evaluation of both above-the-line assets and below-the-line assets. By utilizing the mathematical techniques learned in this chapter, you will arrive at a value for the underlying assets of any given company. Therefore, you might be surprised at what appears to you to be an "inflated" price offered for a company by an active acquirer such as Irving Jacobs or Asher Edelman. The reason for the high price they are will to pay might rest with cash flow.

Exactly what is "cash flow"? The classical definition of cash flow is net income, plus depreciation, amortization, and deferred taxes. Referring to Exhibit 4-6, showing Cale Corporation's ("Cale") financials and using the classical definition, the company had a cash flow of $332 million.*

*Adapted from *Forbes*, "Confusing flows the cash flow," by Francesca Lunzer, April 7, 1986, pp. 72–75.

Exhibit 4-6.

19Y5 Financial Review of Cale Corporation

Liquidity

Cale plans to finance its future growth within the chemical industry primarily through internally generated funds and available external sources, including coalitions.

The Corporation maintains committed bank credit facilities. Total U.S. facilities at December 31, 19Y5, were $100 million. Informal bank lines of up to $30 million are ready to fund short-term cash needs. At December 31, 19Y5, none of these credit facilities were utilized. Non-U.S. subsidiaries have facilities with U.S. and non-U.S. banks which currently permit borrowings of up to $164 million or the equivalent in local currency. The Corporation generally does not provide credit support for subsidiary or affiliate borrowings. In October 19Y5, Cale filed a shelf registration statement with the Securities and Exchange Commission covering $100 million of debt securities. The filing permits the issuance of securities on a periodic basis (within a two-year period) in amounts and at rates that are set at the time of the offering. At year-end, the Corporation had not issued debt under the filing.

During 19Y5, Cale sold several businesses for $174 million. The proceeds were added to the Corporation's cash position. In November, the Corporation indicated that it will consider offers to sell its specialty resins and water soluble polymers businesses. The transactions are expected to be completed in 19Y6. In 19Y5, Cale purchased 2.7 million shares of its common stock at a cost of $302 million. By year-end, the Corporation had outstanding authority to purchase 227,700 shares and in January 19Y6 the Corporation announced plans to repurchase an additional 600,000 shares. The Corporation completed the recovery of $389 million before taxes in excess funds from the pension plan. Cash and marketable securities were $369 million at year-end 19Y5 or $203 million above the prior year.

The debt-to-total capitalization ratio declined to 28% from 35% at year-end 19Y4, chiefly because of the early retirement of $100 million of 10⅞% notes due 19Y7 and the conversion of $81 million of outstanding debt into 1.1 million common shares pursuant to original privileges. Consolidated capital spending decreased by $10 million in 19Y5 to $159 million. Capital outlays are projected to be about $550 million during 19Y6–19Y8, with about $170 million in 19Y6. The Corporation believes it unlikely that capital spending in mature products will exceed depreciation levels. Cale invested about $30 million in new business development and technology coalitions in 19Y5 and expects to spend about $60 million during 19Y6–Y8. The quarterly dividend on the common stock was increased by 10 cents per share in the fourth quarter of 19Y5.

Total dividends paid in 19Y5 were $61 million, down $2 million because of the share repurchase program. It is expected that cash from operations over the next three years will be sufficient to cover capital expenditures, share repurchases, dividends and working capital requirements.

Cale liquidity is supported by a large internal cash flow. Net funds from operations totaled $1.9 billion for the 19Y1–Y5 period and financed 132% of the requirements for capital expenditures and dividends.

(millions)	*19Y1*	*19Y2*	*19Y3*	*19Y4*	***19Y5***
Net funds from operations	$363	$272	$413	$408	**$449**

In 19Y5, the $449 million of net funds from operations was $271 million greater than net income of $178 mil-

Exhibit 4-6 continued

lion. The difference is principally due to the $246 million of depreciation expense. The high level of depreciation reflects the Corporation's conservative policy with respect to asset lives (maximum estimated useful life for U.S. machinery and equipment of 9½ years).

Capital Expenditures

Consolidated capital expenditures in 19Y5 were $159 million, down $10 million from 19Y4, and substantially below the peak of $414 million in 19Y1. (Included in the total was the acquisition of the vinyon staple fiber business.) Also included were capital projects for compliance with federal, state and local environmental control regulations amounting to $12 million. Expenditures were directed into new technology and projects that enhanced quality, lowered costs or increased productivity. Expansion occurred in projects offering above-average opportunities, such as the completion of new polyester industrial yarn technology at Charleston, SC, which also increased capacity, and the completion of the first stage of an engineering resin expansion (acetal copolymer) at Dallas, TX. Consistent with the growth strategy, Cale also made additional investments of about $30 million in new business development and technology coalitions. The table below details expenditures by category.

(millions)	*19Y1*	*19Y2*	*19Y3*	*19Y4*	***19Y5***
Consolidated:					
Expansion and new products	$261	$173	$ 19	$ 37	**$ 62**
Maintenance of business	113	71	69	105	**85**
Cost reduction	40	31	17	27	**12**
Total	$414	$275	$105	$169	**$159**

CONSOLIDATED FINANCIAL STATEMENTS

Statements of Income
(millions, except per share)

	19Y3	*19Y4*	***19Y5***
Sales	$3,261	$3,328	**$3,046**
Operating expenses:(a)			
Cost of goods sold	2,683	2,696	**2,555**
Selling and administration	279	266	**261**
Research and development	85	94	**103**
Total operating expenses	3,047	3,056	**2,919**
Operating income	214	272	**127**
Equity in net income of affiliates	34	28	**25**
Interest expense	(77)	(74)	**(52)**
Other income and expense	17	36	**140**
Income before taxes	188	262	**240**
Income tax provision	67	101	**60**
Income before minority interest	121	161	**180**
Minority interest	9	—	**2**
Net income	$ 112	$ 161	**$ 178**
Per share of common stock			
Net income:			
Primary	$ 6.89	$10.87	**$13.70**
Fully diluted	6.52	10.07	**13.18**
Dividends	4.00	4.10	**4.50**

(a) Certain prior years' data restated.

Balance Sheets at December 31
(millions)

	19Y4	***19Y5***
Assets		
Current assets:		
Cash and marketable securities	$ 166	**$ 369**
Receivable from pension plan	370	**—**
Receivables	439	**396**
Inventories	428	**389**
Prepaid expenses	32	**7**

Exhibit 4-6 continued

Total current assets	1,435	**1,161**
Investments in affiliates	200	**228**
Net property, plant and equipment	1,349	**1,217**
Other assets	120	**203**
Total assets	$3,104	**$2,809**
Liabilities and stockholders' equity		
Current liabilities:		
Accounts payable and accrued liabilities	$ 467	**$ 507**
Income taxes payable	319	**304**
Notes payable	6	**15**
Long-term debt due within one year	77	**38**
Total current liabilities	869	**864**
Long-term debt	662	**434**
Deferred pension gain	333	**301**
Deferred income taxes	29	**89**
Interests of others	112	**104**
Stockholders' equity		
Capital stock		
—Cumulative preferred	89	**88**
—Common	306	**387**
Additional paid-in capital	27	**28**
Retained income	878	**995**
Cumulative translation adjustments	(29)	**(15)**
Treasury stock (at cost)	(172)	**(466)**
Total stockholders' equity	1,099	**1,017**
Total liabilities and stockholders' equity	$3,104	**$2,809**

Changes in Financial Position
(millions)

	19Y3	*19Y4*	***19Y5***
Funds from operations:			
Net income	$112	$161	**$178**
Depreciation	213	214	**246**
Gain on sale of structural composites operations	—	—	**(61)**
Amortization of deferred pension gain	—	(37)	**(51)**
Tax provision less taxes paid	53	65	**20**
Changes in:			
Receivables	16	(1)	**38**
Inventories	(25)	17	**27**
Accounts payable and accrued liabilities	87	13	**45**
Prepaid, other	(43)	(24)	**7**
Net funds from operations	413	408	**449**
Investments and other:			
Proceeds from sale of structural composites operations	—	—	**135**
Capital expenditures	(105)	(169)	**(159)**
Capitalized interest	(6)	(9)	**(11)**
Contributions of joint venturer	10	—	**—**
Purchase of minority interest of Fiber Industries, Inc.	(119)	—	**—**
Investment and advances	—	—	**(32)**
Cumulative translation adjustments	(12)	(17)	**14**
Other	6	55	**(49)**
Net investments and other	(226)	(140)	**(102)**
Financial transactions:			
Dividends	(67)	(63)	**(61)**
Notes payable	3	(8)	**9**
Long-term debt including current portion			
Additions	8	4	**10**
Reductions	(42)	(80)	**(277)**
Capital stock (principal stock repurchase in 19Y4 and 19Y5)	3	(151)	**(214)**
Recovery of excess pension assets	—	—	**389**
Net financial transactions	(95)	(298)	**(144)**
Cash and marketable securities:			
At beginning of year	104	196	**166**
At end of year	$196	$166	**$369**

Changes in Retained Income
(millions)

	19Y3	*19Y4*	***19Y5***
Net income	$112	$161	**$178**
Preferred dividends	(4)	(4)	**(4)**
Net income to common stockholders	108	157	**174**
Common dividends	(63)	(59)	**(57)**
Retained income:			
At beginning of year	735	780	**878**
At end of year	$780	$878	**$995**

Individuals and institutions involved in merger and acquisition (m&a) activity have developed a more sophisticated definition of the concept of cash flow. Such parties define cash flow as pretax income (not net), plus depreciation, less maintenance capital expenditures.

Cash Flow Ratio

$$\text{Cash flow} = \text{Pretax income} + \text{Depreciation} - \text{Maintenance capital expenditures}$$

For the purpose of determining the trend of cash over the past few years, you could simply divide the cash flow figure arrived at for each year by the number of shares outstanding in that respective year.

The concept of maintenance capital expenditures is the key change. Maintenance capital expenditures is that part of capital spending required to maintain operations at the current level. While the number is not available in the case of every public company—although the Financial Accounting Standards Board (FASB) is moving in the direction of requiring companies to report this number—the Cale Corporation does disclose it. As Exhibit 4-6 indicates, it was $85 million for 19Y6. Following the revised definition, cash flow would have amounted to $288 million versus the $332 million arrived at using the classical definition of cash flow.

Many professional analysts and entities involved in m&a activity use the revised definition of cash flow because they maintain it gives the most accurate picture of a company's cash-generating ability. In turn, its cash-generating ability determines the amount of debt the company's assets can support and hence, the price a corporate raider would be willing to pay for the company. You will find that by using this revised definition of cash flow what appears to be inflated prices paid for certain takeover companies are really bargain prices. Cash flow is one figure you should calculate any time you are seeking to value a potential asset play. In many instances, you will uncover asset plays that are so because of the cash flow they generate rather than on the basis of their above- or below-the-line assets.

Price-Earnings Ratio

By definition, the price to earnings (P/E) ratio is equal to the market price of the stock divided by the latest 12 months' earnings. In mathematical format, the price to earnings (P/E) ratio is expressed as follows:

$$\text{P/E} = \frac{\text{Market price of the stock}}{\text{Latest 12 months' earnings per share}}$$

For example, refer to the Annual Report and Proxy Statement of the Summerfield Company. Assume that the company's stock was selling at a price of $2.50 per share.

$$\text{P/E} = \frac{\text{Market price of Summerfield Company's stock}}{\text{Latest 12 months' earnings per share of Summerfield Company}}$$

$$= \frac{\$2.50}{.09} = 28$$

What does a P/E ratio of 28 tell you about whether the particular stock represents a buy, sell, or hold? For one thing, the P/E ratio of a stock means something only when it is compared to the P/E ratios of companies in the same or similar field and with the P/E ratio of the overall market. Further, for the P/E ratio of a particular stock to have any meaning it has to be compared with the P/E ratio the stock has had over the past few years. Expressed another way, you should consider the P/E ratio as an expression of market sentiments toward the stock you are seeking to analyze and in no way a reliable measure of the true worth of the company.

In the case of the Summerfield Company, a P/E ratio of 28 means that the company's underlying value, that is, its "net" "net" assets of $4.64 per share, has to have been discovered by other asset-play analysts. This conclusion is based on a couple of facts. First, a typical asset-play situation will sell at a low price to earnings ratio (15 or below) until it is discovered by investment professionals. Second, a price to earnings ratio—or, as professional investors refer to, a "multiple"—of 28 is more characteristic of a growth situation. The ratio techniques that can be applied to growth situations are described in a later section of this chapter.

As to whether with a multiple of 28 times earnings the Summerfield Company still represents a buying opportunity, you have to compare the stock's price and multiple with its underlying assets. Consider the fact that the Summerfield Company has "net" "net" assets of $4.64 per share and a book value of $5.17 per share. A market price of $2.50 per share still represents a discount of $2.14 (47%) from its "net" "net" assets or a discount of $2.67 (52%) from the company's book value per share. There is still a substantial underlying value not reflected in the stock's current market price. Also, the previous example shows that asset plays can be found among stocks trading at under $5 per share as well as stocks trading at over $100 per share.

One last observation should be made with regard to price to earnings ratios. Recent studies have been made comparing the performance of high versus low P/E stocks. These studies found that on the whole low P/E stocks (those typically selling at 15 or below) performed better in the marketplace as opposed to high P/E stocks (these selling at 30 or above). A number of reasons were given for these findings. First, high P/E stocks typically have a high proportion of institutional ownership and are as a consequence more volatile as institutions tend to move more rapidly in and out of individual stocks. Second, a high P/E may mean that the market has already discounted future growth, meaning that the price of the stock already reflects future growth in sales and earnings. Thus, these recent studies reinforce the idea that asset-play investing, with its concentration on underlying assets and low P/E stocks, as opposed to growth and high P/E stocks, offers a better formula for success in the market.

Analytical Techniques Applicable to Growth Situations

While this book is about asset plays, you should be familiar with some of the mathematical techniques for analyzing growth situations. Whereas in the case of asset plays you concentrate on a company's balance sheet, growth situations require that you take apart the company's income statement. In determining if a particular company and its stock represent a growth situation, you will be concerned with such things as the trend in sales, earnings, and expenses, and based on past performance, forecast what the future will bring for the particular company you are seeking to analyze. Second, in analyzing growth situations you have to concentrate on management's ability to achieve its defined goals rather than concern yourself with balance sheet items such as cash, cash equivalents, marketable securities, and real estate. For that matter, many growth companies are characterized by weak balance sheets because the company has to strain its asset base to meet the demand for its products and services. Attending annual meetings and speaking with management (both activities open to subjective judgments) are a basic part of analyzing growth situations, whereas analyzing an asset play relies to a greater degree on number crunching (an objective activity). Finally, in seeking to determine if a particular company represents a growth situation, time should be spent in calculating such things as the rate of return on equity (ROE) and total assets and the growth rate in dividends and earnings (g).

By definition, the ROE is equal to total asset turnover multiplied by leverage and multiplied by net profit margin. In mathematical format, return on equity is expressed as follows:

$$\text{ROE} = (\text{Total asset turnover}) \times (\text{Financial leverage}) \times (\text{Net profit margin})$$

$$= \frac{\text{Sales}}{\text{Total assets}} \times \frac{\text{Total assets}}{\text{Equity}} \times \frac{\text{Income}}{\text{Sales}}$$

Because return on equity is so important to growth-stock analysts, it would be worthwhile to follow through on a sample calculation of a ROE utilizing the data regarding the Summerfield Company contained on page 103.

Sales	=	\$4,267,259
Total assets	=	\$7,655,376
Equity	=	\$7,531,534
Income	=	\$ 134,455

Fitting the given factors into the ROE equation, the ROE for the Summerfield Company is as follows:

$$\text{ROE} = \frac{\$4{,}267{,}259}{\$7{,}655{,}376} \times \frac{\$7{,}655{,}376}{\$7{,}531{,}534} \times \frac{\$134{,}455}{\$4{,}267{,}259}$$

$$= \frac{\$134{,}455}{\$7{,}531{,}534} = 1.90 = 2\%$$

Now that you have calculated the ROE, you are probably wondering what significance it has in any investment decision you might make. The ROE tells you how much a company is earning on its equity, that is, the capital available to the company. As we discovered in examining the financials of the Summerfield Company, it fit into the mold of an asset play because of its high current ratio and quick ratio as well as the inordinate amount of cash it held. Therefore, it is not surprising that the company should have an extremely low ROE in view of the fact that it has substantially curtailed its operations. However, for a company and the stock it represents to be considered a growth situation, it must have a high ROE (20% or better) and the trend of its ROE should be stable and rising.

To understand what return on equity is all about, it is useful to break it into its component parts as the preceding equation does. The three components of a company's ROE are (1) total asset turnover, (2) financial leverage, and (3) net profit margin. This clearly brings home the point that ROE can be improved by greater asset efficiency (turning assets over more rapidly), by altering the company's capital structure (by increasing the amount of money borrowed), and by increasing the company's net profit margin (raising the profit margin by increasing productivity and/or changing the company's product mix). By determining the significance of each of these through a particular company's ROE, you will be able to answer a number of key questions regarding the growth prospects of the particular company, such as where the company's growth is coming from (asset turnover, leverage, or profit margin), how the company's ROE compares with that of other companies in the same or similar industry, whether the pattern of growth will continue in the future, and what steps the company can take to improve its ROE.

Growth Rate (g)

The growth rate of a company and hence the market price of a growth stock depends on two key factors. The rate of return which is earned on the equity retained in the business is the first of these factors. We discussed this factor extensively in the preceding section. The second is the amount of earnings retained in the business. This second factor is referred to by professional investors as the retention rate.

What does the retention rate represent and what does it tell you about whether a particular company is on the growth track? It's a decision of a company's management as to how much of its earnings are retained in the business. Referring to Summerfield Company's financials on page 103, the company had earnings of $134,455 (9¢ per share) for 19Y3. The company's management decided to pay no dividend to its shareholders because of current uncertainty as to the direction of its business.

Growth Rate Ratio

In mathematical format, growth rate (g) is calculated as follows:

$$
\begin{aligned}
g &= \text{ROE} \times \text{RR} \\
&= 1.90 \times 0 = 0 \text{ growth rate}
\end{aligned}
$$

The fact that the growth rate (g) equals 0 is not surprising in the case of the Summerfield Company, as our analysis up to this point has found the company to represent a classic example of an asset play. But what would be the pattern for a growth situation? If it were a true growth situation, management might decide to retain the full 100% of the company's earnings in the business and hence the retention rate would be 100%. Retaining all or close to all (80 to 90%) of a company's earnings means that management feels that the company itself needs the money to finance its growth and its shareholders cannot earn a greater return from some other investment than the company itself.

Again, you should consider the trend in the growth rate preferably for five years as opposed to a single year's results.

Conclusions

Asset-play investing means analyzing a company's balance sheet and identifying substantial hard assets (cash and cash equivalents) or hidden assets (including such things as undervalued real estate, subsidiaries, patents, or stock holdings). There are numerical ratios which are used to determine if a particular company represents the opportunity to buy assets at a discount.

To be a successful asset-play investor you must go beyond the mere "number crunching." The numbers should lead you to the questions that need to be answered before you can decide whether or not to invest in a particular stock. You will develop a "sixth sense" as to the questions that need to be asked and answered as you analyze a number of potential asset plays. Some of the answers to the questions raised from your number crunching can be found in the standard reference sources as well as in the financial press and the research reports prepared by the analysts who follow the particular company; other questions may warrant a telephone call to the company's management.

Asset plays cover a wide segment of stocks. Identifying companies undergoing restructuring or operating in a depressed industry requires you to calculate and understand other numerical concepts such as book value and cash flow.

As discussed in Chapter 2, identifying bankrupt companies as potential asset plays requires the ability to look beyond the numbers to determine the reason(s) for the company going into bankruptcy, appraising the corporation's underlying assets, and determining the likelihood of the company's successful emergence from bankruptcy. As with any of the other categories of asset-play investing, the returns can be substantial if your judgment is correct.

Evaluating Asset Plays–Qualitative Accounting Factors

CHAPTER 5

At this point, you should be comfortable with the "number-crunching" aspect to asset-play investing. But there is another side to number crunching. Whereas in Chapter 4 emphasis was placed on the quantitative side to number crunching, in this chapter we will explain to you the qualitative side of this topic. You will learn that there is more to number crunching than the blind application of a particular ratio. You will learn that number crunching also involves qualitative judgments relative to such things as the quality of a company's financials, whether a particular company asset should be above or below the line (that is, treated as a current or long-term asset), and the impact the selection of a particular approach to valuing inventory (such as FIFO versus LIFO) will have upon your valuation of the company's underlying assets.

Quality of the Figures

In computer jargon, frequent reference is made to GIGO. This stands for "garbage in—garbage out" and has particular significance to anyone seeking to evaluate a potential asset play. What it means is that the reliance you can place on the ratios you calculate depends on the quality of the numbers you are given to work with by a company's management.

What is meant by the "quality of the numbers?" What are some of the clues to tell you how much confidence you should place in a company's financial figures? A key factor is the complexity of a company's financials. Also, the greater the number and the more extensive the footnotes to a company's financials, the greater the time and effort you should spend evaluating them. While neither of these factors should preclude you from investing in a company, their presence means that you should put more effort into determining management's attitude regarding the truthfulness and accuracy of its figures.

Danger Signals Regarding a Company's Financials

There are certain danger signals that should cause an investor to question the credibility of a company's financials. Switching outside accountants on a regular basis, or opinion shopping, is a signal that you should examine closely a company's financials. The fact that a company frequently changes accountants might mean that the company is looking for an accounting firm that is the most flexible and willing to stretch the rules and treat earnings and assets in the most favorable light.

Another signal that should lead you to question a company's financials would be the issuance of a "qualified opinion" by the company's outside accountants. A qualified opinion means that the accountants have raised serious questions about the accuracy and/or completeness of the figures with which they were given to work. In almost every instance, a qualified opinion should cause an investor to reject any idea of investing in that particular company's stock. However, for every rule there are exceptions. For example, closely held, thinly traded companies frequently refuse to divulge information about the profitability of the various segments of their business. This can result in a qualified opinion even though the company's figures are accurate in all respects. Likewise, if a company operates in a very specialized field, such as coffee processing or capital construction, the outside accountants may issue a qualified opinion because they may disagree with the company's approach to valuing inventory or work in progress. A brief look into the matter should tell you whether a particular case is the exception to the rule of not investing in companies with qualified opinions.

A company's sales figures can also be a signal that a problem exists with its figures. This is particularly true in the case of companies that have recently gone public. The sales figures, if properly analyzed, can tell you a lot about a company. In the case of a company which has recently gone public, you should pay particular attention to any marked jump in the company's sales in the year immediately preceding its going public. What you want to determine is if the company's management inflated its sales figures in anticipation of the public offering. An unscrupulous management can make a side agreement with its customers to book large orders prior to a public offering with the understanding that the company would take back the goods once the company had successfully gone public. Such a scenario is most likely to occur in the case of a company where a parent–distributor relationship (franchisee relationship) exists. You should determine both from the prospectus, as well as from speaking to management, the reasons for such a sharp jump in sales and should invest only if you feel that the explanation is accurate.

The pattern of a company's inventory figures can also give you insight into how the company should perform in terms of sales and earnings. Of course, the significance of the inventory figure will vary from industry to industry. For example, in the case of a retail company or apparel manufacturer, the inventory figure will be important both in terms of absolute numbers as well as trend. On the other hand, inventory figures will be relatively unimportant in the case of a service or entertainment company. For those companies for which the inventory figures are important, you should determine if inventory is expanding at a faster rate than the growth in sales. If such is the case, you might find that the company's inventory consists of a substantial amount of unsalable goods.

Finally, a company's bottom-line figures should give you a clue as to the quality of its figures. As an asset-play investor, you should concentrate on the results a company's management produces in the way of earnings. Investors whose orientation is toward growth companies tend to concentrate on what the future will bring. The asset-play investor will look to see whether the growth in sales is being carried down to the company's bottom line. If sales growth is not resulting in greater earnings, either sales are being made for their own sake without regard to profitability, or the company's overhead expenses are too high relative to sales.

FIFO versus LIFO

Undervalued assets are assets whose true value is not reflected in the numbers shown on the company's balance sheet. Undervalued assets can also take the form of undervalued or misstated earnings, and FIFO versus LIFO is one aspect of undervalued earnings.

What comprises undervalued earnings? When should you adjust stated earnings to get an accurate picture of the company's real earnings? How a company values its inventory is an area where the selection of one method over another may result in either overstated or understated earnings.

If prices were unchanging, the selection of the method of valuing inventory would present no problem. However, this is not the case in the real world. A company has a choice of two alternative ways of valuing inventory. It can use either the first-in-first-out (FIFO) method or the last-in-first-out (LIFO) method. If the company decides to utilize FIFO in valuing its inventory, the company's accountants will work on the basis that the units were sold in the same order as they were purchased. In other words, by utilizing FIFO accounting, the company's final inventory will have a unit cost equal to the most recent price. The argument has been made that when prices are changing rapidly—upward in inflationary times, downward in deflationary times—FIFO does not match current costs with current selling prices. It is for this reason that a number of companies decided to utilize last-in-first-out (LIFO) instead of

FIFO. If LIFO is used, the most recent purchase costs are charged against sales before earlier costs. The unit costs of the final inventory would be the earlier price.

From the point of view of the asset-play investor, the selection of the method of valuing inventory—FIFO versus LIFO—will have an impact on the company's stated earnings and hence its value. FIFO includes inventory profits and losses, whereas LIFO does not. Because FIFO includes inventory gains and losses, it means that if FIFO is selected, earnings will be more volatile during swings in the business cycle. But if a company selects the LIFO method of valuing its inventory, it may be understating its earnings. One company may appear to have higher earnings than another for the simple reason that it selected FIFO rather than LIFO. For this reason, it is important to read the footnotes to a company's annual report and, where appropriate, add back in the value of the inventory and adjust the earnings.

Perhaps the best way to understand this concept is through an example. Exhibit 5-1 consists of the financials and footnotes to the annual report of a company that selected LIFO as the method for valuing its inventory. Note 2 on Inventories discloses that:

> "If the first-in-first-out method of valuation had been used, inventories would have been \$5,834,000 and \$6,304,000 higher than reported at December 31, 19Y3 and 19Y2, respectively, and net income would have been higher (lower) by (\$254,000) in 19Y3, \$387,000 in 19Y2 and \$459,000 in 19Y1."

Exhibit 5-1.

Utman Power Company

19Y3 Annual Report

Exhibit 5-1 continued

Consolidated Highlights

	19Y3	19Y2	19Y1	19Y0	19X9
(In Thousands Except Per Share Data)	$	$	$	$	$
Net sales	**35,246**	47,560	54,263	42,992	37,917
Gross profit	**10,164**	14,299	18,352	13,953	12,699
Operating and other expenses	**8,014**	10,593	11,598	8,813	8,263
Income before taxes on income	**2,150**	3,706	6,754	5,140	4,436
Taxes on income	**810**	1,535	2,655	2,075	1,846
Net income	**1,340**	2,171	4,099	3,065	2,590
Percent to sales	**3.8%**	4.6%	7.6%	7.1%	6.8%
Per share:					
Net income	**22.84**	36.45	68.70	51.23	43.30
Dividends declared	**8.31**	9.00	7.65	6.30	5.25
Stockholders' equity	**391.58**	389.26	361.95	300.72	255.79
Working capital	**16,419**	15,010	13,740	12,216	10,776
Total assets	**28,896**	30,837	32,815	25,217	21,505
Long-term debt	**1,078**	1,189	2,205	539	870

NET SALES
(In thousands of dollars)

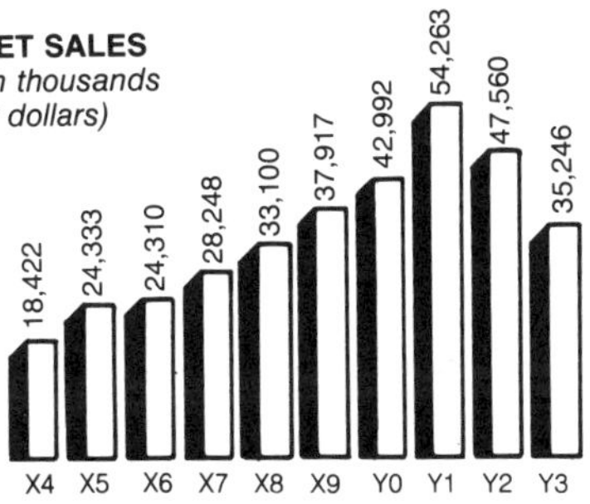

NET INCOME
(In thousands of dollars)

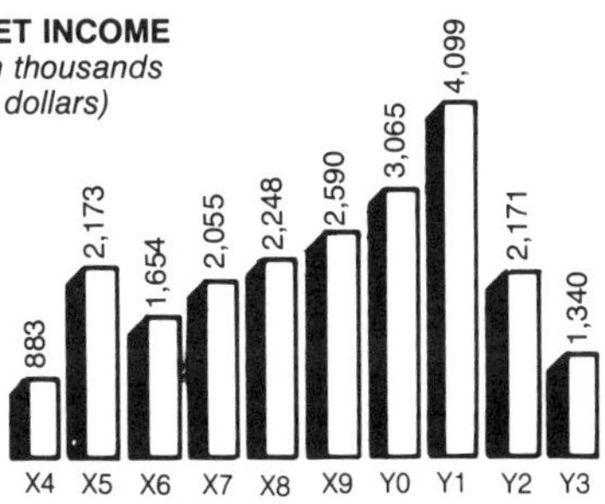

DIVIDENDS DECLARED PER SHARE
(In dollars)

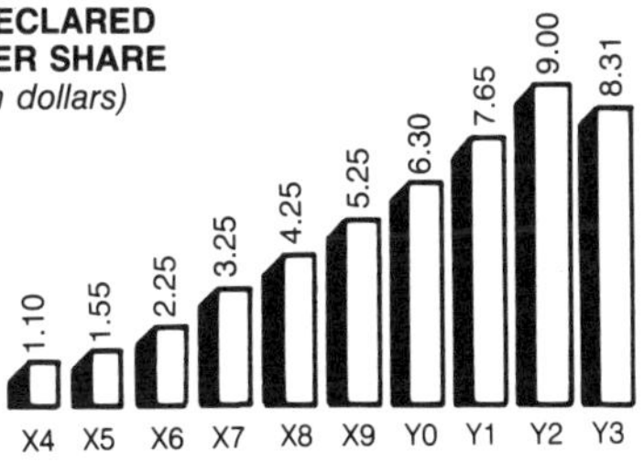

STOCKHOLDERS' EQUITY PER SHARE
(In dollars)

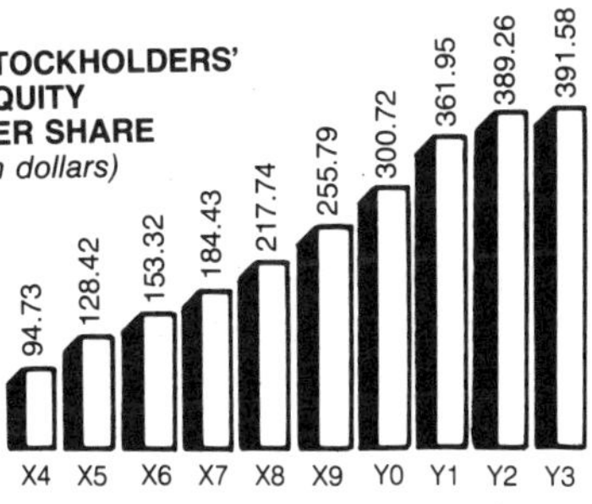

Exhibit 5-1 continued

Letter To The Stockholders

A year of challenges best describes 19Y3. The results for the year were adversely affected by both the increased severity of the recession in our traditional hydrocarbon markets and the strength of the U.S. dollar in worldwide markets.

Net sales decreased 26% to $35,246,000 from the 19Y2 level of $47,560,000, and 35% from the 19Y1 record sales level of $54,263,000. Net income decreased 38% to $1,340,000, $22.84 a share, from $2,171,000, $36.45 a share, in 19Y2, and 67% from record net income of $4,099,000, $68.70 a share, in 19Y1. Dividends per share were $8.31, $9.00 and $7.65 in 19Y3, 19Y2 and 19Y1 respectively. New orders received in 19Y3 were $33,000,000 compared to $40,000,000 in 19Y2. Our backlog of new orders at the end of 19Y3 was $9,000,000, a decline of 25% from the end of 19Y2.

In 19Y3, we noted with deep sadness the passing of Paul H. Otto, chairman of the board of directors. All of us miss him.

In September 19Y3, the board of directors announced the following changes in our management structure. President John B. Fischer was elected chairman of the board; vice president Percy S. Otto was named president and chief executive officer; Ernest Tuft, vice president and treasurer, was elected to the position of executive vice president and treasurer; and Hal A. Kim, controller, was promoted to vice president of finance. Paul E. Otto was appointed to the board, filling the vacancy created by the death of Paul H. Otto.

This year, as in 19Y2, we took the appropriate steps necessary to adjust production and operating expenditures to reflect the decline in the rate of incoming orders. The 19Y3 capital expenditures were $368,000, 76% lower than the previous year. In 19Y4, capital expenditures will be directed primarily toward manufacturing cost reductions.

Despite our reduced level of order entry, we continued to make progress in key areas which will benefit the company in the future. In 19Y3, we began sales of the 20,000 psi high pressure power pump mentioned in last year's annual report. Utman's leadership in technology was exhibited recently through production and testing of a multistage pump designed for oilfield CO_2 injection service. This pump met stringent customer design and test specifications, performing without bearing failure or seizure during a dry test. This was a first in the pump industry and has attracted the interest of customers.

Progress continues in our Chemical Products Division. New fluorocarbon fully lined plug valves were developed in 19Y3 and are scheduled for market introduction in the latter part of 19Y4. Our existing sleeve plug valves were also redesigned. These new valves should also by ready for the market in 19Y4. Economic forecasts for the chemical industry indicate that the rate of capital spending will increase in 19Y4, and as a result of our development work, we fully expect to capitalize on this upturn.

Significant progress continued in the development of our fully integrated

Exhibit 5-1 continued

manufacturing control system. In 19Y3, on-line inventory record control and data base linked structured bills of material were implemented.

As we enter 19Y4, we are fully aware of the difficult challenges we face. We are particularly concerned that for some time to come, our traditional markets will not provide us with the strong basis for growth which we have enjoyed in previous years. With this in mind, in 19Y3 we formed a business planning committee, whose major function is to aggressively pursue new products, markets and profit opportunities. The first products approved by this committee were the new linked and sleeve plug valves mentioned previously. We are currently evaluating a number of other product and market opportunities, several of which will be undertaken in 19Y4.

The year 19Y3, although difficult, was one of success and accomplishment. For this, we are grateful to the Utman Power people who made it happen by their efforts and sacrifices. While we cannot predict when our traditional markets will begin to show signs of recovery, we enter 19Y4 in the strongest financial position in our history and have the people and the products to withstand this recession and to emerge stronger than ever. We are grateful for the efforts of our employees, the support of our stockholders and the guidance of our directors.

PERCY S. OTTO
President and Chief Executive Officer

JOHN B. FISCHER
Chairman

Exhibit 5-1 continued

Consolidated Balance Sheet
Utman Power Company and Subsidiaries

Assets *(In Thousands)*

	December 31,	
	19Y3	**19Y2**
Current:		
Cash and short-term investments	**$ 7,152**	$ 2,502
Accounts receivable, less allowance of $100,000 for possible losses	**6,226**	9,601
Inventories (Note 2)	**6,415**	8,173
Refundable income taxes	**148**	—
Future income tax benefits and other	**96**	97
Total current assets	**20,037**	20,373
Equity in net assets of foreign affiliate	**341**	342
Property and equipment (Note 3):		
Land	**390**	390
Buildings and equipment	**2,889**	2,902
Machinery and equipment	**13,507**	13,526
	16,786	16,818
Less accumulated depreciation	**8,999**	7,644
Net property and equipment	**7,787**	9,174
Other:		
Future income tax benefits	**137**	285
Goodwill and other assets	**594**	663
Total other assets	**731**	948
	$28,896	$30,837

Exhibit 5-1 continued

Liabilities and Stockholders' Equity *(In Thousands)*

	December 31, 19Y3	December 31, 19Y2
Current:		
Accounts payable	**$ 1,975**	$ 2,444
Accruals:		
Taxes on income	**—**	219
Payroll and retirement benefits	**777**	979
Property taxes and other	**755**	705
Current maturities of long-term debt	**111**	1,016
Total current liabilities	**3,618**	5,363
Long-term debt, less current maturities (Note 3)	**1,078**	1,189
Deferred compensation (Note 4)	**1,223**	1,125
Total liabilities	**5,919**	7,677
Commitments (Notes 4, 5, 8 and 9)		
Stockholders' equity (Note 8):		
Common stock, no par value—shares authorized 250,000; issued 59,830 at stated value	**499**	499
Additional paid-in capital	**47**	47
Foreign currency translation adjustment	**(80)**	(27)
Retained earnings	**23,576**	22,723
	24,042	23,242
Less treasury stock, 3,611 and 333 shares at cost	**1,065**	82
Total stockholders' equity	**22,977**	23,160
	$28,896	$30,837

See accompanying notes to consolidated financial statements.

Exhibit 5-1 continued

Income and Stockholders' Equity
Utman Power Company and Subsidiaries

Consolidated Statement of Income *(In Thousands)*

	Year ended December 31,		
	19Y3	19Y2	19Y1
Net sales	**$35,246**	$47,560	$54,263
Cost of sales	**25,082**	33,261	35,911
Gross profit on sales	**10,164**	14,299	18,352
Operating expenses	**8,424**	10,680	11,386
Operating income	**1,740**	3,619	6,966
Other (income) expenses—net (including interest expense of $144,000, $237,000 and $225,000)	**(410)**	(87)	212
Income before taxes on income	**2,150**	3,706	6,754
Taxes on income (Note 7)	**810**	1,535	2,655
Net income	**$ 1,340**	$ 2,171	$ 4,099
Income per share of common stock	**$ 22.84**	$ 36.45	$ 68.70

Exhibit 5-1 continued

Consolidated Statement of Stockholders' Equity ***(In Thousands)***

	Common Stock	Additional Paid-in Capital	Foreign Currency Translation Adjustment	Retained Earnings	Treasury Stock
Balance at					
January 1, 19Y1 ..	$501	$47	$—	$17,458	$ 14
Net income—19Y1	—	—	—	4,099	—
Dividends—$7.65 per share	—	—	—	(457)	—
Treasury stock retired (270 shares)	(2)	—	—	(12)	(14)
Treasury stock purchased (111 shares)	—	—	—	—	19
Balance at					
December 31, 19Y1	499	47	—	21,088	19
Net income—19Y2	—	—	—	2,171	—
Dividends—$9.00 per share	—	—	—	(536)	—
Foreign currency translation adjustment—19Y2	—	—	(27)	—	—
Treasury stock purchased (222 shares)	—	—	—	—	63
Balance at					
December 31, 19Y2	499	47	(27)	22,723	82
Net income—19Y3	—	—	—	1,340	—
Dividends—$8.31 per share	—	—	—	(487)	—
Foreign currency translation adjustment—19Y3	—	—	(53)	—	—
Treasury stock purchased (3,278 shares)	—	—	—	—	983
Balance at					
December 31, 19Y3	$499	$47	$(80)	$23,576	$1,065

See accompanying notes to consolidated financial statements.

Exhibit 5-1 continued

Changes In Financial Position
Utman Power Company and Subsidiaries

Consolidated Statement of Changes in Financial Position *(In Thousands)*

	Year ended December 31,		
	19Y3	**19Y2**	**19Y1**
Funds provided by:			
Net income	**$1,340**	$2,171	$4,099
Items not requiring (providing) funds:			
Depreciation and amortization	**1,791**	1,854	1,561
Future income tax benefits—long-term portion	**148**	(25)	(45)
Deferred compensation	**113**	206	172
Equity in net income of foreign affiliate—net of foreign currency translation adjustment	**(47)**	(36)	(22)
Funds derived from operations	**3,345**	4,170	5,765
Decrease (increase) in accounts receivable	**3,375**	1,445	(711)
Decrease (increase) in inventories	**1,758**	965	(2,487)
Dividend from foreign affiliate	**48**	47	54
Decrease (increase) in other assets	**33**	(6)	(77)
Decrease (increase) in future income tax benefits and other current assets	**1**	105	(100)
Net book value of assets sold	**—**	262	—
Addition to long-term debt	**—**	—	1,705
Total	**8,560**	6,988	4,149

Exhibit 5-1 continued

Funds used for:			
Purchase of treasury stock	**983**	63	19
Decrease (increase) in current maturities of long-term debt	**905**	(345)	(340)
Cash dividends	**487**	536	457
Decrease (increase) in accounts payable	**469**	1,785	(1,222)
Decrease (increase) in accruals	**371**	1,273	(575)
Purchase of property and equipment	**368**	1,561	2,596
Increase in refundable income taxes	**148**	—	—
Liquidation of long-term debt	**111**	1,016	315
Foreign currency translation adjustment	**53**	27	—
Deferred compensation payments	**15**	—	—
Acquisition of a subsidiary (excluding working capital of $284,000):			
Property and equipment	**—**	—	2,212
Excess of cost over values assigned	**—**	—	600
Long-term debt assumed	**—**	—	(276)
Total	**3,910**	5,916	3,786
Increase in cash and short-term investments	**$4,650**	$1,072	$ 363

See accompanying notes to consolidated financial statements.

Exhibit 5-1 continued

Notes To Consolidated Financial Statements
Utman Power Company and Subsidiaries

NOTE 1—Summary of Accounting Policies

Principles of Consolidation

The consolidated financial statements include the accounts of the Company and all wholly-owned subsidiaries. An investment in a 50% owned foreign affiliate is carried at equity. Intercompany transactions and accounts are eliminated.

Foreign Currency Translation

In 19Y2 the Company changed its method of translating the accounts of its Canadian subsidiary and Japanese affiliate into U.S. dollars to conform with the provisions of Financial Accounting Standards Board Statement No. 52. Note 11 discusses this change and its effect on the consolidated financial statements.

Inventories

Inventories are stated at cost not in excess of market. Substantially all domestic inventories are stated on a last-in, first-out (LIFO) cost basis while foreign inventories are stated on a first-in, first-out (FIFO) cost basis.

Property, Equipment and Depreciation

Land, buildings, machinery and equipment are stated at cost. Depreciation for financial reporting purposes is computed over the estimated useful lives of the assets by the straight-line method for additions subsequent to 19Y1 and primarily by accelerated methods for additions prior to 19Y2. The Accelerated Cost Recovery System (ACRS) method is used for 19Y1 and subsequent additions for tax purposes.

Goodwill

The excess of cost over net assets of a subsidiary ($525,000 unamortized at December 31, 19Y3) is being amortized on a straight-line basis over 20 years.

Retirement Benefit Plans

The Company makes contributions to the plans equal to the amounts accrued. Prior service costs are amortized over periods not exceeding 30 years.

Income Taxes

Deferred income taxes are recorded for timing differences between financial and taxable income. Investment tax credits are recorded as a reduction of the current income tax provision. Income taxes are not provided on the undistributed earnings of the Company's Domestic International Sales Corporation ($1,814,000 at December 31, 19Y3) which are considered permanently reinvested.

Net Income Per Share

Net income per share is computed by dividing net income by the weighted average number of shares outstanding during each year.

Exhibit 5-1 continued

NOTE 2—Inventories

Inventories are summarized as follows:

	19Y3	19Y2
	(In Thousands)	
Finished products	**$ 139**	$ 521
Work in process	**5,348**	6,552
Raw materials	**928**	1,100
Total	**$6,415**	$8,173

During 19Y3 inventory quantities were reduced resulting in a liquidation of LIFO inventory quantities carried at lower costs prevailing in prior years. This reduction increased net earnings by $250,000 in 19Y3.

If the first-in, first-out method of valuation had been used, inventories would have been $5,834,000 and $6,304,000 higher than reported at December 31, 19Y3 and 19Y2, respectively, and net income would have been higher (lower) by ($254,000) in 19Y3, $387,000 in 19Y2 and $459,000 in 19Y1.

NOTE 3—Long-term Debt

Long-term debt consists of:

	19Y3	19Y2
	(In Thousands)	
Note payable	**$ 560**	$ 640
Industrial Revenue Bonds	**469**	500
Promissory notes	**160**	1,065
	1,189	2,205
Less current maturities	**111**	1,016
Total	**$1,078**	$1,189

The note payable relates to the land and building occupied by a subsidiary. The note is payable $80,000 annually with interest at 2% below prime, but not less than 14%.

The Industrial Revenue Bonds are payable $15,625 semi-annually, plus interest at 7.75%.

The promissory notes are payable to the former stockholders of a subsidiary with interest at prime, but not less than 9%.

Long-term debt is collateralized by land and buildings having a book value of $1,571,000 and the stock of a subsidiary.

Exhibit 5-1 continued

Maturities of long-term debt are as follows:

Year	Amount (In Thousands)
19Y4	$111
19Y5	271
19Y6	111
19Y7	111
19Y8	111

NOTE 4—Deferred Compensation

The Company has an agreement with an employee providing for payments after termination of employment if conditions of the agreement are met. The Company is also making payments to the estate of a deceased employee according to the terms of an agreement. Deferred compensation expense amounted to $113,000 in 19Y3, $206,000 in 19Y2 and $172,000 in 19Y1. The amount of the commitment to be paid out over a minimum period of 20 years from the respective dates of termination approximated $2,665,000 at December 31, 19Y3.

NOTE 5—Retirement Benefit Plans

The Company has retirement benefit plans covering substantially all employees not covered by collective bargaining agreements. The total retirement benefit expense for the year, including contributions to union administered funds, was $464,000 in 19Y3, $570,000 in 19Y2 and $526,000 in 19Y1. The Company is liable upon withdrawal from or termination of the multi-employer plans for its share of the plan's unfunded vested benefits liability. The Company does not possess sufficient information to determine its portion, if any, of the unfunded vested benefits for the union administered plans.

During 19Y3 the Company froze the pension plan for office and salaried employees and initiated the Utman Power Company Profit Sharing Retirement Plan. Under the plan, the Company's contribution is determined annually by the Board of Directors. The amount charged against income was $340,000 in 19Y3.

A comparison of accumulated plan benefits and plan net assets for the Company administered pension plans is presented below:

	January 1, 19Y3	January 1, 19Y2
	(In Thousands)	
Actuarial present value of accumulated plan benefits:		
Vested	**$2,632**	$2,586
Nonvested	**287**	123
Total	**$2,919**	$2,709
Net assets available for benefits	**$3,265**	$2,824

Exhibit 5-1 continued

NOTE 6—Investment in Foreign Affiliate

Equity in income of the foreign affiliate before U.S. taxes included in the consolidated statement of income was $44,000 in 19Y3, $59,000 in 19Y2 and $22,000 in 19Y1.

NOTE 7—Taxes on Income

The income tax provision consists of:

	19Y3	**19Y2**	**19Y1**
		(In Thousands)	
Current	**$ 662**	$ 1,450	$2,800
Future	**148**	85	(145)
Taxes on income	**$ 810**	$ 1,535	$2,655

The tax effect of significant timing differences is:

	19Y3	**19Y2**	**19Y1**
		(In Thousands)	
Deferred compensation	**$ 45**	$ 95	$ 79
Equity in foreign affiliate	**1**	5	15
Depreciation	**(194)**	(75)	(49)
Lease termination reserve and other	**—**	(110)	100
Total	**$(148)**	$ (85)	$ 145

Income tax expense of $810,000 for 19Y3, $1,535,000 for 19Y2 and $2,655,000 for 19Y1 reflects effective tax rates of 37.7%, 41.4% and 39.3%, respectively. The reasons for the difference between the U.S. Federal income tax rate and the Company's effective income tax rates are:

	19Y3	**19Y2**	**19Y1**
		(In Thousands)	
Computed tax expense	**$989**	$1,705	$3,107
Life insurance proceeds	**(92)**	—	—
Investment and other tax credits	**(52)**	(142)	(256)
U.S. tax benefits from DISC subsidiary	**(22)**	(86)	(154)
Other	**(13)**	58	(42)
Taxes on income	**$810**	$1,535	$2,655

Exhibit 5-1 continued

NOTE 8—Stock Purchase Agreement

The Company has a stock repurchase agreement with the estate of a former stockholder which obligates the Company to repurchase stock if requested by the executor of the estate. The Company's liability cannot exceed $500,000.

NOTE 9—Lease Commitments

The Company leases property and equipment under long-term operating leases which require minimum annual payments as follows:

Year	Amount *(In Thousands)*
19Y4	$610
19Y5	399
19Y6	271
19Y7	150
19Y8	123
19Y9–19Z3	527
19Z4–19Z8	99

Rental expense for all operating leases was $1,054,000 for 19Y3, $1,081,000 in 19Y2 and $894,000 in 19Y1.

Various leases include provisions for renewal, purchase options, and in some instances the payment of property taxes, insurance and related expenses.

NOTE 10—Segment Information

The Company is primarily a manufacturer of industrial pumps. Substantially all manufacturing operations are located in Battle Creek, Michigan. Export sales comprised 18%, 20% and 21% of total sales in 19Y3, 19Y2 and 19Y1, respectively.

NOTE 11—Accounting Changes

During the year ended December 31, 19Y2, the Company changed its policy with respect to translating financial statements of its Canadian subsidiary and Japanese affiliate to conform with the provisions of Financial Accounting Standards Board Statement No. 52.

The Statement requires that adjustments relating to the translation of foreign currency financial statements be accumulated in, and reported as, a separate segment of stockholders' equity rather than being reflected in the income statement.

For the year ending December 31, 19Y1, the accounts of the Canadian subsidiary were translated into U.S. dollars in accordance with Statement of Financial Accounting Standards No. 8. Foreign currency translation loss included in net income was $39,000 in 19Y1.

Effective January 1, 19Y2, the Company changed its method of depreciating newly acquired plant and equipment to the straight-line method for financial reporting purposes. The change was made to make the Company's accounting policies more consistent with those prevailing in the industry.

Exhibit 5-1 continued

Auditors' Report

To the Board of Directors
of Utman Power Company
Battle Creek, Michigan

We have examined the consolidated balance sheets of Utman Power Company and subsidiaries as of December 31, 19Y3 and 19Y2, and the related consolidated statements of income, stockholders' equity and changes in financial position for each of the three years in the period ended December 31, 19Y3. Our examinations were made in accordance with generally accepted auditing standards and, accordingly, included such tests of the accounting records and such other auditing procedures as we considered necessary in the circumstances.

In our opinion, the financial statements mentioned present fairly the consolidated financial position of Utman Power Company and subsidiaries at December 31, 19Y3 and 19Y2, and the consolidated results of their operations and changes in their financial position for each of the three years in the period ended December 31, 19Y3, in conformity with generally accepted accounting principles applied on a consistent basis.

SEIDMAN & SEIDMAN
Grand Rapids, Michigan
February 16, 19Y4

Exhibit 5-1 continued

Officers and Directors

John B. Fischer
Chairman of the Board and Director

Percy S. Otto
President, Chief Executive Officer and Director

Ernest R. Tuft
Executive Vice President and Treasurer

C. Joan Styler
Secretary

George J. Doherty
Vice President of Sales and Engineering

Hal A. Kim
Vice President of Finance

Warren P. William
Vice President of Manufacturing

Mark J. Andrew
Director
Chairman of Executive Committee, The Aro Corp., Bryan, Ohio

James H. Cantor
Director
Vice Chairman, Transamerica Insurance Co. of Michigan, Transamerica Insurance Corp. of America, Battle Creek, Michigan

Gerard V. Ender
Director
Professor Emeritus Mechanical Engineering, University of Michigan, Ann Arbor, Michigan

Paul E. Otto
Director
Group Vice President, Real Estate Division, Great Western Bank & Trust, Phoenix, Arizona

Roy T. Parker, Jr.
Director
Chairman and Chief Executive Officer, The Upjohn Co., Kalamazoo, Michigan

Corporate Offices

200 Captain Ave., S.W.
Battle Creek, Michigan 49016

Plant Locations

Battle Creek, Michigan
Pump and value manufacturing

Burlington, Ontario, Canada
Pump manufacturing

Houston, Texas
Pump repair

Baton Rouge, Louisiana
Pump repair

Subsidiaries and Affiliate

UTMAN POWER INTERNATIONAL, INC., Battle Creek, Michigan
Domestic International Sales Corporation, 100% owned
UTMAN POWER (CANADA), LTD., Burlington, Ontario, Canada, 100% owned
QUICK MOTOR WORKS, INC., Baton Rouge, Louisiana, 100% owned
UTMAN POWER, LTD., Tokyo, Japan, 50% owned

By concentrating on the method of valuation used and reading the footnotes carefully, you would discover that the inventory was worth substantially more than the value for which it was carried on the balance sheet. Furthermore, you would realize that in two of the preceding three years (which represented periods of high inflation), the earnings were lowered by the selection of FIFO as the method for valuing inventory. If you were seeking to value the company from the point of view of being either a merger/acquisition candidate or simply to compare its underlying assets with the price at which its stock is selling, it would be appropriate to add back in the current market value of the company's inventory.

Retirement Plans–Accounting Factors

Up to recently, many investors overlooked the assets contained in the company's pension plan. In the case of many capital intensive "smokestack" types of companies with conservative managements, the typical scenario was for the company's contribution to the pension plan to exceed the actual requirements of the plan. Over a period of years, an excess would be built up in the company's pension plan well beyond the amount of money needed to meet the pension obligations of the company.

Refer back to Exhibit 5-1 for an example of such excess funding in a pension plan. Concentrate on Footnote 5, Retirement Benefit Plans.

What are some conclusions you can draw from reading Footnote 5? First, you can tell that there is excess funding in the company's pension plan from the fact that the company froze the pension plan for office and salaried employees. Many companies have been moved to follow such a course to make themselves less attractive to corporate raiders. The next step for the company would be for it to transfer the excess funding in the pension plan to the company's current assets. The excess funding could be used for immediate corporate purposes such as the financing of plant expansion, acquisition of other companies, or for whatever purpose the corporation's management would deem appropriate.

How can you identify companies that have excess funding in their pension plan? The answer rests with a careful reading of the information contained in a company's annual report and 10K filing. Particular emphasis should be placed on the latter, since it is in its 10K filing that a company will describe in some detail the amount of assets held in its pension plan versus the yearly payout to retired company employees. By comparing pension plan assets to yearly payout, you can develop a feeling as to whether the company has excess funding in its pension plan. Adding this excess funding back into the company's current assets will give you a clearer picture of the company's real worth. Thus, excess funding is an example of a qualitative accounting factor that must be added back in to value a particular company properly.

"Bringing Up" Below-the-Line Assets

Up to this point, you have learned the approach to take toward certain qualitative accounting factors, namely, inventory valuation and pension funding. This section explores the concept of "bringing up" below-the-line assets, another qualitative accounting factor that must be considered in evaluating any potential asset play.

"Bringing up" below-the-line assets usually refers to smaller closely held companies. "Bringing up" assets means that such companies may treat items as long-term assets when they should be considered short-term assets. Whether to treat a particular asset as current or long term represents a qualitative accounting judgment. There is nothing wrong with you second-guessing a company's management and moving a particular asset from below the line (long-term category) to above the line (current category).

There are a number of reasons why a company's management might treat current assets as long-term assets. Management might have an extremely conservative approach to financial reporting. A second reason might relate to the company's fear of making itself too attractive and thus become subject to unwanted interest from the merger and acquisition community.

By treating items as long term rather than current, a company will effectively reduce its current and quick ratios and will cause a casual investor or professional analyst possibly to overlook the company and pass on to another target.

To get a better understanding of what bringing up below-the-line assets is all about, let's examine a particular company where such a situation exists. Exhibit 5-2 consists of the financials of a company with current assets of $19,113,993 versus current liabilities of $3,367,766, and a current ratio of 5.68%. But this is only part of the picture. Let's look at what assets are listed as noncurrent or below-the-line assets and see if they do indeed fit into that category.

Below is a listing of below-the-line assets that might raise some questions in the mind of an asset-play investor:

Marketable equity securities, carried at cost
Investment in Berle-Farview Joint Participation
Note Receivable from Major Brewing
Land Held for Investment

The first of these items, namely, marketable securities, obviously should be included in the category of current assets as opposed to long-term assets. While representing $249,900 in the present year, in the preceding year marketable securities amounted to $7,306,699 (market value of $7,665,862). If included in the prior year's current assets, it would have increased current assets by over 50%.

With regard to the other two items listed before, you would have to do additional work to determine if any portion of these assets should be included in the current asset category. However, Footnote 3 does seem to indicate that at least a portion of the amounts cited should be included in current assets.*

*Note throughout Exhibit 5-2 the sections that have been highlighted (shaded areas) which are of especial importance.

Exhibit 5-2.

FARVIEW

FARVIEW BREWING CORPORATION
19Y6 Annual Report

Exhibit 5-2 continued

FARVIEW BREWING CORPORATION
700 WEST 11TH STREET
VANCOUVER, WA 98660

PRESIDENT'S MESSAGE

DEAR STOCKHOLDER,

We submit this 19Y6 Annual Report to you at a pivotal time in the history of your Company.

On January 17, 19Y7 Peter Kane, President and Chairman of the Board from 19X5 to 19Y5 passed away. Mr. Peter as he was known by the Farview family, directed the Company through this most difficult period with a firm hand, a vision of the future, and an unselfish commitment to the survival of the Company. His death marks the end of an era. He will be missed, not only by the Farview family, but by the entire brewing industry and business community all across the country.

We are pleased to report that your Company was profitable in 19Y6. Despite the continuing pricing pressures and flat consumer demand, the Company recorded an operating profit of slightly over $1,000,000. We are committed to maintaining the same vigilance that has kept your Company profitable and viable notwithstanding the rigors of competition and the marketplace.

During 19Y6, we continued to update the equipment in our Ft. Wayne, Indiana facility. This will result in further operating efficiencies, improvement of our product, and greater profitability. During the coming year, we will be establishing a division within the Company which will focus on the development and redevelopment of our idle land and brewing facilities. Studies are currently underway to determine development possibilities for our Cranston, Rhode Island property. We plan to institute similar activities in Chicago, New Orleans, St. Louis and Galveston.

On March 6, 19Y7, a federal court in New York held that certain activities of the Company were in violation of the antitrust laws. As a result, the Company and Berle Brewing Company were jointly and severally held responsible for Breach of Contract and violations of the Robinson-Patman Act with judgment entered against the Companies in the sum of $15,238,000 which was trebled pursuant to antitrust laws.

Management has been advised by legal counsel that sufficient grounds exist for a successful appeal and that prospects for reversing the judgment are excellent. We expect a decision from the Appellate Court in the latter part of 19Y7. In the meanwhile the Company has posted the required funds to stay the execution of the judgment, pending the Appeal. In order to do so, it was necessary for the Company to reduce its investment in the Berle-Farview Joint Participation by $16,371,270 and to utilize $10,000,00 of its available cash. We do not anticipate that this will result in any cash flow problems during 19Y7.

In conclusion, on behalf of the Directors, I wish to extend our thanks to our very dedicated employees for a job well done and to the Stockholders for their continued support.

LEN IVAN
Chairman of the Board and President

Exhibit 5-2 continued

SELECTED FINANCIAL INFORMATION

	Year Ended December 31,				
	19Y6	**19Y5**	**19Y4**	**19Y3**	**19Y2**
	(In Thousands Except Per Share Data)				
Net sales	**$40,171**	$51,671	$52,534	$55,867	$60,003
Income (loss) before extraordinary item	**56**	(8,193)	2,276	2,134	1,957
Extraordinary item:					
Use of loss carryforward	**970**	—	—	500	1,113
Net income (loss)	**1,026**	(8,193)	2,276	2,634	3,070
Income (loss) per share:					
Income (loss) before extraordinary item	**.01**	(1.23)	.34	.32	.29
Extraordinary item	**.14**	—	—	.08	.17
Net income per share	**.15**	(1.23)	.34	.40	.46
Total assets	**58,397**	59,886	67,579	68,720	60,469
Working capital	**15,726**	7,154	13,601	9,561	6,646

Farview and its subsidiaries and affiliates produce beer and related malt beverages, sold principally under the brand names Farview, Norrogen, Baltone, and Hoffer. Through its affiliation with Berle Brewing Company, the Company also produces and sells aluminum cans for beer and soft drinks.

Management's Discussion and Analysis of Financial Condition and Results of Operations

Results of Operations:

19Y6 vs. 19Y5

Net sales for 19Y6 decreased $11,500,000 or 22.3% as compared to 19Y5. Barrels sold in 19Y6 of approximately 716,400 represent a 218,600 barrel or 23.4% decrease from 19Y5. This decline is consistent with recent experience, and similar declines may occur in the future. The Company intends to concentrate on development and retention of markets for its malt liquor and ale products as these products enjoy high margins and customer identity.

Cost of sales decreased to 90.3% of net sales from 95.2% in 19Y5. This decrease results from the effect of fixed costs being applied to higher volume at Fort Wayne in 19Y6 and increased manufacturing efficiencies at this brewery. Variable per barrel costs of beer produced at Fort Wayne did not change significantly from 19Y5. Barrels sold from the Fort Wayne brewery increased to 564,500 in 19Y6 as compared to 488,500 in 19Y5. Sales of barrels produced under the contract brewing agreement with the Joint Participation decreased to 151,900 as compared to 431,250 in 19Y5. The decline in sales of products produced under the contract brewing agreement results from the shift of pro-

Exhibit 5-2 continued

duction back to Fort Wayne and the overall decline in sales of the Company's products. The settlement of labor relations difficulties and completion of plant refurbishing at Fort Wayne allowed for the production shift back to the Fort Wayne brewery.

Marketing, general and administrative expenses increased to 11.6% of net sales from 6.4% in 19Y5. This increase results primarily from the effect of fixed general and administrative costs being applied to lower volume, continuing employee benefit costs associated with the former Cranston workforce and increased legal costs associated with the Good Brands litigation.

Significant items of other income and expense include earnings from the Joint Participation of approximately $1,804,000, a gain of approximately $1,980,000 from the sale of the Company's former St. Louis office building and a charge of approximately $2,025,000 (for which there is no tax benefit) to realize declines in the market value of certain investments. Joint Participation earnings decreased principally as a result of lower volume at San Antonio. The production shift to Fort Wayne of a significant portion of the Company's brands which had been produced by the Joint Participation in 19Y5 accounted for a major portion of this lower volume at San Antonio.

19Y5 vs. 19Y4

Net sales for 19Y5 decreased $864,000 or 1.6% as compared to 19Y4. Barrels sold in 19Y5 of approximately 935,000 represent a 50,000 barrel or 5.1% decrease from 19Y4. The percentage decline in net sales as compared to the decline in barrels is favorable due to the continued shift in the mix of products to higher priced malt liquor products.

Cost of sales increased to 95.2% of net sales from 89.2% in 19Y4. This increase results from the effect of fixed costs being applied to lower volume at Fort Wayne in 19Y5 and higher costs of obtaining beer under the contract brewing agreement with the Joint Participation. Variable per barrel costs of beer produced at Fort Wayne did not change significantly from 19Y4.

Marketing, general and administrative expenses decreased to 6.4% of net sales from 8.5% in 19Y4, reflecting the results of the Company's continued cost control measures.

Significant items of other income and expense include a $9,000,000 provision to reduce the Company's idle facilities to their net realizable value, a $4,106,000 provision for litigation losses, and earnings from the Joint Participation of approximately $2,291,000. The provision to reduce the carrying value of the idle facilities represents management's belief, based on analysis performed during 19Y5, that an adjustment was necessary to reduce the historical carrying value of the idle facilities to their net realizable value. The provision for litigation includes payments of $215,000 related to cases settled during 19Y5 and a provision of $3,891,000 for lawsuits which were settled in early 19Y6. Joint Participation earnings increased approximately $1,175,000 over 19Y4 due to the increase in the Company's pro rata share of Joint Participation earnings resulting from an additional $6,000,000 cash investment in the Joint Participa-

Exhibit 5-2 continued

tion and increased profitability of the Joint Participation. The Joint Participation's increased profitability results largely from the additional volume generated by the Company's brewing contract with the Joint Participation.

Liquidity and Capital Resources:

The Company's primary source of liquidity is cash generated from operations. Aside from funds generated from operations, the Company generated approximately $3.9 million from the sale of non-current marketable equity securities; $8.5 million from the collection of the note receivable from S&P Company; $1.2 million from the sale of its interest in the New Orleans Saint's football franchise and $2.8 million from the settlement of the 19Y4 sale of its former St. Louis office building. Major uses of cash in 19Y6 included a $1.0 million additional investment in the Joint Participation. Management believes that the current level of operations will generate sufficient funds to meet future liquidity needs and has no intentions of borrowing long- or short-term funds or selling securities to generate funds subject to the resolution of the litigation described in the following paragraph.

On February 18, 19Y7 the United States District Court for the Southern District of New York entered judgment against the Company and Berle Brewing Company and awarded the plaintiff, Good Brands Beverage, Inc. actual and trebled damages of $45,714,000. The judgment results from an action commenced by Good Brands principally as a result of the Company raising prices charged to Good Brands for certain Company products. The Company believes that there is no legal basis for the judgment, which it believes is contrary to the evidence and applicable law. The Company intends to pursue all available remedies to set aside or to reverse the judgment and in this connection will file an appeal with the United States Court of Appeals. The ultimate outcome of this litigation is not presently determinable. Any affirmation of all or a substantial part of the $45,714,000 judgment could have a material adverse effect on the Company's liquidity and financial position.

Impact of Inflation:

The precise effects of inflation upon the Company are difficult to determine. In the past the Company has generally been able to increase prices to offset increases in costs.

Common Stock-Market Prices

The Company's Common Stock is traded in the over-the-counter market and appears on the National Association of Security Dealers Automated Quotation System. The following table presents the range of high and low bid quotations for the Company's Common Stock:

Exhibit 5-2 continued

Quarter Ended	19Y6 High	19Y6 Low	19Y5 High	19Y5 Low
March 31	6¼	5¼	7⅛	5
June 30	8¾	5⅛	6½	5⅞
September 30	8½	6⅞	6⅜	6
December 31	7½	6⅝	6½	6⅛

10-K Report

Farview Brewing Corporation's Annual Report on Form 10-K to the Securities and Exchange Commission for the year ended December 31, 19Y6 provides certain additional information and is available to Farview stockholders upon written request. Copies of the Company's Form 10-K may be obtained by writing to: Corporate Secretary, Farview Brewing Corporation, P.O. Box 0000, Vancouver, Washington 98666.

Board of Directors and Executive Officers

Len Ivan, Executive Vice-President (also President of Berle Brewing Company and Vice President of S&P). Mr. Ivan replaced Mr. Kane as Chairman of the Board of Directors, President and Chief Executive and Financial Officer effective February 21, 19Y6.

Ben Olson, Director, assistant to the Chairman and Secretary (also Vice President and Secretary of S&P since April 19Y2), Assistant to Chairman of S&P, Major Brewing Co., and Berle Brewing Co., since 19Y8.

George Dunn was appointed as a Director effective February 21, 19Y6. Mr. Dunn has been Vice President-Sales of Farview Brewing Corporation since May, 19X8 and has held various sales and marketing positions with the Company.

Executive Offices

700 West 11th Street
Vancouver, Washington 98660

Mailing Address

P.O. Box 0000
Vancouver, WA 98666

Stock Transfer Agent

The Company acts as its own stock transfer agent. The Company charges $7.50 for each new certificate requested plus $7.50 for each old certificate submitted for redemption. The minimum transfer fee is therefore $15.00 although the fee may vary with each transaction depending on the number of certificates involved.

Exhibit 5-2 continued

Registrar

First Interstate Bank
San Francisco, California

Annual Meeting of Stockholders

The Annual Meeting of stockholders will be held on Monday, April 27, 19Y7 at 10:30 a.m. in the offices of the Old Brewery located at 52 New Street, San Francisco, CA 94124.

Exhibit 5-2 continued

Price Waterhouse

Report of Independent Accountants

To the Board of Directors
and Stockholders
Farview Brewing Corporation

We have examined the consolidated balance sheets of Farview Brewing Corporation and Subsidiaries (the "Company") as of December 31, 19Y6 and 19Y5, and the related consolidated statements of operations, stockholders' equity, and of changes in financial position for the years then ended. Our examinations were made in accordance with generally accepted auditing standards and, accordingly, included such tests of the accounting records and such other auditing procedures as we considered necessary in the circumstances. The consolidated financial statements of the Company for the year ended December 31, 19Y4 (before the restatements described in Note 2) were examined by another independent accountant, whose report on such financial statements dated January 22, 19Y5 expressed an unqualified opinion on those statements.

As more fully described in Note 8, on February 18, 19Y7 the United States District Court for the Southern District of New York entered judgment against the Company and Berle Brewing Company, and awarded the plaintiff damages of approximately $46 million. The Company intends to pursue all available remedies to set aside or to reverse the judgment, however the ultimate outcome of this litigation is not presently determinable. In our report dated March 28, 19Y6, our opinion on the 19Y5 financial statements was unqualified; however, in light of the litigation referred to above, our present opinion on the 19Y5 financial statements, as presented herein, is different from that expressed in our previous report.

As described in Note 3, the Company is controlled by S&P Company and its various subsidiaries and has extensive transactions and relationships with members of this controlled group. As a result of these relationships, it is possible that the terms of these transactions are not the same as those which would result from transactions among wholly unrelated parties.

In our opinion, subject to the effect on the 19Y6 and 19Y5 financial statements of such adjustments, if any, that might have been required had the outcome of the litigation discussed in the second paragraph of this report been known, the 19Y6 and 19Y5 consolidated financial statements examined by us present fairly the financial position of Farview Brewing Corporation and Subsidiaries at December 31, 19Y6 and 19Y5, the results of their operations and the changes in their financial position for the years then ended, in conformity with generally accepted accounting principles consistently applied.

PRICE WATERHOUSE

February 27, 19Y7, except as to Note 10.

Exhibit 5-2 continued

FARVIEW BREWING CORPORATION AND SUBSIDIARIES
CONSOLIDATED BALANCE SHEET

	December 31, 19Y6	December 31, 19Y5
ASSETS		
Current assets:		
Cash and cash equivalents (including repurchase agreements of $12,614,000 and $491,000 respectively) (Note 1)	**$14,383,093**	$ 1,263,511
Receivables:		
Trade accounts, less allowance for doubtful accounts of $68,000 in 19Y6 and 19Y5	**2,068,597**	2,203,126
Other receivables	**478,552**	—
Inventories:		
Finished goods	**478,093**	462,005
Raw materials and beer in process	**841,900**	658,666
Packaging materials	**863,758**	634,189
Note receivable from S&P Company (Note 3)	—	8,490,409
Other current assets	—	7,896
Total current assets	**19,113,993**	13,719,802
Property, plant and equipment:		
Land	**450,775**	450,775
Buildings	**4,694,660**	4,694,660
Machinery and equipment	**7,453,143**	7,041,996
Cooperage and pallets	**8,043,592**	8,018,760
	20,642,170	20,206,191
Accumulated depreciation	**(15,215,128)**	(14,689,369)
	5,427,042	5,516,822
Other assets:		
Marketable equity securities, carried at cost (market value—$249,900 and $7,665,862 respectively) (Note 1)	**$ 249,900**	$ 7,306,669
Investment in Berle-Farview Joint Participation (Note 3)	**19,969,383**	17,165,478
Idle facilities (Note 4)	**9,628,003**	9,872,672
Note receivable from Major Brewing Company (Note 3)	**1,953,986**	2,093,179
Note receivable from property sale, net of unrecognized gain (Notes 2 and 8)	—	869,745
Land held for investment, at cost (Note 3)	**1,471,761**	1,471,761
Restricted cash and other	**583,240**	1,870,258
Total other assets	**33,856,273**	40,649,762
Total Assets	**$58,397,308**	$59,886,386

The accompanying notes are an integral part of these financial statements.

Exhibit 5-2 continued

FARVIEW BREWING CORPORATION AND SUBSIDIARIES
CONSOLIDATED BALANCE SHEET

	December 31, 19Y6	December 31, 19Y5
LIABILITIES AND STOCKHOLDERS' EQUITY		
Current liabilities:		
Accounts payable	**$ 1,570,856**	$ 440,585
Accrued liabilities:		
Excise taxes	**202,270**	201,377
Other taxes	**281,356**	542,959
Employee wages and benefits	**535,143**	411,077
Other	**528,591**	857,218
Deposits on containers (Note 1)	**269,350**	220,135
Litigation losses payable (Note 8)	**—**	3,891,413
Total current liabilities	**3,387,566**	6,565,664
Deferred income taxes (Notes 1 and 6)	**3,487,784**	3,487,784
Unfunded pension costs (Note 7)	**2,233,651**	1,512,022
Other liabilities	**1,094,962**	1,243,922
Total liabilities	**10,203,963**	12,809,392
Stockholders' equity (Note 5)		
Preferred stock—par value $100 per share, 6% non-cumulative, convertible:		
Class A—212,500 shares authorized, 100,000 shares issued (including 6,400 treasury shares)	**$10,000,000**	$10,000,000
Class B—212,500 shares authorized, none issued	**—**	—
Common stock—par value $1 per share, 14,100,000 shares authorized; 4,609,275 and 4,586,775 shares issued, respectively (including 59,370 treasury shares)	**4,609,275**	4,586,775
Additional paid-in capital	**10,164,604**	10,097,104
Retained earnings	**24,562,817**	23,536,466
Less treasury stock, at cost:		
Preferred, Class A—6,400 shares	**(640,000)**	(640,000)
Common—59,370 shares	**(503,351)**	(503,351)
Total stockholders' equity	**48,193,345**	47,076,994
Total Liabilities and Stockholders' Equity	**$58,397,308**	$59,886,386

Contingencies (Note 8)

The accompanying notes are an integral part of these financial statements.

Exhibit 5-2 continued

FARVIEW BREWING CORPORATION AND SUBSIDIARIES
CONSOLIDATED STATEMENT OF OPERATIONS

	Year Ended December 31,		
	19Y6	**19Y5**	**19Y4**
Sales	**$47,446,591**	$60,970,988	$61,937,031
Less—excise taxes	**7,275,618**	9,300,479	9,403,004
Net Sales	**40,170,973**	51,670,509	52,534,027
Cost of goods sold	**36,261,199**	49,215,973	46,871,006
Gross profit	**3,909,774**	2,454,536	5,663,021
Marketing, general and administrative expenses	**4,594,975**	3,312,186	4,445,129
Operating income (loss)	**(685,201)**	(857,650)	1,217,892
Equity in earnings of Berle-Farview Joint Participation	**1,803,905**	2,291,303	1,116,393
	1,118,704	1,433,653	2,334,285
Other income (expense):			
Write-down of idle facilities	**—**	(9,000,000)	—
Idle plant expenses	**(742,703)**	(469,585)	—
Litigation losses	**(178,390)**	(4,106,413)	—
Interest and dividends	**1,116,874**	1,325,972	1,698,249
Interest expense	**(45,205)**	(86,035)	(67,172)
Net realized loss on investments	**(2,112,126)**	(289,639)	—
Other, net	**73,795**	698,562	3,685
Gain on property sold (Note 8)	**1,980,402**	—	—
Total other income (expense)	**92,647**	(11,927,138)	1,634,762
Income (loss) before income taxes and extraordinary item	**1,211,351**	(10,493,485)	3,969,047
Provision (credit) for income taxes	**1,155,000**	(2,300,000)	1,693,000
Income (loss) before extraordinary item	**56,351**	(8,193,485)	2,276,047
Extraordinary item—			
Tax benefit from utilization of loss carryforward	**970,000**	—	—
Net income (loss)	**$ 1,026,351**	$(8,193,485)	$ 2,276,047
Income (loss) per common and common equivalent share:			
Income (loss) before extraordinary item	**$.01**	$(1.23)	$.34
Extraordinary item	**.14**	—	—
Net income (loss) per share	**$.15**	$(1.23)	$.34

The accompanying notes are an integral part of these financial statements.

Exhibit 5-2 continued

FARVIEW BREWING CORPORATION AND SUBSIDIARIES
CONSOLIDATED STATEMENTS OF CHANGES IN FINANCIAL POSITION

	Year Ended December 31,		
	19Y6	**19Y5**	**19Y4**
CASH PROVIDED BY (APPLIED TO) OPERATIONS:			
Income (loss) before extraordinary item	**$ 56,351**	$(8,193,485)	$2,276,047
Add (deduct) charges (credits) not affecting cash:			
Depreciation	**529,433**	546,066	1,250,952
Loss on investments	**2,112,126**	289,639	—
Deferred income taxes	**—**	(2,350,000)	1,525,783
Gain on property sale	**(1,980,402)**	—	(42,478)
Write down of facilities	**—**	9,000,000	—
Increase (decrease) in other liabilities	**(148,960)**	332,507	11,900
Increase in unfunded pension cost	**721,629**	193,345	—
Equity in earnings of Berle-Farview Joint Participation	**(1,803,905)**	(2,291,303)	(1,116,393)
Income tax benefit from utilization of loss carryforwards	**970,000**	—	—
Changes in operating working capital:			
Receivables	**(344,023)**	2,017,387	679,748
Inventories	**(428,891)**	1,047,431	1,459,318
Other current assets	**7,896**	25,225	261,442
Loans payable	**—**	—	(2,640,199)
Accounts payable and accrued liabilities	**924,810**	(1,192,511)	(258,335)
Accrued taxes	**(260,710)**	(11,001)	(123,133)
Deposit on containers	**49,215**	(331,692)	(229,127)
Litigation losses payable	**(3,891,413)**	3,891,413	—
Cash provided by (used for) operations	**(3,486,844)**	2,973,021	3,055,525
Other sources of cash:			
Sale of equipment	**244,819**	78,703	919,745
Sale of investments	**5,120,390**	2,605,295	2,587,200
Sale of property	**2,850,000**		
Decrease in notes receivable	**139,193**	480,000	33,119
Stock options and other	**90,000**	37,500	15,084
Decrease in loan to S&P Company	**8,490,409**	—	—
Restricted cash applied to litigation losses	**1,111,271**	—	—
Total cash provided	**14,559,238**	6,174,519	6,610,673

Exhibit 5-2 continued

	Year Ended December 31,		
	19Y6	**19Y5**	**19Y4**
CASH USED FOR:			
Investment in Berle-Farview Joint Participation	**1,000,000**	6,000,000	—
Loan to S&P Company, net	—	8,490,409	—
Increase in notes receivable	—	102,021	869,745
Purchase of equipment	**439,656**	181,700	834,493
Preferred dividends paid	—	561,600	561,600
Increase in other assets	—	28,588	60,209
Increase in restricted cash	—	301,104	—
Total cash used	**1,439,656**	15,665,422	2,326,047
Increase (decrease) in cash and cash equivalents	**$13,119,582**	$(9,490,903)	$ 4,284,626

The accompanying notes are an integral part of these financial statements.

Exhibit 5-2 continued

FARVIEW BREWING CORPORATION AND SUBSIDIARIES
CONSOLIDATED STATEMENT OF STOCKHOLDERS' EQUITY
For the Years Ended December 31, 19Y6, 19Y5 and 19Y4

	Class A Preferred Stock	Common Stock	Additional Paid-In Capital	Retained Earnings	Unrealized Loss on Marketable Equity Securities	Treasury Stock
Balance at December 31, 19Y3	$10,000,000	$4,576,775	$10,069,604	$30,577,104	$ —	$(1,143,351)
Net income				2,276,047		
Cash dividends on preferred stock				(561,600)		
Unrealized loss on marketable equity securities					(492,928)	
Balance at December 31, 19Y4	$10,000,000	$4,576,775	$10,069,604	$32,291,551	$(492,928)	$(1,143,351)
Net loss				(8,193,485)		
Cash dividends on preferred stock				(561,600)		
Shares issued under stock option plan		10,000	27,500			
Change in valuation reserve for marketable equity securities					492,928	
Balance at December 31, 19Y5	$10,000,000	$4,586,775	$10,097,104	$23,536,466	—	$(1,143,351)
Net income				1,026,351		
Shares issued under stock option plan		22,500	67,500			
Balance at December 31, 19Y6	$10,000,000	$4,609,275	$10,164,604	$24,562,817	$ —	$(1,143,351)

The accompanying notes are an integral part of these financial statements.

Exhibit 5-2 continued

FARVIEW BREWING CORPORATION AND SUBSIDIARIES
NOTES TO CONSOLIDATED FINANCIAL STATEMENTS

1. ACCOUNTING POLICIES

Principles of Consolidation

The consolidated financial statements include the accounts of the Company and two wholly-owned subsidiaries. All material intercompany accounts and transactions have been eliminated. The Company's investment in the Berle-Farview Joint Participation is recorded under the equity method (see Note 3).

Cash and Cash Equivalents

Cash equivalents included repurchase agreements with maturities less than 30 days. All repurchase agreements are secured by U.S. Government securities.

Inventories

Inventories are stated at the lower of average cost or market, calculated on a first-in, first-out basis.

Property and Depreciation

Property, plant and equipment is stated at cost. For financial statement reporting depreciation is provided on the straight-line method using estimated useful lives of 5 to 25 years for equipment and 20 to 50 years for buildings. For income tax reporting, accelerated methods are used.

Marketable Equity Securities

Marketable equity securities are carried at the lower of cost or market value. Unrealized losses on marketable equity securities that are considered temporary in nature are recorded as a valuation allowance charged to stockholders' equity. Realized gains or losses on sales of securities are determined based on specific identification of the securities sold. Provisions for investment losses are recorded to reduce the cost basis on securities deemed to have suffered permanent declines in market value.

Container Deposits

Deposit amounts charged to customers for returnable containers expected to be returned are reflected in the balance sheet as a liability to customers. The deposit liability account is reduced when containers are returned.

Pension Cost

Pension costs are actuarially computed and are funded in accordance with the minimum funding requirements of the Employee's Retirement Income Security Act. Unfunded prior service costs are amortized over the estimated remaining service lives of pension plan participants.

Income Taxes

Deferred income taxes are recorded to reflect the differences in reporting certain items for financial statement and income tax purposes, principally accelerated depreciation. Investment tax credits are accounted for on the flow-through method.

Exhibit 5-2 continued

Earnings per Share

Income per share is based on the weighted average number of common and common equivalent shares outstanding during the period. The weighted average number of common and common equivalent shares outstanding in 19Y6, 19Y5 and 19Y4 were 6,660,986, 6,645,056 and 6,628,019, respectively.

2. RESTATEMENT OF 19Y4 AND PRIOR YEARS' FINANCIAL STATEMENTS

During 19Y5, the Company's 19Y4 and prior years' financial statements were restated to 1) eliminate the gain originally recorded in 19Y4 on the sale of the Company's St. Louis office building; 2) restate Joint Participation earnings for the years prior to 19Y5 for interest earned on funds advanced by the Joint Participation to Berle Brewing Company; 3) correct the carrying amount of the cash value of certain life insurance contracts; 4) eliminate extraordinary credits originally recorded in 19Y4 and 19Y3 for utilization of tax loss carryforwards; and 5) reclassify certain restricted funds. The accompanying 19Y4 financial statements are presented as restated.

3. RELATED PARTY TRANSACTIONS

All of the Company's Class A Convertible, Voting, Preferred Stock and 78,700 shares of its common stock are owned by Berle Brewing Company, which in turn is owned by S&P Company and its various subsidiaries. All of these companies are ultimately controlled by the estate of Mr. Peter Kane. This preferred and common stock together represent 49% of the Company's outstanding voting rights and effectively allow S&P Company to control the Company. As described below and elsewhere in this report the Company has extensive transactions and relationships with other members of this controlled group. As a result of these relationships, it is possible that the terms of these transactions are not the same as those which would result from transactions among wholly unrelated parties.

Berle-Farview Joint Participation

In 19X8, the Company and Berle Brewing Company together with its wholly-owned subsidiary Berle Container Company, formed an unincorporated joint venture known as the Berle-Farview Joint Participation ("Joint Participation"). Berle contributed the use of its San Antonio brewery and aluminum can plant and certain other plant assets with a then aggregate stated value of $15,083,238; and Farview contributed $3,000,000 in cash. Income from Joint Participation operations is credited to each partner's capital account in relation to the total capital of the Joint Participation. Although the Joint Participation has a beneficial ownership interest in the properties, assets and funds used in its operations, title to these operating assets vests with Berle. A more detailed description of the contractual and other terms of this venture are provided in the separate financial statements of the Joint Participation.

The Company investment in the Joint Participation at December 31, 19Y6 and 19Y5 was $19,969,383 and $17,165,478, respectively. The Company increased its interest in the Joint Participation by making cash investments of $1,000,000 and $6,000,000 during 19Y6 and 19Y5, respectively. The Company's share of Joint Participation earnings for the years ended December 31, 19Y6, 19Y5 and 19Y4 was $1,803,905, $2,291,303 and 1,116,393, respectively. Joint Participation earnings are credited to the Company based on its pro rata investment in the Joint Participation which was 24.4%, 23.4% and 15.3% at December 31, 19Y6, 19Y5 and 19Y4 respectively.

Exhibit 5-2 continued

The Company has a brewing contract with the Joint Participation whereby 151,900 and 431,256 barrels of the Company's products were produced by the Joint Participation during the years ended December 31, 19Y6 and 19Y5, respectively. The cost to the Company of this production was $54.63 per barrel in 19Y6 and $55.60 per barrel in 19Y5. This cost approximates the Joint Participation's normal brewing costs. Although the Company's production cost per barrel has, in the past, generally been less than that of the Joint Participation, management believes that this 19Y5 production shift was necessary and in the Company's best interests because a) the bottling and other facilities at the Company's Fort Wayne brewery were severely strained in 19Y4 and required refurbishing in 19Y5; and b) labor relation difficulties in 19Y5 dictated the use of alternative production capabilities to assure an uninterrupted supply of the Company's products. These matters have been resolved and a significant portion of the 19Y5 barrels produced under the contract were moved back to Fort Wayne during early 19Y6. Under the terms of this arrangement, the Joint Participation through Berle is responsible for the billing and collection of accounts; bad debts, however, remain the responsibility of the Company. The Company continues to have certain amounts of its products produced under the brewing contract to allow the Company to place its products in markets which cannot economically be served from Fort Wayne.

Revenues associated with the sale and shipment of these Farview products are reflected in the Consolidated Statement of Operations. As explained in Note 8, certain of the Company's dealings with the Joint Participation are the subject of a stockholder lawsuit.

West Coast Distribution and Major Brewing Note

Production and distribution of the Company's brands on the West Coast is governed by an agreement with Major Brewing Company, which is controlled by S&P Company and its various subsidiaries. The agreement with Major was concluded in 19X4, prior to the date the Company was controlled by S&P Company. Barrels produced by Major under this agreement were approximately 15,500 and 22,900 for 19Y5 and 19Y4, respectively, and none in 19Y6.

The agreement with Major also provides for the repayment of a six percent note (in the original principal amount of $2,500,000), accepted in connection with the 19X4 sale to Major of the Company's San Francisco plant. Terms of the note require Major to repay principal and accrued interest only from proceeds of any resale of the plant and equipment by Major and from "production credits," calculated at $1.38 per barrel on the Company's products brewed and shipped by Major. The "production credits" are in addition to the normal price per barrel charged by Major. The plant and the majority of the equipment have not been resold.

Major has not operated the San Francisco plant for several years and had brewed the Company's products at its Vancouver, Washington brewery prior to the closing of this brewery during October, 19Y5. As a result of this closing, Major no longer operates any brewing facilities, and has not produced or shipped any of the Company's products since November, 19Y5. Accordingly, "production credits" are no longer generated to fund repayments of note principal and interest, and the note has been amended to provide for cash funding of interest on a current basis. Interest earned on the note for the years ended December 31, 19Y6, 19Y5 and 19Y4 was $118,569, $123,420 and $118,481, respectively. The principal balance of the note will be repaid upon disposition of the San Francisco Brewery.

Company management believes that the current value of the San Francisco plant and equipment exceeds the principal balance of the note.

Exhibit 5-2 continued

Cranston Brewery

During 19Y3 the Company entered into an agreement with Berle to jointly participate in reopening the Cranston, Rhode Island brewery. In accordance with the agreement, the Joint Participation was ultimately to be responsible for the costs, including labor, associated with the potential reopening. At December 31, 19Y6 this agreement continued to be in effect, however efforts to reopen the brewery were halted during 19Y5. The Joint Participation continued to pay certain employee benefit expenses related to the Company's former Cranston workforce through 19Y5. These employee benefit expenses approximated $647,000 in 19Y5.

As efforts to reopen the Cranston brewery were halted during 19Y5, an agreement was reached with the Joint Participation during the fourth quarter of 19Y6 making Farview responsible for the cost of providing these continuing employee benefits, which approximated $535,000 during 19Y6. The Joint Participation had paid these expenses during 19Y6 but will not be reimbursed by Farview. Accordingly, included in accounts payable at December 31, 19Y6 is $535,000 payable to the Joint Participation.

Land Held for Investment

In 19Y0, the Company sold approximately 41 acres of undeveloped land adjacent to its Cranston, Rhode Island brewery to S&P Company and its various subsidiaries for cash and notes totalling $2,944,000, resulting in a gain of approximately $2,891,000.

In July 19Y3, as provided by the original land sale agreement, the Company exercised its right to enter into an agreement to jointly develop this land with S&P Company. As a result of entering into this agreement the Company acquired, via cancellation of the unpaid balance of the notes taken in connection with the original land sale and receipt of cash, a 50% undivided interest in the land as tenant in common with S&P Company. The Company's cost basis in this land interest, including development costs incurred to date, was $1,471,761 at December 31, 19Y6 and 19Y5 and is classified as "Land Held for Investment."

Material Purchases

During 19Y6 and 19Y5, the Company purchased aluminum cans for approximately $0.2 million and $1.4 million, respectively, from the Joint Participation. During 19Y6 the Company also purchased approximately $1.5 million of aluminum cans and other brewing materials from Parbe Brewing Company ("Parbe," which is controlled by S&P Company and its various subsidiaries). Purchases from Parbe during 19Y5 were nominal. The Company believes that the price paid for these items is equal to or lower than prices which could be obtained from other suppliers.

Loan to S&P Company

During the first quarter of 19Y5, the Company borrowed approximately $15,000,000 from its consolidated pension plan and advanced these funds to S&P Company. S&P Company repaid these amounts to the consolidated pension plan shortly thereafter and, in March of 19Y6, reimbursed the Company for the $277,969 of interest expense incurred as a result of borrowing those funds.

The Company also advanced cash to S&P Company to partially fund the acquisition of Parbe by S&P Company. These advances, which were funded from cash on hand and short-term borrowings, totalled $11,359,531, of which $3,845,573 was repaid during May, 19Y5. The advances are evidenced by an unsecured note, executed in March 19Y6, which bore interest at prime (10¾ to 8½ during 19Y6 and 9½% to 10½% during 19Y5). At

Exhibit 5-2 continued

December 31, 19Y5, the note including accrued interest, plus the interest then due on the funds borrowed from the pension plan totalled $8,490,409. During 19Y6 the Company earned $375,682 of interest on this note. All amounts due under the note were repaid prior to October 1, 19Y6.

Other Transactions with Related Parties

During 19Y6 and 19Y5, the Company sold to Berle and Parbe for $62,000 and $75,000, respectively, certain machinery and equipment from its idle plants. The sales price approximated the net book value of this equipment. During 19Y6, the Company purchased equipment for use in its Fort Wayne brewery from Parbe for $85,000.

Several of the Company's pension plans have been merged into a consolidated pension plan which also covers employees of Berle and Major. The Company funds the consolidated plan only to the extent necessary to provide benefits to Company employees participating in the plan.

Certain officers and employees of Major, Parbe and Berle provide service to the Company at no charge.

4. IDLE FACILITIES

Besides its operating brewery in Fort Wayne, Indiana, the Company also owns brewing facilities in Omaha, Nebraska; Cranston, Rhode Island; Galveston, Texas; New Orleans, Louisiana; and St. Louis, Missouri. It also owns a malting plant in Chicago, Illinois. The Cranston facility has not operated since 19Y3 and while an agreement with Berle exists providing for a joint reopening of this facility, efforts to reopen it were halted during 19Y5. Also during 19Y5, the Company ceased operations at its Omaha brewery. Accordingly, during 19Y5 the Omaha and Cranston plants were reclassified from productive assets to idle facilities.

The Galveston, New Orleans and St. Louis facilities have not operated since 19Y1, 19X8 and 19X7, respectively. These facilities and the Chicago malting plant are also considered idle facilities.

Management believes that during 19Y5 the realizable value of the idle facilities declined below historical carrying value. Accordingly, based on appraisals, management recorded a $9.0 million charge in 19Y5 to reduce the carrying value of these facilities to their estimated net realizable value.

5. STOCKHOLDERS' EQUITY

Class A Preferred Stock

Dividends of the Class A Preferred Stock are payable at $6.00 per share (noncumulative) annually to stockholders of record as of December 31 of the preceding year when and as declared by the Board of Directors, but only to the extent that the net earnings of the Company for the preceding year, after deducting therefrom reserves established by the Board of Directors for capital improvements, are sufficient for such payment. Each share is convertible into 22.5 shares of common stock. Each outstanding share of Class A Preferred Stock has voting rights equal to 45 shares of common stock. At December 31, 19Y6 and 19Y5 S&P Company, through its ownership of Berle, owned all outstanding shares of Class A Preferred Stock.

Unqualified Stock Option Plan

The Company has an unqualified stock option plan authorizing the granting of options to purchase 400,000 shares of common stock at a price equal to 100% of market value at the

Exhibit 5-2 continued

date of grant. The right to exercise any such option commences one year from the date of grant and expires not more than ten years from the date of grant. At December 31, 19Y6, there were 320,750 shares of common stock reserved under the plan and 15,000 exercisable options outstanding.

Stock option activity is summarized below:

	Shares available for grant	Shares Under Option	
		Shares	Price
December 31, 19Y3	296,250	57,000	$3.75–$4.00
December 31, 19Y4	296,250	57,000	$3.75–$4.00
Exercised		(10,000)	$3.75
Cancelled	9,500	(9,500)	$3.75–$4.00
December 31, 19Y5	305,750	37,500	$4.00
Exercised		(22,500)	$4.00
December 31, 19Y6	305,750	15,000	$4.00

6. INCOME TAXES

The provision (credit) for income taxes consists of the following:

	Year Ended December 31,		
	19Y6	19Y5	19Y4
Charge in lieu of federal income taxes	**$ 970,000**	$ —	$ —
Current			
Federal	**—**	—	—
State	**185,000**	50,000	167,217
Deferred	**—**	(2,350,000)	1,525,783
	$1,155,000	$(2,300,000)	$1,693,000

During 19Y6 the Company recognized, as an extraordinary credit, $970,000 of tax benefits resulting from utilization of loss carryforwards. The tax benefit recorded in 19Y5 results from carryback of a portion of the 19Y5 operating loss to 19Y4 and 19Y3 for financial reporting purposes. The amount of such benefits has been limited to the extent that certain elements of the 19Y5 loss may not ultimately result in tax benefits for the Company.

Deferred taxes arise principally as a result of differences in depreciation expense for financial reporting and tax return purposes.

The reconciliation between the statutory tax rate as a percentage of pre-tax income and the effective tax rate is as follows: (No reconciliation is presented for 19Y5 due to the pre-tax loss.)

Exhibit 5-2 continued

	Year Ended December 31,	
	19Y6	19Y4
Federal income tax rate	**46.0%**	46.0%
Net realized capital gains	**(24.2)**	—
Provision for capital loss for financial reporting	**76.9**	—
State taxes net of federal benefit	**8.2**	2.3
Dividend exclusion	**(6.8)**	(5.5)
Surtax exemption	**(1.7)**	(.6)
Life insurance and other	**(3.1)**	.5
	95.3%	42.7%

At December 31, 19Y6 the Company, for tax return purposes, had a net operating loss carryforward available to offset future taxable income of approximately $4,100,000 expiring in 19Z6. For financial reporting purposes the Company has a net operating loss carryforward at December 31, 19Y6 of approximately $3,800,000. In addition, an available investment tax credit carryover of $400,000 will expire for tax purposes from 19Z2 through 2001. Investment tax credit carryovers utilized subsequent to 19Y6 must be reduced by 35%, with one-half of the reduction phased-in during 19Y7.

No federal income taxes were payable for 19Y6, 19Y5 or 19Y4 due to the use of available net operating loss carryforwards of the Company's federal income tax returns.

7. PENSION PLANS

The Company has pension plans covering most of its employees. Pension expense for all plans, including amortization of prior service costs, was approximately $648,000 for 19Y6, $502,000 for 19Y5 and $820,000 for 19Y4.

The present value of accumulated benefits as estimated by consulting actuaries, and the market value of assets of all plans are as follows:

	December 31,	
	19Y6	19Y5
	(thousands of dollars)	
Actuarial present value of accumulated plan benefits:		
Vested	**$34,970**	$34,117
Nonvested	**211**	210
	$35,181	$34,327
Assets available for benefits, including balance sheet accruals	**$28,888**	$30,358

The weighted average assumed rates of return used in computing the actuarial present value of accumulated plan benefits for the Company's various plans ranged from 6% to 7.25% for 19Y6 and from 6% to 9% for 19Y5.

Exhibit 5-2 continued

8. LEGAL PROCEEDINGS

On February 18, 19Y7 the United States District Court for the Southern District of New York entered judgment against the Company and Berle and awarded the plaintiff, Good Brands Beverage, Inc. actual and trebled damages of $45,714,000. The judgment results from an action commenced by Good Brands principally as a result of the Company raising prices charged to Good Brands for certain Company products. The Company, based on advice of counsel, believes that there is no legal basis for the judgment, which it believes is contrary to the evidence and applicable law. The Company intends to pursue all available remedies to set aside or to reverse the judgment and in this connection will file an appeal with the United States Court of Appeals. The ultimate outcome of this litigation is not presently determinable. An affirmation of all or a substantial part of the $45,714,000 judgment could have a material adverse effect on the Company's financial position and results of operations. During 19Y6, 19Y5 and 19Y4, approximately 40%, 41% and 34%, respectively, of the Company's sales were made to Good Brands. Management believes that, in the event its relationship with Good Brands is jeopardized, other willing distributors would be available to handle its products.

In a suit initiated by Trinity Carton Co., the plaintiff alleged existence of an oral lease between the plaintiff and the Company. The alleged actions precipitating this lawsuit occurred prior to the change in ownership and management of the Company in April 19Y5. In March 19Y6, after exhausting all appeals, the Company made a $2.9 million payment to the plaintiff to settle amounts awarded by the court. A provision for this amount was recorded in the fourth quarter of 19Y5 to reflect this settlement.

In February, 19Y6 a stockholder of the Company commenced a derivative action against the Company, Berle, S&P Company and certain directors of the Company. The action alleges that these defendants, via their direction of Company funds into the Berle-Farview Joint Participation and loans to companies controlled by S&P Company and its various subsidiaries to partially fund the acquisition of Parbe Brewing Company by those companies, have among other things, willfully used their power to control the Company's assets and activities to benefit themselves alone, and not the Company and its stockholders. The suit alleges that this abuse of control and breach of fiduciary responsibility has caused a wasting of Company assets and substantial deterioration in Farview's financial position. The complaint seeks relief for the Company and all nondefendant stockholders in the form of an unspecified amount of profits and on an accounting for Company funds transferred to S&P Company and its various subsidiaries. The complaint also seeks costs and other unspecified relief. The Company, based on advice of counsel, believes the action, which is currently in discovery, is without merit and intends to pursue all defenses.

During 19Y5 Planned Industrial Expansion Authority of the City of St. Louis ("P.I.E.") commenced an eminent domain action against the Company in connection with a St. Louis office building which was the subject of a sale agreement in 19Y4. P.I.E. sought to condemn the office building and pay the Company or the building's current owner $2 million in compensation. This action caused the building's lessee to file a claim against the Company, seeking specific performance; alleging that the Company failed to grant the lessee its right of first refusal under the lease when the building was sold in 19Y4. The Company countersued. As a result of these actions the buyer of the building stopped making payments on the note. During 19Y6 the Company accepted a $2,850,000 cash payment from P.I.E. as consideration for the building, recognizing a gain of $1,980,402. The 19Y4 sale agreement was rescinded and the related note receivable held by the Company was cancelled. All litigation involving the Company, P.I.E., the building's lessee

Exhibit 5-2 continued

and the buyer under the 19Y4 sales agreement was resolved at no loss to the Company.

The Company is a party to various other legal proceedings. The Company is contesting these proceedings and management is of the opinion that resolution of these proceedings will not have a materially adverse effect on the Company's financial position.

9. QUARTERLY FINANCIAL DATA (Unaudited)

Unaudited quarterly financial data for 19Y6 and 19Y5 is summarized below (in thousands, except for per share amounts):

	Quarter			
	First	Second	Third	Fourth
19Y6:				
Net sales	$ 8,928	$12,367	$10,512	$ 8,364
Gross profit	883	1,580	859	588
Income (loss) before extraordinary item	434	30	1,996	(2,404)
Per share	.06	.01	.30	(.36)
Net income (loss)	750	53	3,448	(3,225)
Per share	.11	.01	.52	(.49)
19Y5:				
Net sales	$ 13,372	$14,267	$13,927	$ 10,105
Gross profit	759	388	436	872
Net income (loss)	(2,441)	626	523	(6,901)
Per share	(.36)	.09	.08	(1.04)

During the fourth quarter of 19Y6 the Company recorded: a) a charge of approximately $2,025,000 to recognize the permanent decline in market value of a marketable security (fourth quarter bankruptcy); b) a charge of approximately $535,000 for expenses related to its former Cranston workforce (see Note 3) and; c) a charge of $250,000 to write-off certain uncollectible receivables. As a result of the fourth quarter loss, approximately $821,000 of tax related extraordinary credits recorded in prior quarters were reversed during the fourth quarter.

Quarterly amounts for 19Y5 were restated in 19Y5 for the matters described in Note 2.

During the first quarter of 19Y5, the Company recorded a $5.1 million write-down of idle facilities. This write-down was increased to $9.0 million during subsequent quarters, including a $3.4 million charge in the fourth quarter. The additional charge in the fourth quarter is based on appraisal information which became available in early 19Y6.

During the fourth quarter of 19Y5, the Company recorded charges of approximately $3.9 million relating to settlement of legal actions.

10. SUBSEQUENT EVENTS

In connection with the Good Brands judgment (see Note 8) Farview and Berle have each deposited $26,371,270 with the Clerk of the Courts of the United States District Court for the Southern District of New York. These funds include $44.0 million which was obtained by Berle through a four year loan. This loan from another S&P Company subsidiary, which

Exhibit 5-2 continued

had obtained the funds through a bank loan, requires annual principal repayments of $10.0 million in years one through three and a final $14.0 million repayment in year four. Interest is payable monthly at prime in year one increasing to prime plus one-half in year four. The loan is secured by certain of the S&P Company subsidiary's fixed assets and the guarantees of S&P and Berle. Berle deposited its required funds with the Court and used the remainder to repay amounts due to the Joint Participation which in turn repurchased $16,371,270 of Farview's investment in the Joint Participation. This reduced Farview's pro-rata share of the investment in the Joint Participation to approximately 4%. Farview deposited this $16,371,270 plus an additional $10.0 million of cash on-hand with the court.

Exhibit 5-2 continued

Price Waterhouse

To the Partners of the Berle-Farview Joint Participation

We have examined the accompanying statement of assets, liabilities and partners' equity of the Berle-Farview Joint Participation (the "Joint Participation") as of December 31, 19Y6 and 19Y5 and the related statements of operations, partners' equity and of changes in financial position for the years then ended. Our examinations were made in accordance with generally accepted auditing standards and, accordingly, included such tests of the accounting records and such other auditing procedures as we considered necessary in the circumstances.

The accompanying statements of operations, partners' equity and of changes in financial position of the Joint Participation for the year ended December 31, 19Y4, were not audited by us and, accordingly, we do not express an opinion on them.

As more fully described in Note 7, on February 18, 19Y7 the United States District Court for the Southern District of New York entered judgment against Farview Brewing Corporation and Berle Brewing Company and awarded the plaintiff damages of approximately $46 million. The Joint Participation has amounts due from Berle Brewing Company of approximately $61 million at December 31, 19Y6. The Companies intend to pursue all available remedies to set aside or to reverse the judgment; however the ultimate outcome of this litigation is not presently determinable. In our report dated March 28, 19Y6, our opinion on the 19Y5 financial statements was unqualified, however, in light of the litigation referred to above, our present opinion on the 19Y5 financial statements, as presented herein, is different from that expressed in our previous report.

As described in Note 1, the Joint Participation and its partners, Berle Brewing Company and Farview Brewing Corporation are controlled by S&P Company and its various subsidiaries. The Joint Participation and its partners have extensive transactions and relationships with each other and with members of this controlled group. As a result of these relationships, it is possible that the terms of these transactions are not the same as those which would result from transactions among wholly unrelated parties.

In our opinion, subject to the effect on the 19Y6 and 19Y5 financial statements of such adjustments, if any, that might have been required had the outcome of the litigation discussed in the third paragraph of this report been known, the financial statements examined by us present fairly the financial position of the Berle-Farview Joint Participation at December 31, 19Y6 and 19Y5, and the results of its operations and the changes in its financial position for the years then ended, in conformity with generally accepted accounting principles consistently applied.

PRICE WATERHOUSE

February 27, 19Y7, except as to Note 8.

Exhibit 5-2 continued

BERLE-FARVIEW JOINT PARTICIPATION
STATEMENT OF ASSETS, LIABILITIES AND PARTNERS' EQUITY
(Attributable to Joint Participation Operations)

	December 31, 19Y6	December 31, 19Y5
ASSETS		
Current assets:		
Advances to Berle Brewing Company (Note 2)	**$ 61,043,396**	$ 49,094,315
Trade accounts receivable less allowance for doubtful accounts of $29,400 in 19Y6 and 19Y5	**5,378,308**	6,496,153
Other receivables	**2,193,759**	2,558,963
Inventories:		
Raw materials	**1,400,821**	3,128,009
Beer in process	**464,174**	453,259
Packaged beer	**458,092**	716,464
Aluminum cans and other packaging materials	**4,935,147**	6,408,706
Other current assets	**81,767**	81,075
Total current assets	**75,955,464**	68,936,944
Property, plant and equipment:		
Land and buildings	**10,153,052**	10,104,913
Machinery and equipment	**45,924,654**	42,192,080
Other	**1,785,095**	1,804,475
	57,862,801	54,101,468
Accumulated depreciation	**(46,748,550)**	(44,172,445)
Property, plant and equipment—net	**11,114,251**	9,929,023
	$ 87,069,715	$ 78,865,967
LIABILITIES AND PARTNERS' EQUITY		
Current liabilities:		
Accounts payable	**$ 3,459,997**	$ 3,132,589
Excise and property taxes payable	**451,732**	580,237
Accrued vacation pay	**688,979**	601,463
Accrued salaries and wages	**194,725**	195,382
Deposits on containers	**463,747**	506,793
Other current liabilities	**92,134**	647,778
Total current liabilities	**5,351,364**	5,664,242
Partners' equity:		
Berle Brewing Company and Subsidiary	**61,748,968**	56,036,247
Farview Brewing Corporation	**19,969,383**	17,165,478
Total partners' equity	**81,718,351**	73,201,725
	$ 87,069,715	$ 78,865,967

The accompanying notes are an integral part of these financial statements.

Exhibit 5-2 continued

BERLE-FARVIEW JOINT PARTICIPATION STATEMENT OF OPERATIONS

	Year Ended December 31,		
	19Y6	**19Y5**	**19Y4**
			(Unaudited)
Gross sales	**$87,236,775**	$89,759,699	$108,819,567
Less—excise taxes and allowances	**9,014,191**	7,412,561	11,403,333
Net sales	**78,222,584**	82,347,138	97,416,234
Cost of goods sold	**69,955,754**	71,255,916	88,358,355
Gross profit	**8,266,830**	11,091,222	9,057,879
Marketing, general and administrative expenses	**5,112,698**	5,164,522	4,862,403
Operating income	**3,154,132**	5,926,700	4,195,476
Interest income—Berle	**4,362,494**	3,462,027	3,092,388
Net participation income	**$ 7,516,626**	$ 9,388,727	$ 7,287,864

The accompanying notes are an integral part of these financial statements.

BERLE-FARVIEW JOINT PARTICIPATION STATEMENT OF PARTNERS' EQUITY FOR THE YEARS ENDED DECEMBER 31, 19Y6, 19Y5 AND 19Y4

	Berle Brewing Company and Subsidiary	**Farview Brewing Corporation**	**Total**
Balance at December 31, 19Y3*	**$42,767,352**	$ 7,757,782	$50,525,134
Net participation income*	**6,171,471**	1,116,393	7,287,864
Balance at December 31, 19Y4*	**48,938,823**	8,874,175	57,812,998
Investment, cash	**—**	6,000,000	6,000,000
Net participation income	**7,097,424**	2,291,303	9,388,727
Balance at December 31, 19Y5	**56,036,247**	17,165,478	73,201,725
Investment, cash	**—**	1,000,000	1,000,000
Net participation, income	**5,712,721**	1,803,905	7,516,626
Balance at December 31, 19Y6	**$61,748,968**	$19,969,383	$81,718,351

*Unaudited

The accompanying notes are an integral part of these financial statements.

Exhibit 5-2 continued

BERLE-FARVIEW JOINT PARTICIPATION
STATEMENT OF CHANGES IN FINANCIAL POSITION

	For the Year Ended December 31,		
	19Y6	**19Y5**	**19Y4**
			(Unaudited)
Sources of funds:			
Net participation income	**$ 7,516,626**	$ 9,388,727	$ 7,287,864
Add item not affecting advances to Berle:			
Depreciation expense	**2,606,891**	2,712,400	2,799,507
Changes in working capital:			
Accounts receivable	**1,483,049**	(229,223)	(861,436)
Inventories	**3,448,204**	(2,398,127)	(668,444)
Other current assets	**(692)**	(41,803)	(6,928)
Accounts payable	**327,408**	1,315,473	(1,655,148)
Accrued salaries and wages	**(657)**	(143,953)	333,840
Deposits on containers	**(43,046)**	250,696	82,735
Other liabilities	**(596,583)**	267,597	32,434
Funds provided by operations	**14,741,200**	11,121,787	7,344,424
Investment by Farview	**1,000,000**	6,000,000	—
Total sources of funds	**15,741,200**	17,121,787	7,344,424
Uses of funds:			
Increase in property, plant and equipment, net	**3,792,119**	3,435,778	930,214
Total uses of funds	**3,792,119**	3,435,778	930,214
Net increase in advances to Berle Brewing Company	**11,949,081**	13,686,009	6,414,210
Advances to Berle Brewing Company, beginning of year	**49,094,315**	35,408,306	28,994,096
Advances to Berle Brewing Company, end of year	**$61,043,396**	$49,094,315	$35,408,306

The accompanying notes are an integral part of these financial statements.

Exhibit 5-2 continued

BERLE-FARVIEW JOINT PARTICIPATION
NOTES TO FINANCIAL STATEMENTS

1. DESCRIPTION OF THE JOINT PARTICIPATION

In 19X8 Farview Brewing Corporation ("Farview") and Berle Brewing Company together with its wholly-owned subsidiary Berle Container Company (together "Berle") formed an unincorporated joint venture known as the Berle-Farview Joint Participation ("Joint Participation). Berle contributed the use of its San Antonio brewery and aluminum can plant and certain other assets with a then aggregate stated value of $15,083,238; and Farview contributed $3,000,000 in cash. The purpose of the Joint Participation is to provide a means for Farview to share in Berle's brewing, can manufacturing and related operations. The agreement, as amended in 19X9 provides that:

(a) Berle and Farview will associate together as partners under the name Berle-Farview Joint Participation.
(b) The management of the Joint Participation vests exclusively with Berle.
(c) Title to all assets, properties and funds transferred to or generated by the Joint Participation vests with Berle. Farview's interest is limited to an undivided beneficial ownership interest in the net equity of the Joint Participation. The Joint Participation is entitled to beneficial ownership of the assets, properties and funds used in its operations.
(d) The Joint Participation agreement can be terminated by either partner at the end of any calendar year upon not less than 90 days' notice.
(e) Either partner may at any time increase or decrease its investment in the Joint Participation via cash investments or distributions.
(f) Net participation income is credited to each partner's capital account in relation to the total capital of the Joint Participation.

All of Farview's Class A Convertible, Voting, Preferred Stock and 78,700 shares of its common stock are owned by Berle Brewing Company, which in turn is owned by S&P Company and its various subsidiaries. All of these companies are ultimately controlled by the estate of Mr. Peter Kane. This preferred and common stock together represent 49% of Farview's outstanding voting rights and effectively allow S&P Company to control Farview.

The Joint Participation, through Berle, is engaged in the production and sale of beer and related malt beverages and the manufacture of aluminum cans. Cans manufactured are used to package the Joint Participation's products with the remainder sold to various related and unrelated parties. The Joint Participation also operates an aluminum can recycling center.

In the event the Joint Participation incurs a loss, the entire loss is charged against Berle's equity account, however, Berle is entitled to recovery any such loss from subsequent Joint Participation income prior to Farview receiving its proportionate share of any subsequent income. Also, if the Joint Participation incurs a loss in any given year, S&P Company has agreed to pay Farview a rate of return on Farview's equity account equal to 120% of the average prime rate for that year.

Upon termination of the Joint Participation, Farview's equity account, if any, will be distributed in cash with the remaining Joint Participation net assets distributed to Berle.

Exhibit 5-2 continued

2. ACCOUNTING POLICIES AND BASIS OF PRESENTATION

As described in Note 1, Berle holds title to the Joint Participation assets and acts as trustee for these assets, and the Joint Participation has only a beneficial ownership interest. The accompanying statement of assets, liabilities and partners' equity for the Joint Participation reflects those assets and liabilities of Berle which relate to Joint Participation operations. Likewise, the accompanying statement of operations presents those operations of Berle which are subject to Joint Participation. These operations consist of the brewing, can manufacturing and related operations of Berle.

Advances to Berle Brewing Company

The Joint Participation does not maintain any bank accounts or cash funds; all receipts and disbursements are handled by Berle. "Advances to Berle Brewing Company" represents the Joint Participation's operating funds held by Berle. Interest for Berle's use of these funds is charged by the Joint Participation at prime. Summarized financial information for Berle is presented in Note 3.

Inventories

Inventories are stated at the lower of average cost or market, calculated under the first-in, first-out method. Raw materials consist principally of bulk aluminum, but also include brewing ingredients.

Property, Plant and Equipment

Property, plant and equipment is stated at cost. Depreciation is provided over the estimated useful lives (equipment, 5 to 15 years; buildings 20 to 40 years) of the assets using various methods.

Container Deposits

Deposit amounts charged to customers for returnable containers expected to be returned are reflected in the balance sheet as a liability to customers. The deposit liability is reduced when containers are returned.

Pension Plans

Although the Joint Participation has no employees, it bears all employee related costs of the Berle employees who conduct the affairs of the Joint Participation. Certain of these employees are covered by a defined benefit pension plan which includes certain Farview employees and employees of other companies controlled by S&P Company. Berle is allocated a portion of the cost of this plan based on the number of its employees covered by the plan. Certain other Berle employees are covered by multi-employer pension plans for which Berle makes per hour contributions as specified in union contracts.

Income Taxes

The Joint Participation records no provision for income taxes. The partners include their respective shares of Joint Participation income in their tax returns.

Exhibit 5-2 continued

3. SUMMARY FINANCIAL INFORMATION—BERLE BREWING COMPANY AND SUBSIDIARY

Summary financial information for Berle Brewing Company and Subsidiary as of December 31, 19Y6 and 19Y5 is presented below.

	December 31,	
	19Y6 (Unaudited)	**19Y5 (Unaudited)**
ASSETS		
Cash	**$ 155,582**	$ 207,178
Advances to S&P Company	**19,743,619**	
Marketable securities, at cost	**6,731,062**	35,897,629
Real estate, net	**3,278,921**	3,929,437
Investment in Berle-Farview Joint Participation	**61,748,968**	56,036,247
Investment in Farview Brewing Corporation, at cost:		
Class A Preferred Stock	**9,360,000**	9,360,000
Common Stock	**236,100**	236,100
Other assets	**1,589,080**	1,729,408
	$102,843,332	$107,395,999
LIABILITIES AND STOCKHOLDER'S EQUITY		
Notes payable	**$ 4,400,000**	$ 4,400,000
Advances from Berle-Farview Joint Participation	**61,043,396**	49,094,315
	65,443,396	53,494,315
Stockholder's equity	**37,399,936**	53,901,684
	$102,843,332	$107,395,999

(1) The market values of these securities at December 31, 19Y6 and 19Y5 were $8,354,000 and $44,010,000, respectively. At December 31, 19Y5 securities with a market value of $28,332,000 were held by Seattle First National Bank as collateral for a loan to S&P Company made in connection with the acquisition of Pabst.

(2) Berle Brewing Company is a member of the consolidated federal income tax filing group of S&P Company and, as such, is jointly and severally liable for any group tax liabilities. One member of the group is presently contesting a claim by the Internal Revenue Service for substantial additional taxes.

4. RELATED PARTY TRANSACTIONS

The Joint Participation and its partners, Berle and Farview, are under the common control of S&P Company and its various subsidiaries. (See Note 1.) As described below and elsewhere in this report, the Joint Participation and its partners have extensive transactions and relationships with each other and with other members of the controlled group. As a result of these relationships, it is possible that the terms of these transactions are not the same as those which would result from transactions among wholly unrelated parties.

Exhibit 5-2 continued

Farview Brewing Contract

The Joint Participation has a brewing contract with Farview whereby 151,900 and 431,256 barrels of Farview's products were produced by the Joint Participation during the years ended December 31, 19Y6 and 19Y5, respectively. The cost to Farview of this production was $54.63 per barrel in 19Y6 and $55.60 per barrel in 19Y5. This cost approximates the Joint Participation's normal brewing costs. Under the terms of this arrangement, the Joint Participation, through Berle, is responsible for the billing and collection of accounts; bad debts, however, remains the responsibility of Farview. This contract was originally entered into to allow for refurbishing of Farview's Fort Wayne brewery and to assure an uninterrupted supply of Farview's products in light of labor relation difficulties at Fort Wayne. These matters have been resolved and a significant portion of the 19Y5 barrels produced under the contract were moved back to Fort Wayne during early 19Y6. Farview continues to have certain amounts of its products produced under the brewing contract to allow placement of Farview products in markets which cannot economically be served from Fort Wayne.

Amounts paid by Farview to the Joint Participation for products produced under the brewing contract are treated as reductions of Cost of Goods Sold in the accompanying Joint Participation financial statements.

Farview Employee Costs

During 19Y3 Farview entered into an arrangement with Berle to jointly participate in reopening the Cranston, Rhode Island brewery. In accordance with the agreement, the Joint Participation was ultimately to be responsible for the costs, including labor, associated with the potential reopening. At December 31, 19Y6 this agreement continues to be in effect, however efforts to reopen the brewery were halted during 19Y5. The Joint Participation continued to pay certain employee benefit expenses related to Farview's former Cranston workforce through 19Y5. These employee benefit expenses approximated $647,000 in 19Y5.

As efforts to reopen the Cranston brewery were halted during 19Y5 an agreement was reached during the fourth quarter of 19Y6 making Farview responsible for the cost of providing these continuing employee benefits, which approximated $535,000 during 19Y6. The Joint Participation paid these expenses during 19Y6 but will now be reimbursed by Farview. Accordingly, included in other receivables at December 31, 19Y6 is $535,000 receivable from Farview.

Sale of Cans

Included in Joint Participation operations are sales of cans to Farview. These sales are made under terms similar to terms of sales with unrelated parties and totalled approximately $0.2 and $1.4 million in 19Y6 and 19Y5, respectively.

Advances to Berle

During 19Y6, 19Y5 and 19Y4 interest earned on advances to Berle (see Note 2) totalled $4,362,494, $3,462,027, and $3,092,388, respectively.

5. SIGNIFICANT SALES AND PURCHASES

During 19Y6 and 19Y5, sales of cans to one customer amounted to approximately $16.3 million and $24.1 million or approximately 19% and 27% of total gross sales, respectively. In addition, during 19Y6 and 19Y5 the Joint Participation purchased bulk aluminum from one vendor totalling approximately $12.9 million and $24.5 million or approximately 19% and 30.3% of total purchases, respectively.

Exhibit 5-2 continued

6. OTHER RECEIVABLES

Other receivables at December 31, 19Y6 and 19Y5 are comprised principally of amounts due from sales of scrap aluminum and brewing by-products. Also included are approximately $1,028,000 and $333,000, respectively, due from related parties.

7. LEGAL PROCEEDINGS

On February 19, 19Y7 the United States District Court for the Southern District of New York entered judgment against Farview and Berle and awarded the plaintiff, Good Brands Beverage, Inc. actual and trebled damages of $45,714,000. The judgment results from an action commenced by Good Brands principally as a result of Farview raising prices charged to Good Brands for certain Farview products. Farview, based on advice of counsel, believes that there is no legal basis for the judgment, which it believes is contrary to the evidence and applicable law. Farview intends to pursue all available remedies to set aside or to reverse the judgment and in this connection will file an appeal with the United States Court of Appeals. The ultimate outcome of this litigation is not presently determinable. As the Joint Participation has amounts due from Berle of approximately $61 million at December 31, 19Y6 an affirmation of all or a substantial part of the $45,714,000 judgment could have a material adverse effect on the Joint Participation's financial position and results of operations.

8. SUBSEQUENT EVENTS

In connection with the Good Brands judgment (see Note 7) Farview and Berle have each deposited $26,371,270 with the Clerk of the Courts of the United States District Court for the Southern District of New York. These funds include a $44.0 million loan that was obtained by Berle from another subsidiary of S&P Company which had obtained the funds through a bank loan. This loan requires annual principal repayments of $10.0 million in years one through three and a final $14.0 million repayment in year four. The bank loan is secured by certain of the S&P Company subsidiary's fixed assets and the guarantees of S&P Company and Berle. Berle deposited its required funds with the Court and used the remainder of the funds to repay amounts due the Joint Participation which in turn repurchased $16,371,270 of Farview's investment in the Joint Participation. This reduced Farview's pro-rata share of the investment in the Joint Participation to approximately 4%. Farview deposited this $16,371,270 plus $10.0 million of cash on-hand with the Court.

Conclusions

In Chapter 4 you learned some of the numerical techniques and ratios that are used to identify asset plays. In this chapter, some of the qualitative aspects to identifying asset plays were cited. After reading both of these chapters, you have probably come to realize the extent to which a company's financials cannot be taken at face value. Analyzing any company's financial records goes beyond the mere application of some ratios; it requires looking beyond the numbers.

Successful Asset-Play Investors

CHAPTER 6

Up to now, this book has dealt with the "mechanical" aspects to asset-play investing. But there is another interesting and important component of asset-play investing, namely, the "players" of the game. By examining the philosophy and approach to investing taken by selected professional asset-play investors, you should be able to obtain a better grasp of the whole picture. The best way to learn about investing is by studying successful investors.

Who are these successful investors? What traits do they have in common? Successful asset-play investors vary considerably in age, personality, and investment style. Furthermore, each player brings a different perspective to the investment process based on personal background and experience. By studying their individual techniques, you can learn some of their tricks for locating asset plays, some of the particular places in the investment arena where asset plays are to be found, and the thinking patterns that such investors bring to the whole process of investing and portfolio management.

If there is a common thread that all successful asset-play investors share, it is that they are basically loners. Many of their investing ideas run contrary to those of other market professionals since they hold positions for long periods of time and tend not to follow market fads and glamour stocks. But their success points out that it can pay handsomely to act on one's own instinct. Let's begin with examining some of the "players" in the game of asset plays.

Benjamin Graham

Benjamin Graham was the man who originated the concept of asset-play investing. He is considered to be the father of security analysis—applying logic to the investing process.

After graduating from Columbia University in 1914, Graham worked on Wall Street as a messenger rather than pursue the teaching career for which he had been trained. His classical education with its emphasis on mathematics and logical thinking would prove useful for him in future years. Within a short period of time, he advanced from messenger to the position of statistician—what today are called security analysts—and wrote a number of articles on financial topics. By 1920, Graham had become a partner in the firm of Neuburger, Henderson & Loeb. In 1926, he founded the Benjamin Graham Joint Account, which he managed for a share of the profits and which grew to $2.5 million by 1929.

During this period of time, Graham formulated his investment philosophy. While earlier investment managers concerned themselves with the quality and character of a company's management, Graham was the first statistician to emphasize a mathematical/quantitative approach to evaluating a company. He was a pioneer in developing and utilizing many of the financial ratios described in this book.

Graham and the accounts he managed did not escape the effects of the Crash of 1929. He saw the assets of the Joint Account decline 70% between 1929 and 1932. Beginning in 1928 and continuing through 1956, he taught an evening course at Columbia University's Business School based on the quantitative approach to investing that he continued to develop and refine over the ensuing years on Wall Street. Many of today's leading asset-play analysts and portfolio managers were students of Graham. In 1934, he was co-author of a book entitled *Security Analysis* with Professor David L. Dodd, which is regarded as the bible of modern-day security analysis. He wrote a popularized version of his theories in *The Intelligent Investor,* which was published in 1949.

At the cornerstone of the Graham/Dodd investment philosophy is the concept of value. The mathematical techniques which Graham emphasized in all his writings and which are highlighted in this book call for the investor to look behind the numbers reflected in a company's financials. Furthermore, he maintained that an "intelligent investor" should not be a follower but rather a leader. He rejected the growth stocks of his day and maintained that by scanning the Standard & Poor's *Stock Guide,* which contains basic financial information on thousands of stocks, an investor applying the ratios Graham developed could identify many opportunities to buy assets at a discount. In large part, Graham found his bargain stocks among the niches and corners of the investment world rather than among the glamour stocks of the day. While Graham's philosophy encompassed investing in risk arbitrage, liquidations, convertible hedges (buying a convertible bond or preferred stock and selling short the common into which it converts), and buying control of entire companies—things that are beyond the scope of the individual investor—buying bargain stocks at less than their net current assets or less than their underlying assets remains a viable alternative for the average investor. Finally, Graham emphasized diversifications of investments, although he did not always practice this in his own approach to investing.

Just how successful Graham was in applying his asset-play technique to real-life situations can be shown by a couple of examples. In the process of reviewing the filings pipeline companies had to make with the Interstate Commerce Commission in the late 1920s, Graham discovered the Northern Pipeline Company. According to his calculations (which involved using the same ratios described in this book), Northern Pipeline had quick assets of $95 per share which compared favorably with the

$65 per share at which the stock was then selling. Also, at a market price of $95 per share Northern had a 9% yield. Based on his number crunching, Graham's partnership went on to accumulate 38% of Northern's common stock, and at the next meeting of Northern's Board of Directors, Graham was elected to the Board. Graham was able to persuade the Board to pay out $50 per share and what remained was still worth some $50 per share. Thus, within the matter of a year or so, Graham was able to realize $100 on an investment of $65 per share. Again, the key point is that Graham was unconcerned about what the company's business was or the capability of its management; his only concern was in identifying undervalued assets and buying them before they were recognized as such by the marketplace. Graham was able to repeat this process again and again allowing himself and his partners to recover from the 1929 Crash and prosper until the partnership was eventually liquidated.

Another prominent example of Graham's ability to recognize undervalued situations was his partnership's investment in 1948 of $720,000 in Government Employees Life Insurance Company (GEICO). GEICO was first brought to his attention by a stockbroker whose business was to sell stock in start-up companies to funds and partnerships spread around the country. GEICO's business involved selling automobile insurance by mail to government employees. Graham saw beyond the stockbroker's spiel and recognized the special niche in which GEICO operated and the degree to which its customers (generally concerned and careful drivers having few accidents) and the growing numbers of government employees would cause the company to grow and expand at a tremendous rate over the years. The 50% interest which Graham purchased in GEICO for $720,000 in 1949 would grow to about $500 million when spun off to the partners in the fund. While his investment in GEICO did run counter to Graham's rule regarding diversification of investments, it shows the degree that one can profit from the utilization of many of the ratios and number-crunching techniques described in this book.

Graham's approach still works in today's world of computers and greater market efficiency. While computers have speeded up the research process, and in many respects the marketplace is more efficient today in that undervalued situations stay that way for a shorter period of time, the fact that there are still a number of highly successful professional asset-play investors (some well known and other not so well known to the investing public) proves that investing in "value" has a place in today's marketplace. At this point, it might be appropriate to meet with and explore the investment approach of a number of the present-day disciples of Graham.*

Warren Buffett

Warren Buffett probably represents the best known professional asset-play investor of today. Those individuals who had invested $10,000 at the time Buffett set up his initial investment partnership in 1956 would have seen their investment grow to $300,000 by the time the partnership was dissolved in 1969. Even more striking is the fact that despite a number of severe bear markets during this period, Buffett's partnership never had a down year.

As the son of an ultra-conservative Republican Congressman from Nebraska, Buffett grew up in Washington, D.C. and has spent the better part of his life in Omaha, Nebraska. Buffett's father became a stockbroker after he left public life, but was never greatly concerned with the acquisition of wealth or with the management of assets. However, his son demonstrated an interest in the stock market from an early age and learned from some of his early mistakes. For example, at age eleven, Buffett purchased three shares of Cities Service preferred at $38. His sister soon followed suit and purchased a like amount of shares. When the stock promptly declined to $27, his sister questioned him daily about the stock's performance or lack of. When it recovered to $40, Buffett sold his and his sister's stock. The stock promptly went to $200 per share and left Buffett with the lasting desire to "run his own shop" rather than function as an employee of an organization.

While a student at the University of Nebraska in 1949, Buffett read a book which was to have a dominant influence on

*Train, John, *The Money Masters,* Penguin Books, New York, N.Y., 1981.

his approach to investing. The title of the book was *The Intelligent Investor* and its author was Benjamin Graham. As a result of reading this book, Buffett decided to pursue his studies at Columbia University where he would be able to meet with and learn from Graham. This was the beginning of a relationship which was to last until Graham's death and included a period (1954–56) when Buffett worked for the Graham-Newman Corporation.

Buffett learned much during the two years he worked for Graham. He was able to perfect his skill at number crunching, or analyzing the quantitative aspects of a company's financials. Graham did not believe in qualitative analysis—getting to know about a company's products, how it conducted its business, or its future outlook—but Buffett did. For that matter, Graham did not believe in meeting with a company's management. While some of the professional asset-play investors you will meet later in this chapter subscribe to Graham's quantitative approach to investing, Buffett's approach to investing does include qualitative elements.

It was in part because of this difference in investment approach that Buffett moved back to Omaha in 1956 and set up his investment partnership at age twenty-five. The partnership was funded with $100,000 of his own money. Operating his own shop, Buffett was able to concentrate on combining the quantitative techniques learned while working with Graham in his own qualitative approach to investing. Buffett felt that an investor should concentrate his purchasing power in a few stocks rather than across the board; purchase what is unpopular at the present time, and hence, illiquid, and be willing to hold a position for a long period of time. Buffett went beyond the number crunching and argued that a company should be viewed as a living thing. He maintained that an investor should seek out companies having a strong business franchise. By a strong business franchise, Buffett meant that the company should occupy a dominant position in a special market niche. For example, Buffett invested heavily in the American Express Company in 1964 when its stock declined greatly in reaction to the Salad Oil Scandal. He did this because he felt that the company had a strong business franchise in two areas. On the one hand, its credit card business appeared to be immune to the effects of either the scandal or to an increase in the cost to the consumer of the card. On the other hand, from its traveler's business it had the use of billions of dollars of cash "float" from the time the checks were purchased until they were used by the purchaser. That Buffett was correct in his judgment has been borne out by the subsequent market performance of American Express's stock.

As in the case of the American Express Company, Buffett found many of what he refers to as "gross profit royalty" companies in consumer-oriented industries. Most of his very successful investments have been made in such areas as television, newspapers, advertising agencies, and entertainment. The one common theme that runs through his investments is the purchasing at a discount of companies having a strong business franchise. While it is interesting to examine Buffett's approach toward investing, bear in mind that to be a successful investor—whether on an individual basis or as a professional investor—it is necessary to spend many hours in examining a variety of situations from a quantitative and qualitative viewpoint before you will be able to identify those companies worth investing in. And Buffett acknowledges that it is more difficult to identify such situations in today's market.

Tweedy, Browne & Co.

Whereas Warren Buffett has sought to blend the quantitative and qualitative aspects to asset-play investing, the principals of Tweedy, Browne & Co. maintain that they are the last of the investment advisers to adhere strictly to the Benjamin Graham approach to investing. They thus consider themselves to be principally involved in the identifying and purchasing of undervalued securities.

Tweedy, Browne & Co. had its start in the 1920s when the founder of the firm, Bill Tweedy, began attending the annual meetings of many small, closely held companies. In an attempt to increase business, he sought to obtain the shareholders' lists of such companies and would offer to buy and sell as little as 50 or 100 shares of the stocks of the companies. In many cases,

Tweedy was the only buyer in town and for this reason could purchase the stock at a discount from the company's underlying assets. In those cases where it was not possible to sell immediately the stock thus acquired, Tweedy would put the stock into the company's investment account. As a consequence, over time the firm has built up a valuable portfolio of stocks.

Furthermore, as an outgrowth of Bill Tweedy's activities, the firm has come to assume an important position in a particular area of the investment marketplace, namely, functioning as a market maker in literally thousands of inactively traded stocks. In some ways their approach to investing and market making can be likened to the activities of an art or antique dealer who stands ready to bid on a particular piece (in this case, the stock of a little-known company) whenever it is offered to him. The firm keeps files on all the companies in which it makes a market, and when the firm receives a call from a potential seller it can very easily update its calculations and be ready to bid on the stock.

How does Tweedy, Browne & Co. calculate what they will bid for a particular stock? What kinds of companies do they follow? The firm seeks to buy the stock of companies at two-thirds of net current assets, allowing for every possible charge or adjustment. They become sellers when the price of the stock is again at 100% of net current assets. Obviously, the stocks that Tweedy, Browne & Co. trade in tend to have mediocre managements, but the firm feels that in most instances the discount the marketplace applies to such companies is excessive. Likewise, the firm has found that buying a stock selling at a multiple (price to earnings ratio) of 6 or 7 times earnings has worked out better as opposed to stocks selling at 2 or 3 times earnings because the lower multiple frequently implies that the company has some serious problem. Typically, Tweedy, Brown & Co.'s portfolio consists of 30% representing net current asset investments, 30% in companies in which it has acquired a control position, and 30–40% in completely inactive companies, with some of these representing hidden asset situations.

Why the activities of Tweedy, Browne & Co. are interesting has to do with the firm's performance over time. TBK (Tweedy, Brown & Co's trading/investment vehicle) has compiled over the past 20 years a growth rate of better than 15% per year, which compares favorably with the record of other brokerage firms/investment advisers. The assets under management have likewise expanded from something like $30 million to well over $1 billion.

Furthermore, the individual investor is provided with a convenient way of following the activities of such entities as TBK Partners. This is through following the 13D filings such entities are required to make with the SEC once they acquire 5% or more of the stock of a publicly traded company.

Herzog, Heine Geduld, Inc.– Mutual Shares Corporation et al.

Another family of funds which operates from the point of view of identifying and investing in asset plays is the Mutual Shares Corporation family of funds. Founded by Max Heine in the late 1940s and presently run by his handpicked successor, Michael Price, the fund is in the Graham-Dodd mold and typically never pays above the calculated breakup figure for a stock.

To understand the investment techniques utilized by Mutual Shares Corporation, you have to explore its founder's background. Emigrating from Germany in the late 1930s, Max Heine approached investing in a systematic manner. Rather than relying on chance, he looked for a reason and value before investing either for himself or for his clients. In the late 1930s, Max Heine found that prime railroad bonds were going for 10 cents on the dollar. In his judgment they represented an opportunity to buy assets at a discount, and he was a substantial buyer of such bonds. As the economy moved out of the Great Depression and entered World War II, many of the nation's railroads began to show substantial earnings and their bonds rapidly appreciated in value. Heine became one of Wall Street's premier bankruptcy analysts and was able to apply profitably the skills gained in the 1930s to the evaluation of many of the major bankruptcies (for example, Penn Central Co.) of the 1960s and 1970s as well as the evaluation of the potential takeover/restructuring candidates of the 1980s.

What are some of the techniques used by Mutual Shares

management which you can apply to the selection of securities in which to invest? The Fund's management avoids the so-called Nifty Fifty (well-known companies heavily owned by institutions) and concentrates on "bottom fishing." This means that the Fund's management reviews bankruptcy filings; follows the activities of closely held, thinly traded companies; and seeks to identify companies with substantial current assets, hidden assets, or valuable business franchises. While analyzing bankruptcy situations may be beyond the ability of the average investor, certainly all of the other aforementioned categories lend themselves to the application of the numerical techniques and analytical techniques described in this book.

As in the case of the other players who were described previously in this chapter, you are probably wondering how Mutual Shares Corporation has performed in the recent past. Mutual Shares trailed the S&P 500 in three of five years recently, but it did rank in the top half of all funds in 1986 with a 16.5% gain. However, Michael Price offers no apologies for the fund's performance. He maintains that the fund's Graham-Dodd approach supports his stocks in weak or declining markets. To support this thesis, he points to 1984 when the S&P 500 increased 6.2% and Mutual Shares rose 14.5%.†

Charles Royce–
Royce Value and Pennsylvania Mutual Funds

Charles Royce is another well-known advocate of the Graham-Dodd approach to investing. His two biggest mutual funds in 1986 posted relatively modest gains of 10.9% and 6.3% respectively; the same funds (Royce Value and Pennsylvania Mutual Funds) each rose more than 43% in 1983 and 1984.

Royce gives a number of reasons for the most recent performance of the funds he manages. For one thing, the big action in the market has been in the large capitalized companies. Institutional and foreign investors are more comfortable with these stocks because their names are household words throughout the world. Likewise, many of the large capitalized companies have been the subject of takeovers and/or restructuring to a greater degree than the small capitalized companies. A combination of these factors has worked to limit the price appreciation of small capitalized companies during the past year.

Why does Royce continue to advocate investing in small capitalized stocks? One reason is that as a value-orientated investor, Royce believes in investing for the long term rather than chasing each year's fad stocks. Furthermore, he likes smaller companies because he believes that over time they have more opportunities to grow and promise higher returns.

What are the techniques Royce uses to identify potential asset plays? For the most part, he relies on many of the same techniques described in this book, namely, the application of a variety of numerical ratios to identify undervalued assets. Royce adds one caveat to this—the willingness to pay more for assets that generate sustainable high returns. This has led Royce to invest in companies such as Frank Paxton Co., a lumber distributor; Showboat, Inc., a casino operator; Kimball International, Inc., a maker of pianos and office furniture; and Old Republic International, an insurance company.†

Ron Brierley–
Brierley Investments Ltd., Industrial Equity Ltd., et al.

So that you don't think asset-play investing is the exclusive domain of the American investor, it is appropriate to explore the investment approach utilized by Ron Brierley, a forty-nine-year-old Sydney-based New Zealander. Brierley is Chairman of New Zealand's Brierley Investments Ltd., Australia's Industrial Equity Ltd., and Hong Kong's Industrial Equity Pacific Ltd. Brierley has some $700 million invested in about 40 British stocks and another $300 million invested in about 70 U.S. stocks. How successful he has been in identifying potential asset plays is shown by the fact that $1,000 of New Zealand money invested 26 years ago in Brierley Investments Ltd. would be worth $9.2 million in New Zealand money today.

Brierley got his start at age nineteen by publishing from his

†Carey, David, "The Sons of Ben Graham," *Financial World,* May 5, 1987, pp. 110–112.

home in Wellington, New Zealand, a monthly stock market letter called *Stocks and Shares*. Brierley went public in 1971 raising $72,000 in New Zealand money from the subscribers to his newsletter and from fellow members of an investment club in which he was active. His New Zealand company now has approximately 113,000 shareholders (3½% of New Zealand's population) and 80% of the stock is in public hands. While Brierley owns relatively small amounts of his companies' stock (1 to 5% worth approximately $135 million), Brierley is probably atypical among professional investors in that he has done more for his shareholders than for himself.

Brierley's approach to investing has been likened to Warren Buffett's. Brierley characterizes himself as an investor and emphatically denies that he is an asset-stripper, liquidator, or greenmailer. However, he acknowledges that he is not hesitant to put pressure on the managements of the companies he invests in if he does not like the way the company is being run.

Under the leadership of Brierley, his family of funds was able to grow by buying into dozens of neglected New Zealand and Australian companies. As with the other professional asset-play investors, Brierley concentrated his search for undervalued assets by examining the balance sheets of countless companies, applying the same ratios described in this book, and holding for the long term. Brierley has observed that "once upon a time you could sit down and look at a company's basis statistics, and some fairly substantial anomalies would emerge just from that intensive measuring of price against true value. Nowadays the pressure of investment competition has narrowed the gap in most instances. But there's still a more subtle value or potential that, fortunately, the computers don't reflect."‡ His faith in the validity of asset-play investing is proven by his recent presence in the American marketplace where he feels that it is still possible to locate asset-play situations, particularly among the lesser known and inactively traded securities.

Conclusions

1. The typical professional asset-play investor relies on the same analytical tools available to the individual investor that

‡Jaffe, Thomas, "Market Letter Writer Makes Good," *Forbes*, February 23, 1987, pp. 32–34.

are described extensively in this book. Time and experience rather than computer hardware/software are the main requirements to be a successful asset-play investor.

2. For the most part, professional asset-play investors tend to be long-term holders and concentrate their investment dollars in less well known or closely followed stocks.
3. In many instances, professional asset-play investors favor companies dominating a particular industry niche.
4. In recent years many professional asset-play investors have moved to take a more active role in the management of the companies in which they invest.
5. It is up to the individual to decide whether to make his or her own investment decisions or to work with a professional investor. If you lack the time or interest in managing stock investments, an alternative would be to purchase shares in a "value-orientated" fund. Furthermore, by following the 13D filings made with the SEC by professional asset-play investors, you can learn which stocks are attracting the interest of such investors.

Techniques for Purchasing Stock in Asset-Play Companies

CHAPTER 7

In preceding chapters to this book you were made aware of the principal sources for potential asset plays and the major players involved in the world of asset-play investing. But there is another important element to asset-play investing: the steps to follow in buying a particular asset-play stock. This is referred to as "taking a position." In this chapter you will learn some of the "tricks of the trade" utilized by professional investors.

Locating a Brokerage Firm and Registered Representative Dealing in Asset-Play Stocks

Books have been written on the subject of how to select a brokerage firm. Likewise, much has been written on the steps to be followed in selecting the particular registered representative most compatible with your investment goals and aims. It is crucial to select the right brokerage firm and registered representative since good ideas and skillful execution of orders are crucial to the success of an investor in asset plays.

Brokerage Firm versus a Service Firm

There are key differences between a discount brokerage firm and a full service firm. Once you are familiar with these differences, you will know what to expect from each and what type of firm best suits your investment needs.

With a discount brokerage firm, you are paying solely for speed and accuracy in the execution of orders. Such firms do not provide you with investment ideas nor do they furnish the "handholding" typically associated with full service brokerage firms. Because there are marked differences between commissions charged and the quality of service furnished, it is worthwhile to shop around before you select a particular discount broker. Also, many market veterans utilize the services of both a full service and discount broker. The registered representative of a full service brokerage firm bringing you an acceptable investment idea is rewarded with the purchase order. On the other hand, if you uncover the asset play on your own, it is probably most appropriate to utilize a discount brokerage firm, particularly in those cases where it is easy to acquire stock.

Another important aspect to the selection of a full service brokerage firm is to establish an account with a brokerage firm acting as a market maker in one or more of the asset plays you currently own or are interested in. Establishing an account with such a market maker is particularly important if you are thinking of acquiring a large number of shares and investing a significant amount of money. By opening an account with a market maker, you will be able to purchase shares with the broker acting as principal rather than agent. Thus, you will be able to purchase the shares you want at the asked price (bid) and not have to pay commission on the transaction. As a fringe benefit, since the brokerage firm you are dealing with is a market maker, it should have some knowledge about the company and the way the stock trades. Table 3-2 (see page 96) is a listing of those brokerage firms which are market makers in asset-play stocks.

The Float and Its Significance in Acquiring Positions in Asset-Play Stocks

The float is an important concept to anyone interested in asset-play stocks. Despite its importance, you will find that few individual investors are familiar with the concept.

The float of a stock refers to the number of shares available in the marketplace. To calculate a stock's float you have to subtract from the number of shares outstanding the number of shares owned by insiders (that is, officers, directors, and 5% shareholders), institutions (that is, mutual funds, bank trust departments, and insurance companies), and shares held in the company's treasury. The Standard & Poor's *Stock Guide* will provide you with the number of institutional owners and the number of shares they own; the company's proxy statement will give you the number of shares owned by insiders; and the balance sheet will tell you whether any of the company's stock is held in its treasury.

The following is a step-by-step example of how to calculate a stock's float.

How to Calculate the Float of XYZ's Common Stock

Number of shares outstanding	9,000,000
Number of shares owned by insiders	3,000,000
Number of shares owned by institutions	3,000,000
"Float" or number of freely traded shares	3,000,000

Why a Stock's Float Is Important to Asset-Play Investors

Professional investors frequently refer to the fact that a particular stock is "thinly traded" or "trades by appointment only." Such a stock has a small float. In today's institutional environment, if a company has a float of 5 or 6 million shares, most professional investors would regard the stock as having a small float. In the extreme case, some small, inactively traded companies have a float amounting to less than 100,000 shares. It is among such companies that you can find some of the best buying opportunities.

What does the size of a stock's float tell you about the nature of the owners/investors in the company's stock? For the most part, institutional investors require that a stock have liquidity before they will invest in it. By definition, a stock is liquid if it can be easily bought and sold without unduly disturbing its price. Also, there should be enough shares available in the public marketplace so that an institution can make a meaningful investment. Hence, for the most part, thinly traded stocks are unattractive investment vehicles for institutional investors. Thus, in the area of asset-play investing, the individual investor enjoys an advantage over the institutional investor because the individual investor has the freedom to take a position in a number of asset plays which institutions, by their very nature, are precluded from investing in. Only later when the asset play has increased the size of its float by either selling additional shares or splitting its stock will institutions find it appropriate to purchase shares. In effect, institutional investors will be buyers at the time individual investors will be selling this particular asset play and looking to move on to another undiscovered situation.

Institutionalization of the Marketplace

Typically, asset-play investors will not invest in stocks in which institutions own a significant portion of the outstanding shares. The argument is made that institutional domination of a particular stock will increase the price volatility of the stock and result in the stock being overpriced compared to the underlying assets. Also, because institutional favorites typically carry a higher price-earnings ratio, they are more vulnerable to any downturn in the overall market. Recent studies have shown that low price-earnings stocks have historically outperformed high price-earnings ratio stocks.

Leverage and Investing in Asset Plays

With any security transaction, as investor is faced with the decision whether to purchase the particular security for cash or to buy on margin. Those investments made for cash are executed through the customer's cash account while all transactions that are financed or bought on margin are executed through the customer's margin account. The rules governing how much of a security transaction can be financed are spelled out in the margin requirements set forth in Regulation T, which is administered by the Federal Reserve Board. Since 1976, the initial margin requirement has been set at 50%. At the rate of 50%, 50¢ in cash has to be put up for every $1 of securities purchased.

There are other factors relating to purchasing stock on margin which you should be aware of. First, all securities purchased on margin are held by the brokerage firm with which you do business and remain under their control. A second aspect to trading on margin is that should you be wrong in your judgment as to how the particular stock you buy will perform (that is, the price of the stock falls rather than rises), you may be called upon to put up additional cash or securities. Such an occurrence is referred to as receiving a margin call. Thus, any investor purchasing stock on margin should have some assets in reserve to meet any such call.

There is another important consideration you have to keep in mind when contemplating the buying of stocks on margin: not all asset-play stocks are marginable. It is possible to buy on margin all stocks listed on an exchange as well as those over-the-counter securities named on the Federal Reserve Board's List of Over-the-Counter Marginable Securities. Because they have a small number of shares outstanding and/or a limited number of shareholders, some asset-play stocks cannot be purchased on margin. What this means to the individual investor is that in some instances such an investor is precluded from utilizing margin, a form of leverage or borrowing, when purchasing certain asset-play stocks. Obviously leverage is an extremely useful tool in the hands of an astute investor in that it gives an investor added buying power and can magnify the returns which can be obtained from a successful investment.

This does not mean that the individual investor in asset plays is totally excluded from utilizing leverage. For one thing, such an investor can use the marginable securities in the portfolio to finance the purchase of the stock of nonmarginable asset-play stocks. Alternatively, an asset-play investor can arrange to use such stock as collateral for what bankers refer to as a nonpurpose loan. Essentially, a nonpurpose loan is for any purpose other than the purchase of securities but is collateralized by securities. If agreeable to the particular bank, such securities need not be marginable. Hence, asset-play stocks can potentially be utilized to finance such things as the purchase of real estate, cars, home improvements, and many other purposes for which money is borrowed.

Whether you decide to utilize leverage or not will depend to a large measure on your particular financial situation, attitude toward debt, and projections as to what return the particular investment will generate and how long it will take for the investment to prove successful. You must also realize that leverage is a two-edged sword that can magnify losses as well as gains.

Trading Patterns and the Spread

Purchasing shares of many asset-play stocks or "acquiring a position" requires that the individual investor be familiar with the way such stocks are traded.

As was mentioned previously, many asset-play stocks have a small "float," that is, a limited number of shares available in the marketplace, and are inactively traded. Furthermore, there may be only three or four brokerage firms making a market in a particular asset-play stock. Also, many asset-play stocks are not followed by security analysts and are not tracked by institutional or professional investors. While these factors contribute to the stock representing an opportunity to buy assets at a discount, they also frequently result in such stocks having an atypical trading pattern.

Atypical Trading Patterns

By atypical trading patterns, it is meant that there is a wide spread (that is, as much as 10 to 20%) between the bid and asked price for such a security. Also, such stocks are traded inactively, and when traded, hundreds rather than thousands of shares switch hands. To better understand an atypical trading pattern, you need some standard with which to compare it. It therefore would be worthwhile to spend some time describing the manner in which the majority of over-the-counter stocks are bought and sold.

The Pink Sheets. The Pink Sheets are the mechanism through which buyers and sellers of such stocks are brought together. For a company to gets its stock listed in the Pink Sheets, the company has to find a brokerage firm interested in making a market, that is, trading its stock. The same procedure is followed whether the company is going public for the first time or trading is being resumed after it has been out of the Pink Sheets for a period of time. Before it can begin to trade the stock, the proposed market maker is required to file a listing application with the National Quotation Bureau, Inc., a copy of which is forwarded to the SEC for that agency's review. Figure 7-1 is a sample of a typical listing application.

The most important element of the listing application is the provision that current financial information (two years of annual reports) be furnished when the listing application is filed. It is not possible to get a company's stock listed in the Pink Sheets if such current financial information is not available. The responsibility of the SEC for reviewing listing applications is only to the extent that the application is complete and the proper information has been submitted. The agency in no way passes judgment on the investment merits of the particular company seeking to get listed in the Sheets. However, if the financials or other data contained in the listing application are found to be false or misleading, the company and/or the brokerage firm submitting the listing application may be subject to prosecution for violating the federal securities laws.

Once a stock is listed for trading in the Pink Sheets, typically other brokerage firms besides the original or listing brokerage firm will begin trading the stock. For these other brokerage firms to become market makers is a much simpler process. Subsequent market makers just have to advise the National Quotation Bureau, Inc. that they wish to become market makers in the particular stock. However, all market makers are required to maintain a "due diligence file" on every stock in which they

Figure 7-1.

National Quotation Bureau incorporated

No quotation will be published until the broker-dealer seeking to insert the quotation furnishes the information requested in Parts 1 and 2 below, and if necessary, the information in Part 3, and duly executes and delivers this form.

PART 1

A. Exact name of the issuer and predecessor (if any).

B. State of incorporation.

C. Address of principal executive offices.

D. Complete title and class of security to be quoted.

E. Par or stated value of security.

F. Name and address of any transfer agent.

G. Number of shares outstanding of the security as of the end of the issuer's most recent fiscal year.

H. Price at which security is to be initially quoted. Bid______________Asked____________

PART 2

Check the item below which indicates the exemption from Rule 15c2-11 of the Securities Exchange Act of 1934 (the "34 Act") upon which you rely in submitting your quotation.

☐ A. The issuer has filed a registration statement under the Securities Act of 1933 (the "33 Act") which became effective less than 90 calendar days prior to the date hereof, and such registration statement has not been the subject of a stop order which is still in effect, and the undersigned has in its records a copy of the prospectus specified by Section 10(a) of the 33 Act; or

☐ B. The issuer has filed a notification under Regulation A of the 33 Act which became effective less than 40 calendar days prior to the date hereof, and the offering circular provided for under Regulation A has not become the subject of a suspension order which is still in effect, and the undersigned has in his records a copy of such offering circular; or

☐ C. (i) The issuer is required to file reports pursuant to Section 13 or 15d of the 34 Act, or is an issuer of a security covered by Section 12(g) (2) (B) or (G) of the 34 Act; and

(ii) the undersigned has a reasonable basis for believing the issuer is current in filing the reports required to be filed at regular intervals pursuant to Section 13 or 15d of the 34 Act, or, in the case of insurance companies, exempted from Section 12(g) of the 34 Act by subparagraph 12(g) (2) (G) thereof, the annual statement referred to in Section 12(g) (2) (G) (i) of the 34 Act; and

(iii) the undersigned has in his records the issuer's most recent annual report (on Form 10-K) filed pursuant to Section 13 or 15d of the 34 Act; or the annual statement of an insurance company not subject to Section 12(g) of the 34 Act; together with any other reports required to be filed at regular intervals under such provisions of the 34 Act which have been filed by the issuer after such annual report or annual statement; or

☐ D. The security of the issuer on which you are submitting a quotation has been the subject of both bid and asked quotations in an interdealer quotation system at specified prices on each of at least 12 days within the previous 30 calendar days with no more than four business days in succession without such a two-way quotation; or

(OVER)

The Harborside Financial Center 600 Plaza Three Jersey City, NJ 07311 (201) 435-9000

NQB FORM 211

☐ E. The security of the issuer of which you are submitting a quotation is admitted to trading on a national securities exchange (as registered under the 34 Act) and has been traded on such an exchange on the same day as, or on the business day next preceding, the day the quotation is published or submitted; or

☐ F. The security of the issuer of which you are submitting a quotation is a security of a foreign issuer exempt from Section 12(g) of the 34 Act by reason of compliance with the provisions of Rule 12(g) 3-2(b) thereunder.

☐ G. None of the above.

If you have checked A or B above, supply a copy of the prospectus or offering circular to National Quotation Bureau with this Form 211.

If your answer was "G. None of the above", please supply the information specified in Part 3.

PART 3

A. Describe the nature of products or services offered by the issuer.

B. Describe the nature and the extent of the issuer's facilities.

C. Indicate the name of the Chief Executive officer and members of the Board of Directors of the issuer.

D. Attach a copy of the issuer's most recent balance sheet and profit and loss retained earning statement.

E. Attach similar financial information for such part of the two preceding fiscal years as the issuer or its predecessor has been in existence

F. State whether the undersigned, or any person associated with the undersigned, is affiliated directly or indirectly with the issuer.

G. State whether the quotation is being published or submitted on behalf of any other broker-dealer. If so, state the name of such broker or dealer.

H. State whether the quotation is being submitted or published directly or indirectly on behalf of the issuer or any director, officer or any person, directly or indirectly, the beneficial owner of more than 10% of the outstanding units or shares of any equity security of the issuer. If so, state the name of such person and the basis for any exemption under the Federal securities laws for any sales of such securities on behalf of such person.

____

Broker-Dealer Firm Must Be A NQB Subscriber

I certify that I have examined this form and, to the best of my knowledge and belief, it is true, correct and complete. I authorize the National Quotation Bureau, Incorporated to furnish a copy of this questionnaire and any or all of the information contained in this form to the Securities and Exchange Commission or any other regulatory agency.

Name of Broker-Dealer employee to contact regarding information contained herein______________________ **Phone**__________

Name and Signature of Broker-Dealer Partner or Officer______________________

Firm Name______________________ **Date**__/__/__
(NQB SUBSCRIBER)

Address______________________ **Zip**________

make a market. Such a file contains current financial information, news releases, and so forth. The purpose of such a file is to ensure that every market maker is current on the affairs of every company in which it makes a market. Also, a market maker is required to meet certain capital requirements depending on the number of stocks in which it trades.

What are some of the reasons other brokerage firms follow the lead of the listing broker into a particular stock? First, market makers are continually looking for new stocks to trade and "scan" the Pink Sheets on a daily basis for new listings. Second, certain market makers tend to trade the same kinds of stocks. For example, some market makers are active in penny stocks, others in foreign stocks, and still others in asset-play stocks. If one of these brokers were to go into the Sheets in a particular stock, it is almost certain that other asset-play market makers would follow suit. It is for this reason that it is useful for the individual investor to review the Pink Sheets periodically.

Over-the-counter stocks and NASDAQ. Significant changes have occurred in the way in which over-the-counter (OTC) stocks in general are traded. These changes began in 1971 with the introduction of NASDAQ. Most investors are familiar with NASDAQ as the service which displays OTC stock prices on Quotron and other display screens. Prior to the development of NASDAQ, traders had to consult the Pink Sheets indicating each market maker's bid and asked price for the prior day as well as the phone number for each market maker. The second significant change in the way OTC stocks are traded came about in 1982 with the introduction of the NASDAQ National Market System. This system helped "legitimize" the OTC marketplace by providing last sale prices for certain selected over-the-counter stocks for the first time. Both institutional and individual investors felt more at home with the OTC marketplace resulting in a jump in both price and volume. A record 28.7 billion shares were traded on NASDAQ in 1986 representing a marked increase from the 1.7 billion shares in 1976. NASDAQ's share of the combined trading volume of the OTC market, NYSE, and Amex rose to 42% from the 22% it accounted for in 1976.

NASDAQ and the National Market System have had a far-reaching impact on the way over-the-counter stocks are bought and sold. In the case of NASDAQ listed stocks, the spread between the bid and asked price has in many cases narrowed to as little as 5%. Current and accurate trading data has fostered competition between market makers and lead to a more liquid OTC market. Furthermore, it is in general easier to execute a transaction in the over-the-counter market because data such as closing price, current bid and asked price, and size of the market (that is, number of shares offered versus number of shares wanted) are instantaneously available to any broker seeking to buy or sell a particular stock, whether on his own behalf or for a client.

Not every over-the-counter stock is listed for trading on NASDAQ or included as part of the National Market System. To be eligible for trading on NASDAQ, a company has to meet certain criteria as to assets, earnings, number of shareholders, and number of shares available for trading. Many asset-play companies do not meet the requirements as to the number of shareholders and/or the float, and hence are excluded from NASDAQ even though their management may seek to have their stock listed on the system. Also, the managements of many asset-play companies do not want to have their stock listed for trading on NASDAQ. The desire to run the company without interference from small shareholders, fear of an unfriendly takeover, or the desire to take the company private in the future are the major reasons why many asset-play companies do not seek a NASDAQ listing. Not being on the system means that it will be more difficult to acquire or dispose of a block of the company's stock and the spread between the bid and asked price may be larger. It also means that by being a Pink Sheet number rather than being listed on NASDAQ the stock may represent a real opportunity to buy assets at a discount as long as the stock remains undiscovered.

Six Key Factors to Consider before Investing in Asset Plays

What are some of the "tricks" to trading in asset-play stocks? Obviously, what you learn from reading this book can in no way replace the knowledge you would gain from working as a trader on the over-the-counter desk of any brokerage firm. But there are certain concepts and techniques that you as an individual investor can apply to trading and investing in asset-play stocks.

1. The Number of Market Makers in an Asset-Play Stock Will Tell You Much About the Stock's Trading Pattern

If there are three or less market makers in a particular stock, almost certainly there are few shares available in the marketplace. It is very likely that the spread between the bid and the asked price will be substantial. For example, in such a case the market makers might be bidding (that is, seeking to buy) stock at $16 per share and asking (that is, offering to sell) stock at $19 per share for a substantial spread of $3 per share between the bid and asked price. Such a substantial spread (19% as opposed to the 5% characteristic of NASDAQ listed stocks) means that it will be difficult to acquire a position as well as to liquidate such a position once acquired. But if the stock appears to be substantially undervalued based on your evaluation of the company's financials, and you are buying with the intention of owning the stock for a period of time, the fact that there are only a few market makers and the spread is substantial should not dissuade you from buying the stock. Also, as an individual investor purchasing a limited amount of shares you have an advantage over institutional investors who have to be concerned that their large-scale buying will disturb the market and will result in a widening of the spread, an increase in the price of the stock, or both.

2. Watch for the Appearance of New Market Makers

The appearance of a new name in an asset-play stock is a significant development that will have an impact on the price and trading pattern of that particular stock. If the new market maker is a major brokerage firm or a known and respected asset-play market maker (see Table 3-2 on page 96), it can be interpreted to mean that institutional interest has developed in the particular stock. The mere presence of a new market maker may cause the price of the stock to rise as long-time market makers check their pricing of the stock and because the new market maker has to purchase stock to build up its trading position.

3. A Two-Sided Market Is Important

Two-sided market means that market makers are both bidding and asking for stock. In the case of a two-sided market it should be relatively easy to buy and sell stock. However, as you scan the Pink Sheets you will see instances in which market makers are bidding only for stock or, in a fewer instances, offering only stock. This is referred to as a one-sided market. Likewise, you will also find stocks in which only the names of the market makers appear with no reference made either to a bid or asked price. Professional traders refer to this as appearing in "name only." It means that the market makers are unwilling to quote a price in the Pink Sheets because stock is not available (that is, in their inventory) or they are uncertain as to how to price the particular stock. From the individual investor's perspective the fact that there is a one-sided market or a name-only quote in the Sheets means that it may be difficult, if not impossible, to buy or sell stock. Also, in buying such thinly traded stock, you have to be patient. Internal or external developments such as the offering of additional stock, splitting of the company's stock, or the acquisition of the company will eventually occur and result in an accurate valuation of the company's assets. Again, if the company's financials justify investing in its stock, there are certain techniques which you as an individual investor can utilize to acquire a position in such a stock. These techniques are discussed in the next section.

4. Know the Techniques Professional Investors Use

After you become familiar with the techniques for identifying undiscovered asset plays, you will undoubtedly find that in the case of one or more of the stocks you are interested in there is only a one-sided market or a name-only quote. This does not mean that you cannot purchase shares of that particular asset-play stock. However, to a large measure your success or failure depends on your own ingenuity.

The first technique professional investors utilize and which is available to you is to have your broker "go into the sheets" for you. What is meant by the term "going into the sheets" is that your broker applies to the National Quotation Bureau to have himself listed as an additional market maker in the particular stock you want to buy shares of. Essentially, the broker is acting on your behalf and will advise you of any stock that is offered to him from whatever source. In many instances, such an approach is successful in turning up stock where conventional methods have failed.

Certain other techniques are available to the individual investor seeking to acquire a position in stocks which are quoted on a name-only basis. One such technique is to contact the management of the company directly and see if the corporation's officers are aware of any individual or institutional shareholders who are interested in selling any of their shares. Typically, managements will react in one of two ways. Some managements will discourage your interest and advise you to look elsewhere to invest your money. Other managements may be flattered by your interest in their company and may indeed find a source of stock for you. In any event, such an approach should quickly answer your question as to whether there is any stock available. If the answer is in the negative, you can quickly turn your attention to other stocks.

Another technique relies on the investor's ingenuity. It consists of tracking down educational and charitable institutions that may have received shares of the company's stock as a donation or contacting former employees who may have received shares as part of a profit sharing plan.

5. Know the Relationship Between a Company and the Brokerage Firms Which Make a Market in Its Stock

Many investors are not aware of the nature of the relationship between a company and its market makers and the role market makers play in how a stock performs in the marketplace. Typically, the brokerage firm which takes a company public becomes its initial market maker. This is one of the reasons why it is so crucial for a company to select the brokerage firm with the best reputation and the strongest capital base as its underwriter. Furthermore, the underwriter (that is, initial market maker) will attract a particular group of market makers. For example, if Merrill Lynch is the underwriter of the company and hence its initial market maker, it is a certainty that firms such as Goldman Sachs, Pru-Bache, and the like will also make a market in the company's stock. Firms of similar size and reputation tend to follow the lead of each other and become market makers in the same stocks. Thus, the underwriter a company selects will determine the caliber of the brokerage firms making a market in its stock and hence the type of individuals and institutions that will be active in its stock.

There are other aspects to the relationship between a company and its market makers. Since many asset-play stocks are not followed by security analysts, investment bankers, or institutions, the only contact such companies have with the financial community is through conversations with the brokerage firms making a market in their stock. In many instances, market makers will keep themselves informed as to corporate developments and will be the first to call the company should there be any influx of large buy or sell orders. Also, the market makers may look to the company as a potential buyer of any large block of stock which comes on the market based on the theory that the company would be interested in preventing its stock from being unduly depressed. Likewise, the market makers may look to the company as a source of stock to fill a large buy order or to build up its own inventory position. For that matter, a particular market maker may be selected by the company to act as its unofficial agent in connection with a stock repurchase program. The relationship between a company and its market makers can be very close, and market makers play a variety of roles with the companies in which they make markets. If you can determine the nature of the relationship between a company and its market makers, you will be better able to determine if the company represents a real buying opportunity or whether the market for its stock is too closely controlled by the company acting in concert with the market makers.

6. Use Timing and Dollar Cost Averaging as Techniques for Investing in Asset-Play Stocks

Timing is an important consideration in connection with any form of investing and is something you have to consider once the decision is made to purchase a particular stock. Timing is particularly important in the case of asset-play stocks, since such stocks for the most part represent long-term commitments.

Individual investors usually buy as many shares of a particular stock as they can afford at one time. The majority of investors fail to consider that the best way of acquiring a position is to think in terms of a buying program. Rather than purchasing as many shares as you can afford at one time, you should start in a small way buying as little as 50 shares. Then follow the stock's price movements. Over time as you become more familiar with the company, the price range in which the stock trades, and develop a "feel" for the stock, you will be ready to add to your position until you reach the desired number of shares.

Also, buying into a stock over a period of time will enable you to utilize another trading technique—dollar cost averaging. This technique calls for the investment of a fixed amount of dollars in the selected stock at defined intervals of time. For example, once an investor has selected a particular asset-play stock he or she is interested in accumulating, the decision might be made to purchase $2,500 worth of stock every three months. If a discount brokerage firm is used, the transactional costs should be relatively low. The benefits come from the fact that the purchases would be made at an average price, rather than the yearly high or low price. Like other mechanical trading procedures, dollar cost averaging is designed to eliminate emotion from the investing process but does not guarantee a profit in every case in which it is used. The selection of the right stock is still the deciding factor as to whether money is made or lost.

Index

N

O

P

Q

R

S

T